JAMESTOWN LITERATURE PROGRAM
Growth in Comprehension & Appreciation

Reading & Understanding
Short Stories

LEVEL I

About the Cover and the Artist

The design on the cover of this book is a quilt called Leaf Symmetry I, *created by quilt artist Nancy Whittington of Chapel Hill, North Carolina. Nancy bases the designs of her quilts on geometric motifs found in nature. Her work has been widely exhibited in both regional and national exhibitions.*

Books in the Program

Short Stories, Level I	*Cat. No. 861*
Hardcover Edition	*Cat. No. 861H*
Teacher's Guide	*Cat. No. 871*
Nonfiction, Level I	*Cat. No. 862*
Hardcover Edition	*Cat. No. 862H*
Teacher's Guide	*Cat. No. 872*
Plays, Level I	*Cat. No. 863*
Hardcover Edition	*Cat. No. 863H*
Teacher's Guide	*Cat. No. 873*
Poems, Level I	*Cat. No. 864*
Hardcover Edition	*Cat. No. 864H*
Teacher's Guide	*Cat. No. 874*
Short Stories, Level II	*Cat. No. 881*
Hardcover Edition	*Cat. No. 881H*
Teacher's Guide	*Cat. No. 891*
Nonfiction, Level II	*Cat. No. 882*
Hardcover Edition	*Cat. No. 882H*
Teacher's Guide	*Cat. No. 892*
Plays, Level II	*Cat. No. 883*
Hardcover Edition	*Cat. No. 883H*
Teacher's Guide	*Cat. No. 893*
Poems, Level II	*Cat. No. 884*
Hardcover Edition	*Cat. No. 884H*
Teacher's Guide	*Cat. No. 894*

JAMESTOWN LITERATURE PROGRAM
Growth in Comprehension & Appreciation

Reading & Understanding
Short Stories

LEVEL I

JAMESTOWN PUBLISHERS
a division of NTC/CONTEMPORARY PUBLISHING COMPANY
Lincolnwood, Illinois USA

JAMESTOWN LITERATURE PROGRAM
Growth in Comprehension & Appreciation

Reading & Understanding Short Stories
LEVEL I

Developed by Jamestown Editorial Group
and Helena Frost Associates, Gaynor Ellis, Editor

Cover and text design: Deborah Hulsey Christie
Photo Research: Helena Frost Associates
Illustrations:
Chapters 1, 2, 8, 12, Yee Chea Lin
Chapter 7, Sandra Speidel
Chapters 3, 4, 9, Jan Naimo Jones
Chapters 5, 11, Mou-Sien Tseng
Chapters 6, 10, Tom Sperling

ISBN: 0-89061-486-5 (softbound)
ISBN: 0-89061-689-2 (hardbound)

Published by Jamestown Publishers,
a division of NTC/Contemporary Publishing Company,
4255 West Touhy Avenue,
Lincolnwood (Chicago), Illinois 60646-1975 U.S.A.

Manufactured in the United States of America.

7 8 9 0 QB(HC) 12 11 10 9 8 7 6 5 4

Acknowledgments

Acknowledgment is gratefully made to the following individuals and publishers for permission to reprint the stories in this book.

"The Big Wave" by Pearl S. Buck. Copyright ©1947 by the Curtis Publishing Company. Copyright ©1948 by Pearl S. Buck. Adaptation and abridgement of complete text of *The Big Wave* by Pearl S. Buck (John Day Company). Reprinted by permission of Harper & Row, Publishers, Inc.

"From Mother . . . with Love" by Zoa Sherburne. Reprinted by permission of Ann Elmo Agency, Inc.

"Through the Tunnel" by Doris Lessing. Copyright ©1954 by Doris Lessing. Reprinted by permission of Jonathan Clowes, Ltd., London (Canadian rights) on behalf of Doris Lessing. Copyright ©1955 by Doris Lessing. From *The Habit of Loving* by Doris Lessing (Thomas Y. Crowell). Originally appeared in *The New Yorker.* Reprinted by permission of Harper & Row, Publishers, Inc.

"A Mother in Mannville" by Marjorie Kinnan Rawlings. Copyright ©1936 by the Curtis Publishing Company; copyright renewed ©1964 Norton Baskin. From *When the Whippoorwill.* Reprinted by permission of Charles Scribner's Sons.

"The Secret Life of Walter Mitty" by James Thurber. From *My Life—and Welcome to It* by James Thurber, published by Harcourt Brace Jovanovich, Inc. Copyright ©1942 by James Thurber. Copyright ©1970 by Helen W. Thurber and Rosemary A. Thurber.

"Of Missing Persons" by Jack Finney. Copyright ©1955 by the Hearst Corporation; copyright renewed ©1983 by Jack Finney. Reprinted by permission of Don Congdon Associates, Inc.

"The Rule of Names" by Ursula Le Guin. Copyright ©1964, 1975 by Ursula K. Le Guin. Reprinted by permission of the author and the author's agent, Virginia Kidd.

"As the Night, the Day" by Abioseh Nicol. Copyright ©1965 by Oxford University Press. Reprinted by permission of Harold Ober Associates, Inc.

"The Necklace" by Guy de Maupassant. From *The Complete Short Stories of Guy de Maupassant,* published by Doubleday & Company, Inc., 1955.

"Zlateh the Goat" by Isaac Bashevis Singer. From *Zlateh the Goat and Other Stories,* by Isaac Bashevis Singer. Copyright ©1966 by Isaac Bashevis Singer. Reprinted by permission of Harper & Row, Publishers, Inc.

"Men in a Storm" by Jorge Ferretis. From *The Spanish American Short Story,* Seymour Martin, editor/translator. Copyright ©1980 by The Regents of the University of California. Reprinted by permission of the University of California Press.

Contents

To the Student

In this book you will read twelve short stories. They present a wide range of topics, styles, times, and places. Some are narratives about people struggling with everyday kinds of challenges. Others are fantasies that take you far outside the everyday world. Some are from English-speaking cultures; others are from Africa, Latin America, and Europe and have been translated into English.

Why do people read stories? Most people become involved with the characters and events. However, stories can also be understood and enjoyed for other reasons. How does the writer get you involved? Does he or she arrange events in a certain order? Does the writer use words in a particular way? How does the author feel about the characters? What message does the story offer? Those are a few of the questions that you can ask yourself to get the most out of what you read.

Each chapter in this book contains one story. Information is provided at the beginning of each selection to introduce you to the story and the author. Knowing the background of the author provides insight into his or her work.

The lesson at the end of each chapter teaches skills that will help you to understand what you read. These skills will also help you to enjoy your future readings.

The last feature of the book is a glossary that includes all the literary terms introduced in the book. As you read, you will find several literary terms underlined in each chapter. The first time a term appears in the text, it is underlined and defined. In the glossary, a page reference following each term indicates where the term first appears.

UNIT ONE

Stories of the Real World

The Big Wave
PEARL S. BUCK

The Short Story: An Overview

From Mother . . . with Love
ZOA SHERBURNE

Plot

Through the Tunnel
DORIS LESSING

Conflict

A Mother in Mannville
MARJORIE KINNAN RAWLINGS

Character and Characterization

The short story is the youngest form of literature. Poetry and drama date back thousands of years. The first novel was written almost one thousand years ago in Japan. Short stories, however, did not appear until the 1800s. By that time, more and more people were learning to read and write. As a result, newspapers and magazines became popular. In order to attract readers, those publications began to include short pieces of fiction. As the demand for short stories grew, writers experimented with the new form of literature.

A short story is a work of fiction that can usually be read at one sitting. Although short stories are fictional, some writers base their stories on actual people or events. They may set them in real towns or cities. Their characters may take part in actual historical events. Such stories are called realistic fiction because the characters and events seem like those of real life.

Much realistic fiction centers on experiences that all people face—the death of a loved one, the desire to succeed, or the importance of friendship. Although a writer might be inspired by a real person or event, the story itself will be a product of the writer's imagination. The writer will, for example, make up the appearances of the characters and invent personalities for them. Also, the writer can weave events and characters into a story. While stories of the real world may sound as though they could have happened, they are still the creations of a writer's mind.

Many people enjoy reading realistic fiction because it is close to their own experiences. They like to hear about how other people handle crises or succeed in difficult situations. Even if a story tells about people from another time or place, the message of how people overcome hardships or share feelings can be universal—recognizable to anyone.

The four stories that you will read in Unit One take place in various places in the world. The characters all sound as though they could have existed. The stories include events that are true-to-life, and the language of the stories is familiar to us today.

Chapter 1

Selection ***The Big Wave***

PEARL S. BUCK

Lesson *The Short Story: An Overview*

About the Selection

Today, we often think that we can tame the forces of nature. Huge bridges span the great rivers of the world. Miles of highways cut through regions that were once thick forests or impassable deserts. Canals channel waters from one sea to another. Despite those successes in making nature serve our purposes, we do not control all its forces. Think of how often you read about earthquakes, floods, or electrical storms causing destruction to life and property. Remember the scenes on the television news showing blizzards, hurricanes, and tornadoes.

"The Big Wave" is a story in which the destructive forces of nature play a large role. The story takes place in Japan, a country that has more than its share of natural disasters because of its location. Japan is a chain of islands east of China off the coast of Korea. The islands are mountainous. In fact, they are the highest peaks of several underwater mountain ranges.

Japan is part of an area called the Ring of Fire because of the volcanoes and earthquakes that erupt and shake the region, often with terrible results. Winds and underwater earthquakes can cause tidal waves—great towering waves that sweep inshore. Over the centuries, the Japanese have often experienced such destructive forces. Many Japanese have learned to recognize the early signs of volcanic activity and earthquakes that might result in tidal waves.

Although the seas that surround Japan pose a danger, they also provide the Japanese with a living. The Japanese depend on the resources of the seas for food. Fishing is essential to their survival. Because Japan is so mountainous, farmland there is limited. However, the Japanese have learned to farm the mountainsides, even as they keep a careful watch on nearby volcanoes.

In "The Big Wave," you will see the different ways of life of two boys. Kino, a farmer's son, lives on a mountain. Jiya (GEE-yah), a fisherman's son, lives in a village near the ocean. The two boys become friends. Yet Kino cannot understand Jiya's attitude toward the sea. To Kino, the sea is a calm, beautiful place to explore. To Jiya, it is a place of danger.

Pearl S. Buck, the author of the story, wrote many works of fiction, including sixty-five books and hundreds of short stories. Many of her stories take place in China or Japan. Although Buck was born in the United States in 1892, she was taken to China by her missionary parents when she was only five months old. She grew up in China, learning to speak Chinese before she learned English. She did not return to the United States until she was seventeen. Later, she went back to China where she taught in Chinese schools for many years.

The 1920s and 1930s were a turbulent time in China. The manuscript for Buck's first novel was destroyed by revolutionaries in 1927. Her second novel, *East Wind: West Wind,* was published in 1930. Pearl Buck's most famous novel is *The Good Earth.* It tells of the hardships faced by a Chinese peasant, Wang Lung, and his family. Buck won a Pulitzer Prize for *The Good Earth,* and in 1938 she was awarded the Nobel Prize for literature.

Pearl Buck's writings about China and Japan have long been popular in the West. Through her stories, she helped Westerners to understand some of the traditions and customs of those ancient cultures. She often portrayed peasant families, showing their successes and their failures in the struggle to survive.

The ways of life that Pearl Buck described in her stories and novels have changed in both China and Japan. Airplanes, automobiles, television, and other inventions of the modern world have affected even tiny villages. People are no longer as isolated from the rest of the country as they once were. Despite those great changes, farm families in China, Japan, and other parts of Asia still struggle against the harsh forces of nature.

Lesson Preview

The lesson that follows "The Big Wave" gives an overview of the major elements of a short story. You will learn how short stories differ from longer pieces of fiction, such as novels. Although short stories differ greatly from one another, they do share some features. For example, every story has a time and a place. It has characters and action. The differences among short stories depend on how the individual writer sets up and develops those basic features.

"The Big Wave" is quite short. However, it has all the major elements of a short story. The questions that follow will help you identify those elements. As you read, think about how you would answer these questions.

1 Where does the story take place?

2 Who are the main characters in the story? What do you learn about them?

3 Do the main characters face any problems or challenges? If so, what are they? How are they solved?

4 What action does the story involve?

5 What larger ideas about life does the author suggest through this story? What can you take put it in your life.

Vocabulary

Here are some difficult words that appear in the selection that follows. Study the words and their definitions, as well as the sentences that show how the words are used. This will help you get the most from your reading.

thatched covered with a roofing made of straw and rushes. *We stayed in an old cottage with a thatched roof that leaked when it rained.*

darted moved suddenly. *The rabbit darted into its hole to avoid the fox.*

tolled rang. *The church bells tolled every hour on the hour.*

fathoms units of measurement for the depth of water. *The shipwreck lay many fathoms beneath the surface of the ocean.*

scroll a roll of parchment or paper with writing or pictures on it. *In the antique store, we found a lovely old scroll painted by a famous Chinese artist.*

kimono traditional loose-fitting outer garment worn by Japanese men and women. *In Tokyo, you will see most people in Western dress, although some older women still wear the kimono.*

The Big Wave

PEARL S. BUCK

Kino lived on a farm that lay on the side of a mountain in Japan. The mountain rose so steeply out of the ocean that there was only a strip of sandy shore at its foot. Upon this strip was a small fishing village where Kino's father sold his vegetables and rice and bought fish.

Kino often looked down upon the thatched roofs of the village. The village houses faced one another, and those which stood beside the sea did not have windows toward it. Since Kino enjoyed looking at the waves, he often wondered why the village people did not, but he never knew until he came to know Jiya, whose father was a fisherman. Jiya's house did not have a window toward the sea either. "Why not?" Kino asked him. "The sea is beautiful."

"The sea is our enemy," Jiya replied.

"How can you say that?" Kino asked. "Your father catches fish from the sea and sells them, and that is how you live."

Jiya shook his head. "The sea is our enemy," he repeated.

It was hard to believe this. On hot sunny days Kino and Jiya threw off their clothes and swam far out toward a small island which they considered their own. Actually it belonged to an old gentleman whom they had never seen except at a distance. Kino longed to sleep on the island some night, but Jiya was never willing. Even when they spent only the afternoon there he looked often out over the sea.

"What are you looking for?" Kino asked one day.

"Only to see that the ocean is not angry," Jiya replied.

But certainly the ocean was not angry now. The sun sparkled deep into the clear water, and the boys swam over the silvery surface of rippling waves. Beneath them the water was miles deep. When Kino dived he went down, down, down, until he struck icy-still water.

Today when he felt the coldness grasp his body he understood why Jiya was afraid, and he darted upward again to the sun. On the beach he threw himself down and was happy again. But Jiya looked often at the sun. When he saw it sinking toward the west he called to Kino: "Come quickly. We must swim home."

After supper that evening Kino turned to his father. "Why is Jiya afraid of the ocean?" he asked.

"The ocean is very big," Kino's father replied. "We do not understand the ocean."

"I am glad we live on the mountain," Kino went on. "There is nothing to be afraid of on our farm."

"But one can be afraid of the land too," his father replied. "Do you remember the volcano we visited last autumn?"

Kino did remember. They had gone to visit a great volcano twenty miles away. Kino had looked down into the yawning mouth of the volcano and he had not liked it. Great curls of yellow smoke were rolling about it, and a white stream of melted rock was crawling slowly from one corner.

"Must we always be afraid of something?" Kino asked.

His father looked back at him. "No," he replied. "I did not mean that. It is true that on any day, an ocean may rise into storm and a volcano may burst into flame. We must accept this fact, but without fear. We must say, 'Some day I shall die, and does it matter whether it is by ocean or volcano, or whether I grow old and weak?' "

"I don't want to think about such things," Kino said.

"It is right for you not to think about them," his father said. "Enjoy life and do not fear death. That is the way of a good Japanese."

There was much in life to enjoy. In the winter Kino went to a school in the fishing village, and he and Jiya shared a seat. In the summer Kino worked on the farm, helping his father. Even his little sister, Setsu, and the mother helped when the rice seedlings had to be planted and when the grain was ripe and had to be threshed.

Sometimes if it were not seedtime or harvest Kino went fishing with Jiya and Jiya's father. "I wish my father were a fisherman," he would say. "It is stupid to plow and plant and cut the sheaves, when I could just come out like this and reap fish from the sea."

Jiya shook his head. "But when the storms come, you would wish yourself back upon the earth," he said.

On days when the sky was bright and the winds mild, the ocean lay so calm and blue that it was hard to believe that it could be cruel and angry. But when the deep water moved and stirred, ah, then Kino began to be glad that his father was a farmer and not a fisherman!

And yet it was the earth that brought the big wave. Deep under the deepest part of the ocean, fires raged in the heart of the earth. And at last the fires grew so strong that they forced their way through the mouth of the volcano. That day Kino saw the sky overcast halfway to the zenith. "Look, Father!" he cried. "The volcano is burning again!"

His father gazed anxiously at the sky. "It looks very angry," he said. "I shall not sleep tonight."

All night Kino's father kept watch. When it was dark, the sky was lit with red and the earth trembled under the farmhouse. Down at the fishing village, lights in the little houses showed that other fathers watched too.

When morning came, the sky was red, and even here upon the farm, cinders fell from the volcano.

In the house the mother took down everything from the walls that could fall or be broken. Her few good dishes she packed into straw in a basket and set them outside.

"Shall we have an earthquake, Father?" Kino asked as they ate breakfast.

"I cannot tell, my son," his father replied. "Earth and sea are struggling together against the fires inside the earth."

No fishing boats set sail that hot summer morning. The sea lay dead and calm, but when Kino looked at it he felt afraid.

No one stirred from home that day. Kino's father sat at the door, watching the sky and the oily sea, and Kino stayed near him. He did not know what Jiya was doing, but he imagined that Jiya, too, stayed by his father.

Early in the afternoon the sky began to grow black. The air was as hot as though a forest fire were burning. The glow of the volcano glared over the mountaintop, blood-red against the black. All at once a deep-toned bell tolled over the hills.

"What is that bell?" Kino asked his father.

"It is the bell in the temple inside the walls of Old Gentleman's Castle," his father replied. "Old Gentleman is calling people to come up out of the village and find shelter within his walls."

"Will they come?" Kino asked.

"Not all of them," his father replied. "Parents will try to make their children go, but the children will not want to leave their parents. Mothers will not want to leave fathers, and the fathers will stay by their boats. But some will want to be sure of life."

"I wish Jiya would come up to our farm," Kino said. "Do you think he will see me if I stand on the edge of the terrace and wave my girdle cloth?"

"Try it," his father said.

So Kino took off the strip of white cloth which he wore instead of a belt and he waved it high above his head. Far down the hill, Jiya saw the two figures and the waving strip of white. For Jiya was already on his way up the mountain toward Old Gentleman's Castle. He was crying as he climbed, and trying not to cry. He had not wanted to leave, but his father said, "If the ocean yields to the fires, you must live after us."

"I don't want to live alone," Jiya said.

"It is your duty to obey me, as a good Japanese son," his father told him.

So Jiya had run out of the house, crying. Now when he saw Kino, he decided that he would go there instead of to the castle, and he began to hurry up the hill to the farm.

Kino's father put out his hand to help Jiya climb over the stone wall of the terrace, and Kino was just about to shout out his welcome, when suddenly a hurricane wind broke out of the ocean. Kino and Jiya clung together and wrapped their arms about the father's waist.

"Look, what is that?" Kino screamed.

The purple rim of the ocean seemed to lift and rise against the clouds. Under the deep waters of the ocean, the earth had yielded at last to the fire. It groaned and split open, and the cold water fell into the middle of the boiling rocks. Steam burst out and lifted the ocean high into the sky in a big wave.

The wave rushed toward the shore, green and solid, frothing into white at its edges.

"I must tell my father!" Jiya screamed. But before Jiya could scream again, the wave reached the village and covered it fathoms deep in swirling wild water. Upon the beach where the village had stood, not a house remained.

Jiya gave a wild cry, and Kino felt him slip to the ground. Jiya was unconscious. What he had seen was too much for him. His family and his home were gone.

Kino's father gathered Jiya into his arms and carried him into the house. "It is better that he is unconscious," he said gently. "Let him remain so until his own will wakes him. I will sit by him."

"What shall we say to Jiya when he wakes?" Kino asked his father.

"We will not talk," his father replied. "We will give him warm food and let him rest. We will help him to feel he has a home still."

"Here?" Kino asked.

"Yes," his father replied.

"I don't think Jiya can ever be happy again," Kino said sorrowfully.

"Yes, he will be happy some day," his father said. "Life is always stronger than death. Soon now he will open his eyes, and we must be there, you to be his brother, and I to be his father. Call your mother, too, and little Setsu."

So they went back into the house. Jiya's eyes were still closed, but he was sobbing in his sleep. Kino ran to fetch his mother and Setsu, and they all gathered about the bed, kneeling on the floor.

In a few minutes, Jiya's eyelids fluttered and then he opened his eyes. He did not know where he was. He looked from one face to the other as though they were strangers.

None of them said anything for a long time. They continued to kneel about him, waiting. But Setsu could not keep quiet. She clapped her hands and cried, "Jiya has come back!"

The sound of her voice made him fully awake. "My father—my mother," he whispered.

Kino's mother took his hand. "I will be your mother now, dear Jiya," she said.

"I will be your father," Kino's father said.

"I am your brother now, Jiya," Kino faltered.

"Jiya will live with us!" Setsu said joyfully.

Then Jiya understood. He got up from the bed and walked to the door. He looked down the hillside to the beach where the fishing village had stood.

Kino's heart ached for his friend-brother. Kino's mother was wiping her eyes, and even little Setsu looked sad. She stood beside Jiya and took his hand and stroked it. "Jiya, I will give you my pet duck," she said.

But Jiya could not speak. He kept on looking at the ocean.

"We ought all to eat something," Kino's mother said. "I have a fine chicken for dinner."

"I'm hungry," Setsu cried.

"Come my son," Kino's father said to Jiya.

Jiya was not hungry, but when Kino begged him he took up his chopsticks and ate some of the meat and rice. His mind was still unable to think, but his body was young and strong and glad of the food.

When they had all finished, Kino said. "Shall we go up the hillside, Jiya?"

But Jiya shook his head. "I want to go to sleep again," he said.

Each day Jiya was still tired. He did not want to think or to remember. He only wanted to sleep. One day when the work was over and Jiya still had not waked, Kino and his father sat together on the threshold. "Father, are we not very unfortunate people to live on this island?" he asked.

"Why do you think so?" his father asked in reply.

"Because the volcano is behind our house and the ocean is in front, and when they make the earthquake and the big wave, we are helpless. Often many of us are lost."

"To live in the midst of danger is to know how good life is," his father replied.

"But if we are lost in the danger?" Kino asked anxiously.

"To live in the presence of death makes us brave and strong," Kino's father replied.

"What is death?" Kino asked.

"Death is that great gateway," Kino's father said. His face was not at all sad.

"The gateway—where?" Kino asked again.

Kino's father smiled. "Can you remember when you were born?"

Kino shook his head. "I was too small."

Kino's father laughed. "I remember very well when you were born," he said. "And oh, how hard you thought it was to be born! You cried, and you screamed."

"Didn't I want to be born?" Kino asked.

"No," his father told him, smiling. "You wanted to stay where you were, in the warm dark house of the unborn. But the time came to be born, and the gate of life opened."

"Did I know it was the gate of life?" Kino asked.

"You did not know anything about it, and so you were afraid," his father replied. "But see how foolish you were! Here we were waiting for you, your parents, already loving you and eager to welcome you. And you have been very happy, haven't you?"

"Until the big wave came," Kino replied. "Now I am afraid again because of the death that the big wave brought."

"You are only afraid because you don't know anything about death," his father replied. "Some day you will wonder why you were afraid, as today you wonder why you feared to be born."

While they were talking the dusk had deepened, and now, coming up the mountainside, they saw a flickering light. "I wonder who comes?" Kino exclaimed.

In a few minutes they saw that their visitor was Old Gentleman coming from the castle. "Is this the house of Uchiyama, the farmer?" Old Gentleman asked.

At this Kino's father stood up, and so did Kino. "Please, Honored Sir," Kino's father said. "What can I do for you?"

Old Gentleman came forward. "Do you have a lad here by the name of Jiya?"

"He lies sleeping inside my house," Kino's father said.

"It is my habit when the big wave comes to care for those who are orphaned," said Old Gentleman. "Three times the wave has come, and three times I have searched out the orphans and widows, and I have fed them and sheltered them. I have heard of this boy Jiya and I wish to do even more for him. I will make him my own son."

"But Jiya is ours!" Kino cried.

"Hush," his father replied. "We must think of Jiya's good. We are only poor people." Then he said to Old Gentleman, "Sir it is very kind of you to propose this for Jiya. I had planned to take him for my own son, now that he has lost his parents, but I am only a poor farmer and I cannot pretend that my house is as good as yours. Tomorrow when he wakes, I will tell him of your kind offer. He shall decide."

"Very well," Old Gentleman said. "But let him come and tell me himself, so that I know how he feels."

As soon as Kino woke the next morning he remembered Jiya and the choice he had to make. After breakfast Kino went to the field to weed the cabbages, but his father stayed in the house to talk to Jiya.

For a long time Kino stayed in the field, working alone. Then, when the sun was nearing zenith, he heard his father calling. He got up at once and walked along the part between the terraces until he reached the doorway. There his father stood with Jiya.

"I have told Jiya that he must not decide until he has seen all that Old Gentleman can give him for a home," Kino's father said. "Jiya, you know how our house is—these four rooms and the kitchen, this little farm upon which we have to work so hard for our food. We have only what our hands can earn for us."

Then he turned to Kino again. "You are to go with Jiya, and when you see the castle you must persuade him to stay there, for his own sake."

So the two boys went down the mountainside to the castle. The gate was open and the garden was most beautiful. A gardener was sweeping the green moss, but he left his work to lead them to the house. There they took off their shoes and followed the gardener through a great door. Inside this they met a manservant who dismissed the gardener and said to the boys, "Follow me."

So they followed him through a wide passageway. On both sides of this passageway panels slid back to show beautiful rooms, and in each room were a vase of flowers, an exquisite scroll, a few pieces of dark polished furniture. Neither Jiya nor Kino had ever seen such a house.

Then far in the distance they saw Old Gentleman sitting beside a small table. The table was set in front of the open sliding panel that looked into the garden, and Old Gentleman was writing.

When the two boys came near he looked at Jiya. "Well," he said. "Will you be my son?"

Jiya turned very red. He had not expected to have the question put to him so directly.

Old Gentleman saw he found it hard to speak. "Say yes or no," he told Jiya.

"No," Jiya said. "I thank you, but I have a home—on the farm," he added.

For a moment Kino was filled with pure joy. Then he remembered the small farmhouse, the four little rooms and the old kitchen. "Jiya," he said solemnly, "remember how poor we are."

Old Gentleman was smiling a half-sad little smile. "They are certainly very poor," he said to Jiya. "And here, you know, you would have everything."

Jiya looked about him. Then he shook his head again.

Old Gentleman took up his brush again. "Very well," he said. "I will do without a son."

The manservant motioned to them and they followed, and soon they were out in the garden.

"How foolish you are," the manservant said to Jiya. "You would have everything here."

"Not everything," Jiya replied.

They went out of the gate and across the hillside and back to the farmhouse. Setsu came running to meet them, the sleeves of the bright kimono flying behind her, and her feet clattering in wooden sandals.

"Jiya has come back home!" she cried.

And Jiya, seeing her happy little face, opened his arms and gave her a great hug. For the first time he felt comfort creep into his heart.

Their noonday meal was ready, and Kino's father came in from the field. And when he had washed, they all sat down to eat. "How happy you have made us," he told Jiya.

"Happy indeed," Kino's mother said.

"Now I have my brother," Kino said.

Jiya smiled. Happiness began to live in him again. The good food warmed him, and his body welcomed it. Around him the love of the people who received him glowed like a warm and welcoming fire upon the hearth.

Sept 14, 98. homework

Reviewing the Selection

Answer each of the following questions without looking back at the story.

Recalling Facts

1. When Kino looks down on the houses in the fishing village, he notices that none of them has
   - ☐ a. vegetable gardens.
   - ☑ b. doors facing the mountain.
   - ☐ c. windows facing the ocean.
   - ☐ d. thatched roofs.

Understanding Main Ideas

2. Kino's father has a realistic outlook on life that has been shaped by
   - ☐ a. Old Gentleman.
   - ☑ b. the land where he lives.
   - ☐ c. the type of work he does.
   - ☐ d. Jiya.

Placing Events in Order

3. Kino and Jiya go to Old Gentleman's house
   - ☐ a. before the big wave strikes.
   - ☑ b. after the big wave strikes.
   - ☐ c. before Old Gentleman says that he wants Jiya to be his son.
   - ☐ d. before Jiya meets Kino's parents.

Finding Supporting Details

4. Kino's father encourages his son to
   - ☑ a. enjoy life and not to fear death.
   - ☐ b. become rich like Old Gentleman.
   - ☐ c. fear volcanoes and the ocean.
   - ☐ d. be a fisherman.

Recognizing Words in Context

5. " 'It is stupid to plow and plant and cut the sheaves, when I could just come out like this and <u>reap</u> fish from the sea.' " In this context *reap* means
   - ☐ a. sell.
   - ☑ b. gather.
   - ☐ c. count.
   - ☐ d. plant.

Interpreting the Selection

Answer each of the following questions. You may look back at the story if necessary.

Making Inferences

6. At the end of the story, Kino's father wants Jiya to
   - ☑ a. live with Old Gentleman.
   - ☐ b. stay on the farm.
   - ☐ c. move back to the fishing village.
   - ☐ d. go to a better school.

Generalizing

7. As a result of the big wave, both Kino and Jiya
   - ☐ a. become fearful of nature for the first time in their lives.
   - ☑ b. learn to accept life in the midst of danger.
   - ☐ c. lose their parents.
   - ☐ d. realize that farming is safer than fishing.

Analyzing Character

8. Kino's father shows his understanding of life when he
   - ☐ a. predicts the earthquake.
   - ☐ b. suggests that Kino wave to Jiya.
   - ☑ c. says that Jiya will be happy again someday.
   - ☐ d. tries to persuade Jiya to return to his village.

Comparing

9. At the beginning of "The Big Wave," Jiya is
   - ☐ a. happier than Kino.
   - ☑ b. more serious than Kino.
   - ☐ c. a better student than Kino.
   - ☐ d. a better swimmer than Kino.

Drawing Conclusions

10. At the end of the story, it appears that
    - ☐ a. Jiya and Kino will no longer be friends.
    - ☐ b. Jiya will marry Setsu.
    - ☐ c. Jiya will forget about his family.
    - ☑ d. Jiya will learn to be happy with Kino's family.

The Short Story: An Overview

What is a short story? How does it differ from a novel? What are the main elements of a short story?

The chief difference between a short story and a novel is length. A short story can usually be read at one sitting, although short stories do vary in length. Some are only two or three pages long. Others are ten or twenty times that length. Novels, on the other hand, are book-length works of literature.

In both short stories and novels, writers build on four main elements: setting, character, plot, and theme. The fourth element, theme, grows out of the first three. However, whereas in a novel the author has almost unlimited space, a short-story writer must develop a unified work in a relatively short space.

In this lesson, you will learn about each of the four elements in a story. You will also see how the author, Pearl Buck, combines the elements to produce a successful story.

Setting

"The Big Wave" begins: "Kino lived on a farm that lay on the side of a mountain in Japan." In that short sentence, Pearl Buck begins to describe the story's setting. Setting is the time and place of the action of a story. In "The Big Wave," setting is important because the place—the environment—plays a major role. It provides the action that is at the heart of the story.

In the first two paragraphs, the author sets the stage on which the action is to take place. Buck describes the mountain where Kino lived, the fishing village at the foot of the mountain, and the sea beyond.

1. On a piece of paper, sketch a map or a diagram based on the details about setting given in the first two paragraphs of "The Big Wave." Indicate where Kino and Jiya live.

Besides telling *where* a story takes place, the setting includes *when* the story takes place. In some stories, the writer gives you an exact date or mentions an event that lets you know the time. In "The Big Wave," however, Pearl Buck does not give a specific date or year. You must figure out the approximate time. Notice how the people in the story live. What entertainments do they have? How do they work? What do those details suggest about the time of the story?

2. Think about what you know about Japan today. Compare your understanding of what Japan is like to the setting in "The Big Wave." Do you think this story is set in the past, present, or future? What clues can you find in the story to support your answer?

By describing the setting, a writer can give you a feeling about what will happen in the story. The feeling may be calm or troubled, happy or sad. The writer can then add details about the setting to change the feeling. For example, at the beginning of "The Big Wave," Buck describes a setting that seems peaceful—a scenic mountain, a quiet fishing village, and a calm ocean. Buck then adds dialogue, or conversation between two or more characters, to show more about the setting.

"The sea is beautiful," Kino points out early on. "The sea is our enemy," Jiya replies. From that dialogue, you learn not only that the sea is important to the story but also that it is dangerous. It is both a place of sparkling-clear water where the boys swim and a frightening natural force.

3. Skim the first three pages of the story. List two details of setting that create a troubled feeling in the story.

Setting is important to all the stories in this book. As you read each story, think about when and where it is taking place. Identifying the setting helps you to understand the world in which the characters live.

Character

Character is the second main element in a short story. Characters are the people, animals, things, or even machines that act or speak in a story. In most stories, you will find both major and minor characters. Major characters are those that have the most important roles. They are involved in the major action of the story, so you often learn a great deal about their personalities. The thoughts and actions of those characters have great meaning for the story.

Minor characters play supporting roles. They may make comments that enlighten the major characters. Sometimes, they help to move the action along in some other way, such as by revealing a new thought or idea to the reader. In some stories, a minor character might be discussed but never appear in the action.

4. List all the characters in "The Big Wave." Put a star next to each major character.

The author of a short story creates well-developed characters in a variety of ways. The most obvious way is to describe the character's physical appearance. Another technique is to detail the character's words, thoughts, and actions. Still another method is to reveal the character's personality through what other characters say or think about him or her.

Pearl Buck gives little physical description of the characters in "The Big Wave." Instead, she lets you learn about the characters from what they say, think, and do. In addition, she tells you what others think and say about the characters. For example, when Jiya says, "The sea is our enemy," he shows his fear of the sea. His actions also show that fear. When the boys go swimming one afternoon, Jiya keeps looking at the sun. When it starts to set, he calls to Kino to go home. Later, Kino discusses Jiya's fear of the ocean with his father. The discussion between Kino and his father reveals many things about both father and son.

> "The ocean is very big," Kino's father replied. "We do not understand the ocean."
>
> "I am glad we live on the mountain," Kino went on. "There is nothing to be afraid of on our farm."
>
> "But one can be afraid of the land, too," his father replied. "Do you remember the volcano we visited last autumn?"

In that passage, Kino wants to assure himself of a safe, secure home. But Kino's father suggests that such security is not possible either on the sea or on the land. He accepts the dangers posed by nature and is teaching his son to do the same. By listening to what characters say, you learn more about them.

5. Find a scene in the story in which you learn about a character from his or her words, thoughts, or actions, or from what others say and think. Describe the situation and explain what you learn about the character.

Plot

The characters of a story are involved in the plot—the sequence of events. The plot is made up of all the actions and events in the story. At the center of every plot are one or more conflicts, or struggles, of one kind or another.

In "The Big Wave," one conflict is the struggle between the people and the forces of nature, such as the ocean. Of course, the people cannot physically fight against the ocean. The conflict centers on the people's will to survive and enjoy life despite the destructive power of nature. Another conflict is Jiya's need to decide whether he will live with Kino's family or with Old Gentleman.

Like the plots in most stories, the plot of "The Big Wave" builds to a climax—the point of greatest interest or highest tension. Usually, the climax is the turning point in a story. As a result of the climax, the fortunes of the main characters change either for the better or for the worse.

In "The Big Wave," as in many other stories, the main character faces one or more crises before the story reaches its climax. Each crisis has an effect on the main character. As the earth begins to tremble and his father orders him to safety, Jiya faces a major crisis. "I don't want to live alone," he says. Jiya's father replies, "It is your duty to obey me, as a good Japanese son." Reluctantly, Jiya obeys his father.

6. How does Jiya behave in the days right after his family is killed? In time, how do his feelings change? Why do you think they change?

After Jiya moves in with Kino's family, the plot moves on toward the climax. The new crisis poses what may be an even more difficult situation for Jiya than the earlier one when his father ordered him to obey. This time he must make his own decision.

7. Think about the plot of "The Big Wave." What is the climax of the story? How do Jiya's circumstances change as a result of the climax?

8. Look back over Kino's role in the plot. Do you think he changes during the story? Explain your answer.

Theme

The fourth element of a short story is <u>theme</u>—the underlying message or meaning of the story. Through the theme, the writer can share his or her insights about life.

Writers seldom state a theme outright. Generally, you must infer the theme by looking at the setting, characters, and plot. From those elements, you can usually figure out what the writer is saying about the human condition.

Like many other stories, "The Big Wave" has more than one theme. The major theme is that people should enjoy and appreciate life even if they must face danger. That theme becomes clear in two conversations between Kino and his father. Even before the big wave, Kino wonders why his family and Jiya's family live in such a dangerous place, where they are threatened by volcanoes and the ocean.

9. Reread the conversation on page 10 that begins, " 'Must we always be afraid of something?' Kino asked." Look carefully at the father's responses to the boy's comments. What does Kino's father say about how Kino should face the dangers of life?

In another conversation, after the big wave destroys the fishing village, Kino and his father again touch on that theme. Kino has seen the destructive power of nature and is suffering for his friend, Jiya.

> "Father, are we not very unfortunate people to live on this island?" he asked.
>
> "Why do you think so?" his father asked in reply.
>
> "Because the volcano is behind our house and the ocean is in front, and when they make the earthquake and the big wave, we are helpless. Often many of us are lost."
>
> "To live in the midst of danger is to know how good life is," his father replied.

Kino's father then goes on to explain why danger and even death are not as frightening as the boy seems to think.

10. How does that conversation between Kino and his father support the theme of the story?

A second, or minor, theme concerns the importance of family. At the beginning of the story, you learn about the two boys and their families. Although you see Jiya's father only once, it is at a momentous point. The father orders Jiya to leave the fishing village and escape danger so that the boy will live even if disaster strikes and his parents are killed. Jiya does not want to obey but does so when his father insists that it is his duty. According to the strong family traditions of Japan, a son must obey his father.

Yet the family also brings warmth and love, as you see in Kino's home. Kino's family welcomes Jiya as a son and as a brother. When Old Gentleman makes an offer to adopt the boy, Kino and his family are saddened at the thought of losing him. Jiya turns down the offer, and Old Gentleman's manservant says, "How foolish you are. . . . You would have everything here." Jiya replies, "Not everything."

11. What do you think Jiya means by his reply? How do his reply and the scene that follows it reinforce what Buck is saying about family?

A successful short story is one that you cannot put down until you finish it. Although you may not notice the story's elements while you are reading, the author has established a setting, developed interesting characters, and caught you up in the plot. If you stop to think about the story afterward, you can pick out its themes. As you read the other stories in this book, remember to look for those elements. Think about how they work together in each story.

Questions for Thought and Discussion

The questions and activities that follow will help you explore "The Big Wave" in more depth and at the same time develop your critical thinking skills.

1. **Extending an Idea.** "The Big Wave" is set in Japan, where volcanoes, earthquakes, and tidal waves pose a threat to the people. Think about the major theme of the story. Can the theme apply to people in other lands? Explain your answer. Everyon has some kind of difficulty and one has to face it and enjoy the beautiful of his life.

2. **Taking a Position.** Compare what Kino's family can offer Jiya to what Old Gentleman offers him. Do you think Jiya made the right choice? Explain your answer. Yes, he wouldn't be happy if he lived with the oldman.

3. **Applying a Quotation.** "The only thing we have to fear is fear itself." That famous statement was made by President Franklin D. Roosevelt during the Great Depression in the United States. Yet it echoes a theme in "The Big Wave." What does Roosevelt's statement mean? How does Roosevelt's statement apply to "The Big Wave"?
   Fear can make you hesitate. discourge you

4. **Analyzing a Description.** Pearl Buck creates vivid images in her story even though she uses very little description. Early on, Jiya looks to see "that the ocean is not angry." Later, Kino's father says about the volcano,

"It looks very angry." What images does the word *angry* create in each case? Find another example in which the author draws a clear picture with just a few words.

Writing About Literature

Several suggestions for writing projects are given below. You may be asked to complete one or more of these projects. If you have any questions about how to begin a writing assignment, review Using the Writing Process , beginning on page 337.

1. **Creating a New Ending.** Think about how "The Big Wave" might have ended if Jiya had chosen to live with Old Gentleman. Write a new ending for the story. Be sure to show how Kino would have felt. Use dialogue to show what Kino's father might have said to his son.
2. **Describing a Natural Occurrence.** On the day of the big wave, Kino's father says, "Earth and sea are struggling against the fires inside the earth." Describe that struggle in scientific terms. Do research in library sources to find out the causes of earthquakes and volcanoes.
3. **Creating Dialogue.** Imagine that you are sent to interview Jiya when he is an adult. Prepare at least five questions to ask him. Include his replies as part of your dialogue.
4. **Writing a Letter.** Imagine that you are Kino and are writing a letter to your cousin telling about the events of the story. First decide what events to include. Then write the letter. In your conclusion, explain what you have learned as a result of those events.

For Sept. 18

Chapter 2

Selection *From Mother . . . with Love*

ZOA SHERBURNE

Lesson *Plot*

About the Selection

What are some qualities you expect from a close friend or family member? You might answer that you expect the person to be willing to listen and to be understanding. You expect the person to be someone you can depend on if you are in trouble. Maybe, too, you expect the person to laugh and share fun times with you.

Both children and adults look for that kind of close friendship. Often, our strongest ties are with parents, brothers, sisters, or other members of our families. But what happens if the ties are broken? Friends can be separated if one moves away or goes to a different school. Family members, too, can be divided for various reasons, including death.

In the story "From Mother . . . with Love," a girl named Minta has a close friendship with her mother. Minta is an only child. She loves and admires her mother, who is always thoughtful and willing to have a good time. Despite the age difference, the two are alike in some ways.

As the story begins, Minta is excited about going to MaryHill, the boarding school that her mother attended as a girl. Because her mother has had a serious operation, Minta has delayed her plans to enter MaryHill. She did not mind the delay because she wanted to help and be with her mother while she was recovering.

As an only child, Minta has a special relationship with both her parents. Usually, parents try to protect their children from the harsher side of life. In this story, however, Minta seems to take on the responsibility of protecting her parents. She tries to keep both her father and her mother from learning what she feels might be hurtful to them.

"From Mother . . . with Love" takes place in the United States. The scenes of family life will be familiar to you even though the story was written about thirty years ago. Despite the differences in time and place between this story and "The Big Wave," which was set in Japan, the two stories have some ideas in common. Like Jiya in "The Big Wave," Minta has strong family ties. She, too, faces a tragic loss and changes as a result of it.

Zoa Sherburne, the author of this story, began writing at an early age. But it was only after she married and had several children that she began to write seriously for publication. From a night-school course in commercial writing, Sherburne went on to sell several short stories to magazines in the early 1950s.

Sherburne's first novel, *Almost April,* was published in 1956. Since then she has published more than fifteen novels and over three hundred short stories and nonfiction articles. Many of her stories, though fiction, are based on real experiences.

Lesson Preview

The lesson that follows "From Mother . . . with Love" focuses on plot. As you read in Chapter 1, plot is the sequence of events in a story. In some stories, the plots are complex and involve a number of related events. In others, the plots are simple and are made up of only a few events. "From Mother . . . with Love" has a fairly simple plot. Like all stories, the plot centers on the conflict, or struggle, faced by the main character.

The action in a story falls into distinct parts as the plot builds to its climax. Usually, the author does not tell you when one part ends and another begins. However, you can identify the different parts by what takes place in them.

The questions that follow will help you recognize the important elements of plot in "From Mother . . . with Love." As you read, think about how you would answer these questions.

1. Who is the main character? What is the main character like?
2. When and how does the author introduce the information that is essential to the plot?
3. Does the tension increase as you read the story? If so, when and why does it increase?
4. What is the climax, or turning point, of the story?
5. How does the story end? How does the main character change as a result of the events in the story?

Vocabulary

Here are some difficult words that appear in the selection that follows. Study the words and their definitions, as well as the sentences that show how the words are used. This will help you get the most from your reading.

poignant deeply moving; having a sharp and deep effect on the feelings. *As the girl boarded the plane, she turned to her parents for the poignant moment of farewell.*

pungent having a sharp or stinging taste or smell. *Somehow the food cooked on an outdoor fire seems to have a more pungent odor than food cooked indoors.*

engrossed completely absorbed. *I was so engrossed in reading the new mystery that I didn't hear the knock at the door.*

constrict to make smaller or narrower; contract. *He felt the muscles in his arms constrict as he lifted the weights.*

complacently with a feeling of satisfaction at what one has done. *The girl smiled complacently as she easily answered the test questions.*

reprovingly in a scolding manner. *The boy spoke reprovingly to his younger brother about his poor grades.*

From Mother . . . with Love

Zoa Sherburne

The day that Minta Hawley grew up was a crisp golden day in early September.

Afterwards she was to remember everything about that day with poignant clarity. She remembered the slapping sound the waves made, the pungent smell of the logs burning, even the gulls that soared and swooped overhead; but most of all she remembered her father's face when he told her.

It began like any other Saturday, with Minta lying in bed an extra hour. Breakfast was always lazy and unhurried on Saturday mornings. The three of them in the breakfast room—Minta's father engrossed in his paper; her mother flying around in a gaily colored housecoat, mixing waffles and frying bacon; Minta setting the table.

They talked, the casual happy talk of people who love each other and don't have to make conversation. About neighborhood doings . . . about items in the paper . . . about the clothes Minta would need when she went away to school in a couple of weeks.

It was after the dishes were finished that Minta's father asked her if she would like to go down to the beach for a little while.

"Low tide," he said. "Might get a few clams."

Minta nodded agreement, but her mother made a little face.

"Horrors, clam chowder for another week!"

"Sure you wouldn't like to go, Mary?" Minta's father asked. "The salt air might help your headache."

"No. You two run along. I'll curl up with an apple and a television program." She yawned and stretched, looking almost as young as Minta.

Minta ran upstairs and got into her heavy shoes and jeans. "Shall I call Sally and ask her if she wants to go?" she yelled, leaning far over the bannister.

"Let's just go by ourselves this time," her father answered rather shortly.

He was silent as they drove toward the beach, but it wasn't the companionable silence that Minta had come to expect from him. There was something grim about it.

"He's going to talk to me about school," Minta told herself. "He's going to try to talk me out of it again."

It was funny the way her father had acted when she announced her intention of going to MaryHill this term. It had always been such an accepted thing; her mother had graduated from MaryHill and it followed that Minta should be enrolled there as a matter of course.

Last year was different. With Mother just recovering from that operation it was natural that he should expect Minta to stay home; she had even *wanted* to stay. But now going to MaryHill was something special. She would live in a dormitory and be part of all the campus fun. It wasn't as if MaryHill were clear across the country, either, she'd probably be getting home every month or so . . . and there were the Christmas holidays . . . and then spring vacation.

Minta's chin was lifted in a stubborn line as her father parked the car and went around to get the shovels and pail from the trunk.

jolly - cheerful.

It wasn't like him to be so stubborn, usually he was jolly and easy-going and inclined to leave such matters entirely up to Minta's mother.

She followed him down to the beach, her boots squishing in the wet sand. The tide was far out and farther up the beach she could see bent figures busily digging along the water's edge.

A scattered beach fire smoldered near the bank and Minta poked it into place and revived it with splinters of driftwood until she had coaxed back a steady warming blaze. When she sat back on her heels to smile up at her father she felt her throat constrict with a smothering fear. His eyes looked the way they had when . . .

When?

Suddenly she remembered. He was looking at her and trying to smile, just the way he had looked at her the time her appendix burst and they were taking her to the hospital. She could almost hear the wail of the ambulance siren and feel the way he had held her hands tightly, trying to make it easier. His eyes had told her then, as they told her now, that he would a thousand times rather bear the pain than watch her suffer.

It seemed like a long time that she knelt there by the beach fire, afraid to move, childishly willing herself to wake from the nightmarish feeling that gripped her.

He took her hand and pulled her to her feet and they started walking up the beach slowly, not toward the group of people digging clams, but in the other direction, toward the jagged pile of rocks that jutted out into the bay.

She heard a strange voice, her own voice.

"I thought . . . I thought you wanted to talk to me about school, but it isn't that, is it, Father?"

Father.

She never called him Father. It was always "Dad" or "Pops" or, when she was feeling especially gay, "John Henry."

His fingers tightened around hers. "In a way it is . . . about school."

And then, before the feeling of relief could erase the fear he went on. "I went to see Dr. Morton last week, Minta. I've been seeing him pretty regularly these last few months."

She flashed a quick frightened look up at him. "You aren't ill?"

"No." He sighed and it was a heartbreaking sound. "No. It isn't me. It's your mother. That's why I don't want you to go to MaryHill this year."

"But . . . but she's feeling so much better, Dad. Except for these headaches once in a while. She's even taking on a little weight—" She broke off and stopped walking and her hand was steady on his arm. "Tell me," she said quietly.

The look was back in his eyes again but this time Minta scarcely noticed it, she was aware only of his words, the dreadful echoing finality of his words.

Her mother was going to die.

To die.

Her mother.

To die, the doctor said. Three months, perhaps less. . . .

Her mother who was gay and scatterbrained and more fun than anyone else in the world. Her mother who could be counted on to announce in the spring that she was going to do her Christmas shopping early *this* year, and then left everything until the week before Christmas.

No one was worse about forgetting anniversaries and birthdays and things like that; but the easy-to-remember dates, like Valentine's Day and St. Patrick's Day and Halloween were always gala affairs complete with table favors and three-decker cakes.

Minta's mother wore the highest heels and the maddest hats of any mother on the block. She was so pretty. And she always had time for things like listening to new records and helping paste pictures in Minta's scrapbook.

She wasn't ever sick—except for the headaches and the operation last year which she had laughingly dismissed as a rest cure.

"I shouldn't have told you." Her father was speaking in a voice that Minta had never heard from him before. A voice that held loneliness and fear and a sort of angry pain. "I was afraid I couldn't make you understand, why you had to stay home . . . why you'd have to forget about MaryHill for this year." His eyes begged her to forgive him and for some reason she wanted to put her arms around him, as if she were much older and stronger.

"Of course you had to tell me," she said steadily. "Of course I had to know." And then—"Three months, but Dad, that's *Christmas.*"

He took her hand and tucked it under his arm and they started walking again.

It was like walking through a nightmare. The steady squish-squish of the wet sand and the little hollows their feet made filling up almost as soon as they passed.

He talked quietly, explaining, telling her everything the doctor had said, and Minta listened without tears, without comment.

She watched his face as though it were the face of a stranger.

She thought about a thousand unrelated things.

Last winter when he had chased her and her mother around the back yard to wash their faces in the new snow. She could still see the bright red jacket her mother had worn . . . the kerchief that came off in the struggle . . . the way the neighbors had watched from their windows, laughing and shaking their heads.

She remembered all the times they had gone swimming this past summer. Minta and her father loved to swim but her mother had preferred to curl up on a beach blanket and watch them.

"You have the disposition of a Siamese cat," Minta had accused her mother laughingly. "A cushion by the fire in the winter and a cushion in the sun in the summer. . . ."

"And a bowl of cream nearby," her mother had agreed instantly.

She was always good-natured about their teasing.

But in spite of her apparent frailty and her admitted laziness she managed to accomplish an astounding amount of work. Girl Scouts, PTA, Church bazaars, Red Cross. People were always calling her to head a committee or organize a drive. Young people congregated in her home. Not just Minta's gang, but the neighborhood youngsters. She had Easter egg hunts for them; she bought their raffle tickets and bandaged their skinned knees.

It was like coming back from a long journey when her father stopped talking and they turned back toward the car.

"So that's why I can't let you go away, Midge." Her father's voice was very low and he didn't seem to realize that he had called her by the babyish name she had discarded when she started to first grade. "It isn't just your mother I'm thinking about . . . it's me. I need you."

She looked at him quickly and her heart twisted with pity. He did need her. He would need her more than ever.

In the car she sat very close to him.

"We didn't get the clams," she reminded him once, but he only nodded.

Just before they reached home he reached over and took her hand in a tight hurting grip.

"We can't tell her, Minta. The doctor left it up to me and I said not to tell her. We have to let her have this last time . . . this last little time . . . without that hanging over her. We have to go on as if everything were exactly the same."

She nodded to show that she understood. After a moment she spoke past the ache in her throat. "About school. I'll . . . I'll tell her that I decided to wait until next year. Or that I'm afraid I'd be lonesome without the gang. I've been sort of . . . sort of seesawing back and forth, anyway."

It seemed impossible that life could go on exactly as before.

The small private world peopled by the three of them was as snug and warm and happy as though no shadow had touched them.

They watched television and argued goodnaturedly about the programs. Minta's friends came and went and there was the usual round of parties and dances and games. Her father continued to bowl two evenings a week and her mother became involved in various preholiday pursuits.

"I really must get at my Christmas shopping," she mentioned the day she was wrapping trick-or-treat candy for Halloween.

Minta shook her head and sighed gustily.

Her mother started this "I-must-get-at-my-Christmas-shopping" routine every spring and followed it up until after Thanksgiving but she never actually got around to it until two or three days before Christmas.

It was amazing that Minta could laugh and say, "Oh, *you* . . ." the way she did year after year.

It was a knife turning in her heart when her mother straightened up from the gay cellophane-wrapped candies and brushed a stray wisp of taffy-colored hair back from one flushed cheek.

"Don't laugh," she said, pretending to be stern. "You know you're just exactly like me."

It was a warming thought. She *was* like her mother. Inside, where it really mattered she was like her mother, even though she had her father's dark eyes and straight black hair, even though she had his build and the firm chin of all the Hawleys.

She wanted to put her arm around her mother and hug her, hard. She wanted to say, "I hope I am like you. I want to be."

But instead she got up and stretched and wrinkled her nose.

"Perish forbid," she said, "that I should be such a scatterbrain."

She was rewarded by the flash of a dimple in her mother's cheek.

It seemed to Minta, as week followed week, that the day at the beach had been something out of a nightmare: something that she could push away from her and forget about. Sometimes she looked at her father, laughing, teasing them, or howling about the month-end bills and she thought, "It didn't happen . . . it isn't true."

And then at night she would lie sleepless in her room, the pretty room that had been reconverted from her nursery. She watched the moonlight drift patterns across the yellow bedspread and the breeze billow the curtains that her mother had made by hand, because that was the only way she could be sure of an absolute match.

"Yellow is such a difficult color to match," she had explained around a mouthful of pins.

And in the dark hours of the night Minta had known it wasn't a nightmare. It was true. It was true.

One windy November day she hurried home from school and found her mother in the yard raking leaves. She wore a bright kerchief over her head and she had Minta's old polo coat belted around her. She looked young and gay and carefree and her eyes were shining.

"Hi!" She waved the rake invitingly. "Change your clothes and come help. We'll have a smudge party in the alley."

Minta stopped and leaned on the gate. She saw with a new awareness that there were dark circles under her mother's eyes and that the flags of color in her cheeks were too bright. But she managed a chuckle.

"I wish you could see yourself, Mom. For two cents I'd get my camera and take a picture of you."

She ran into the house and got her camera and they took a whole roll of pictures.

"Good," her mother said complacently. "Now we can show them to your father the next time he accuses me of being a Sally-Sit-by-the-Fire."

They piled the leaves into a huge damp stack, with the help of half a dozen neighborhood children. It wouldn't burn properly but gave out with clouds of thick, black, wonderfully pungent smoke.

Her mother was tired that night. She lay on the davenport and made out her Christmas card list while Minta and her father watched the wrestling matches. It was like a thousand other such evenings but in some unaccountable way it was different.

"Because it's the last time," Minta told herself. "The last time we'll ever rake the leaves and make a bonfire in the alley. The last time I'll snap a picture of her with her arms around the Kelly kids. The last time . . . the last time. . . ."

She got up quickly and went out into the kitchen and made popcorn in the electric popper, bringing a bowl to her mother first, remembering just the way she liked it, salt and not too much butter.

But that night she wakened in the chilly darkness of her room and began to cry, softly, her head buried in the curve of her arm. At first it helped, loosening the tight bands about her heart, washing away the fear and the loneliness, but when she tried to stop she found that she couldn't. Great wracking sobs shook her until she could no longer smother them against her pillow. And then the light was on and her mother was there bending over her, her face concerned, her voice soothing.

"Darling, what is it? Wake up, baby, you're having a bad dream."

"No . . . no, it isn't a dream," Minta choked. "It's true . . . it's true."

The thin hand kept smoothing back her tumbled hair and her mother went on talking in the tone she had always used to comfort a much smaller Minta.

She was aware that her father had come to the doorway. He said nothing, just stood there watching them while Minta's sobs diminished into hiccupy sighs.

Her mother pulled the blanket up over Minta's shoulder and gave her a little spank. "The idea! Gollywogs, at your age," she said reprovingly. "Want me to leave the light on in case your spook comes back?"

Minta shook her head, blinking against the tears that crowded against her eyelids, even managing a wobbly smile.

She never cried again.

Not even when the ambulance came a week later to take her mother to the hospital. Not even when she was standing beside her mother's high white hospital bed, holding her hand tightly, forcing herself to chatter of inconsequential things.

"Be sure that your father takes his vitamin pills, won't you, Minta? He's so careless unless I'm there to keep an eye on him."

"I'll watch him like a beagle," Minta promised lightly. "Now you behave yourself and get out of here in a hurry, you hear?"

Not even at the funeral. . . .

The friends and relatives came and went and it was as if she stood on the sidelines watching the Minta who talked with them and answered their questions. As if her heart were encased in a shell that kept it from breaking.

She went to school and came home afterwards to the empty house. She tried to do the things her mother had done but even with the help of well-meaning friends and neighbors it was hard. She tried not to hate the people who urged her to cry.

"You'll feel better, dear," her Aunt Grace had insisted and then had lifted her handkerchief to her eyes and walked away when Minta had only stared at her with chilling indifference.

She overheard people talking about her mother.

"She never knew, did she?" they asked.

And always Minta's father answered, "No, she never knew. Even at the very last, when she was waiting for the ambulance to come she looked around the bedroom and said, 'I must get these curtains done up before Christmas.' "

Minta knew that her father was worried about her and she was sorry, but it was as if there were a wall between them, a wall that she was too tired to surmount.

One night he came to the door of her room where she was studying.

"I wonder if you'd like to go through those clothes before your Aunt Grace takes them to the church bazaar," he began haltingly. And then when she looked up at him, not understanding, he went on gently, "Your mother's clothes. We thought someone might as well get some good out of them."

She stood up and closed the book and went past him without another word, but she closed the door behind her when she went into her mother's room.

There were some suit boxes by the closet door and Minta vaguely remembered that the women from the bazaar committee had called several times.

Her hands felt slightly unsteady as she pulled open the top dresser drawer and looked down at the stacks of clean handkerchiefs, the stockings in their quilted satin case, the gloves folded into tissue wrappings.

"I can't do it," she told herself, but she got a box and started putting the things into it, trying not to look at them, trying to forget how delighted her mother had been with the pale green slip, trying not to remember.

Once she hesitated and almost lifted a soft wool sweater from the pile that was growing in the suit box. She had borrowed it so often that her mother used to complain that she felt like a criminal every time she borrowed it back again. She didn't mean it though . . . she loved having Minta borrow her things.

Minta put the sweater with the other things and closed the box firmly.

Now, the things in the closet—

Opening the door was almost like feeling her mother in the room beside her. A faint perfume clung to most of her garments. The housecoat . . . the woolly robe . . . the tan polo coat . . . the scarlet jacket . . . her new blue wool with the pegtop skirt.

Minta started folding the things with almost frantic haste, stuffing them into boxes, cramming the lids on and then starting on another box.

At the very back of the closet were the two pieces of matched luggage that had been her mother's last birthday gift from her father. They were heavy when she tried to move them—too heavy.

She brought them out into the room and put them side by side on her mother's bed. Her breath caught in her throat when she opened them.

Dozens and dozens of boxes, all tied with bright red ribbon, the gift tags written out in her mother's careful script. Gaily colored Christmas stickers, sprigs of holly.

To Minta from Mother and Dad . . . to Grace from Mary . . . to John from Mary . . . to the Kelly Gremlins from Aunt Mary . . . to Uncle Art from the Hawley family . . .

"So you knew," Minta whispered the words. "You knew all the time." She looked down in surprise as a hot tear dropped on her hand and she dashed it away almost impatiently.

She picked up another package and read the tag. To Minta from Mother . . . with love.

Without opening it she knew that it was a picture frame and she remembered the way she had teased her mother to have a good photograph taken.

"The only one I have of you looks like a fugitive from a chain gang," she had pointed out. "I can't very well go away to school next year with *that.*"

She put the package back in the suitcase with all the others and carried the cases back into the closet.

Poor Dad, she thought.

"She never knew," she could hear him saying. "Not even at the last."

Minta opened the box beside the bed and took out the sweater and the pale green slip.

"You know perfectly well that you're just exactly like me," she remembered her mother saying.

She brushed the tears away and went down the stairs and out into the cheerless living room.

"I'd like to keep these things, Dad," she said in her most matter-of-fact voice, and she showed him the sweater and slip. "The slip is a little big but I'll grow into it. It . . . it looks like her, I think."

She went around the room, snapping on the lamps, turning on the television that had been silent for so long. She was aware that his eyes followed her, that he could hardly avoid noticing the tear stains on her cheeks.

"I think I'll have an apple," she said. "Want one?"

He nodded. "Sure. Bring me one as long as you're making the trip."

It was natural. It was almost like old times, except that the blue chair by the fireplace was vacant.

She went out into the kitchen hurriedly.

"I'll tell him that I pestered mother to do her shopping early this year," she told herself as she got the apples from the refrigerator. "I'll tell him that it was my idea about the photographs. She wanted him to believe that she didn't know."

The vitamin pills were pushed back on a shelf. She took them out of the refrigerator and put them on the window sill where she would be sure to see them in the morning.

When she came back into the living room she noticed that a light in a Christmas wreath was winking on and off in the Kellys' window across the street.

"I guess we should start thinking about Christmas, Dad." She tossed him an apple as she spoke and he caught it deftly.

She hesitated for just a moment and then walked over and sat down in the blue chair by the fire, as if she belonged there, and looked across at her father, and smiled.

Reviewing the Selection

It is a touching story

Answer each of the following questions without looking back at the story.

Recalling Facts

1. When Minta and her father go to the beach, she is afraid that he will
   - ☒ a. ask her to forget about going to MaryHill.
   - ☐ b. scold her for not finding enough clams.
   - ☐ c. say that he is ill.
   - ☐ d. tell her that her mother is dying.

Understanding Main Ideas

2. "From Mother . . . with Love" is about how Minta
   - ☐ a. talks to her mother about death.
   - ☐ b. learns to love her father.
   - ☑ c. grows into a mature young woman.
   - ☐ d. changes when she goes away to school.

Placing Events in Order

3. The first time Minta cried was
   - ☑ a. before her mother went to the hospital.
   - ☐ b. while her mother was in the hospital.
   - ☐ c. on the day her mother died.
   - ☐ d. at her mother's funeral.

Finding Supporting Details

4. Toward the end of the story, Minta realized that her mother had known she was dying. What evidence lets Minta know this?
   - ☐ a. her mother's green slip
   - ☐ b. some pictures of her mother
   - ☑ c. the wrapped Christmas presents
   - ☐ d. her mother's diary

Recognizing Words in Context

5. " 'You have the disposition of a Siamese cat,' Minta had accused her mother laughingly." In this context *disposition* means
   - ☐ a. appetite.
   - ☐ b. coloring.
   - ☑ c. temperament.
   - ☐ d. fame.

Interpreting the Selection

Answer each of the following questions. You may look back at the story if necessary.

Making Inferences

6. On the night that Minta cried, her mother comforted her as though she were having a bad dream. Why did Minta's mother pretend that her daughter was having a bad dream?
   - ☐ a. She knew that Minta had often had bad dreams as a child.
   - ☐ b. She thought that crying was unhealthy, and she wanted Minta to stop.
   - ☐ c. She knew the crying upset Minta's father.
   - ☑ d. By pretending that Minta had no reason to cry, she could keep their time together as normal as possible.

Generalizing

7. After learning that her mother was dying, Minta was surprised that
   - ☐ a. her mother then lived for so long.
   - ☑ b. life went on as before.
   - ☐ c. her friends could not tell how sick her mother was.
   - ☐ d. no one visited them anymore.

Analyzing Character

8. Which of the following adjectives best describes Minta's character?
   - ☐ a. selfish
   - ☑ b. considerate
   - ☐ c. moody
   - ☐ d. competitive

Comparing

9. By the end of the story, how has Minta changed?
   - ☑ a. She has become more like her mother.
   - ☐ b. She is relieved that her mother's suffering has ended.
   - ☐ c. She is angry about her mother's death.
   - ☐ d. She has become depressed and withdrawn.

Drawing Conclusions

10. After Minta found the suitcases, she went into the living room, turned on the lights and the television, and suggested that she and her father start thinking about Christmas. Those actions showed that Minta
    - ☐ a. thought they should stop mourning for her mother.
    - ☑ b. knew she was just like her mother.
    - ☐ c. had decided to go to MaryHill.
    - ☐ d. was pretending that her mother was still alive.

Plot

Have you ever heard the expression "the plot thickens"? Perhaps someone used it to describe a mystery story. Or you might have read it in a comic strip. The expression means that the story is becoming more suspenseful or that the intrigue is growing more complex. As the plot thickens, events that will have a great effect on the story's main characters follow each other in rapid succession.

That quickening of interest is part of a story's plot. The plot includes all the events of the story, from the beginning to the end. Plot is central to most stories. It always involves a conflict, or struggle, of some kind. The characters in a story carry out the action.

A plot usually has five sections, which you will read about in this lesson. The first is the exposition, in which important background information is given and the conflict is introduced. The exposition leads into the rising action, in which the tension of the story increases and complications build the conflict. The action then heads toward the climax, which is, as you learned in Chapter 1, the point of greatest interest and highest tension. The climax is followed by the falling action, in which the action begins to slow down. The final section of plot is the resolution, or conclusion, in which the conflict ends.

The five sections of the plot can be fit into a diagram, such as the one that follows. As you read this lesson, think about where events in "From Mother . . . with Love" belong on the diagram.

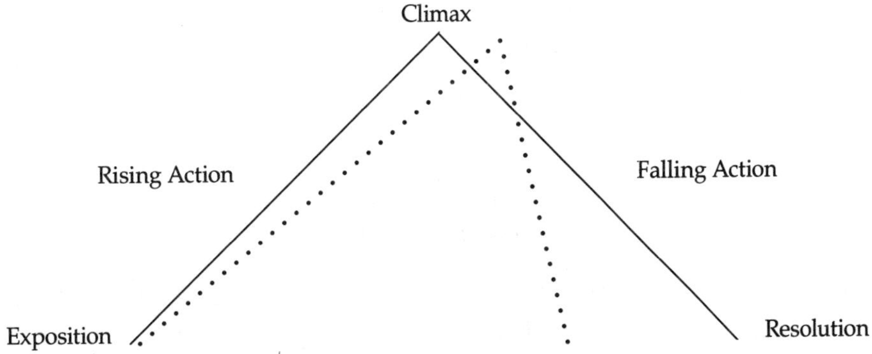

Most plots include the five parts shown in this diagram. However, writers spend differing amounts of time on each part. If a writer spends an equal amount of time developing each stage, the plot could be diagramed as the solid line shows. On the other hand, a story that slowly builds to a climax and then ends suddenly could be diagramed as the dotted line shows.

Exposition

The exposition is usually found at the beginning of a story. It explains the background of the story and introduces the characters. You learn about the characters' personalities, and you get a hint, or sometimes a detailed picture, of the conflict. In "From Mother . . . with Love," the exposition paints a picture of a small, happy family.

1. Look at the beginning of the story. What characters are introduced in the exposition? Write two adjectives that describe the personalities of each. Does the author hint at any problems facing the family? If so, find one or more sentences that suggest those problems.

The exposition also establishes the setting of the story. Often the setting is central to the action. For example, if you know that a story is set in the Arctic during winter, you might expect the main characters to face the dangers of a harsh, cold environment.

In "From Mother . . . with Love," you learn right away that the time is a Saturday in early September. The place is Minta Hawley's home. In the first few paragraphs, the author carefully works in many details that tell you about Minta's home and family.

2. List at least three details about Minta's home life that you learn from the exposition. Then write a sentence or two describing the general atmosphere of Minta's home.

It is a typical, happy family in The state

Rising Action

The second stage of the plot is the rising action. In this stage the problem that the main character must solve comes into focus. Each event adds complications that build the conflict in the story. As a result, the tension increases.

In some stories you can almost feel the change from the exposition to the rising action. For example, the movement from exposition into rising action is fairly clear in "From Mother . . . with Love." The first five paragraphs are largely description without dialogue. Then Mr. Hawley says, "Low tide. Might get a few clams." That dialogue marks the end of the exposition and the beginning of the rising action. At the beach, the tension increases when Mr. Hawley tells Minta what Dr. Morton has said about her mother's condition.

3. Reread the scene that follows Mr. Hawley's suggestion that he and Minta go the the beach. Look at the paragraphs in which Minta and her father are driving to the beach. What words or phrases show that the tension is beginning to build? The silent that was not the companionable silen-

The events of the rising action capture the reader's interest. Sometimes at this stage, you find that you do not want to stop reading a story. You just have to find out what happens next. How will the main character deal with the new complications? How will the story end? The writer has succeeded in involving you in the plot and the characters. Now you move along with the characters, living through events with them.

At the beach with her father, Minta learns that her mother is dying. A thousand thoughts go through her mind as she listens to her father's explanation. Then he tells her how much he needs her. On their way home he says that he wants to keep her mother from knowing how ill she is.

At this point, you know one outcome of the story—Minta's mother will die. But you do not know how Minta and her father will live through the next few months. Nor do you know if they will be able to keep up the pretense that Mrs. Hawley is going to be all right.

Minta wants her mom to be happy.

4. Why do you think Minta agrees to the pretense that all is well with her mother? How does the pretense add to the story's tension?

Minta has to be very careful to preten every thing is alright.

After Minta learns that her mother is dying, she is surprised that her world is still normal. Family life goes on as before. Her friends visit. She and her mother tease each other as usual. Despite the appearance of normality, Minta feels the strain. She must behave as if everything is all right, even though she knows that her mother will die soon.

One night after raking leaves with her mother, Minta's pretense fails. She sobs into her pillow. Her parents hear her crying, but they do not discuss what is really troubling her. Instead, Minta's mother teases her about having a bad dream.

Climax

The rising action leads toward the climax. At the climax, the major problem, or conflict, is most intense. The main character must come to terms with that conflict. Although much of the story focuses on the impending death of Minta's mother, the death itself is not the main problem. Rather, the major conflict involves Minta's struggle to face her mother's death. She pretends for so long that her mother is not dying that she cannot accept the reality of her mother's death.

The climax of "From Mother . . . with Love" occurs when Minta finally comes to grips with her denial of her mother's death. One day her father asks if she will sort and pack her mother's clothes. Minta's emotions are in turmoil as she starts the job. "I can't do it," she tells herself, but then she does it. She goes through her mother's clothes, packing them in boxes. Minta lets herself remember her mother's delight with the pale green slip and how they teased each other over the sweater that Minta used to borrow from her mother. Then she discovers the two suitcases with their all-too-revealing contents—the wrapped Christmas presents.

5. What is significant about the climax? Explain why you think it is so important?

Falling Action and Resolution

After the climax of a story, the action begins to slow down. This section of the plot, called the falling action, shows the effects of the major events. In "From Mother . . . with Love," you see Minta go downstairs and tell her father that she is keeping her mother's sweater and her slip. She then turns on the lights and tries to return a sense of normal life to "the cheerless living room."

The falling action leads into the resolution—the conclusion of the story, in which the conflict ends. In the resolution you see how the main character has grown or changed. In this story the author provides a clear resolution: Sherburne shows that Minta has accepted her mother's death. However, not all stories have a resolution. In some, you must figure out how the conflict might be resolved.

6. Describe three actions that show that Minta has accepted her situation. How do those actions show that Minta has changed?

Plot and the Order of Events

Many short stories present the action in chronological order; that is, the arrangement of events in the order in which they occur. The plot begins at one point in time and moves forward to another. Chronological order is easy for the reader to follow. However, writers do not always write their stories in that order.

A writer may, for instance, use a flashback—a scene, a conversation, or an event that interrupts the present action to show something that happened in the past. The flashback is a memory shown through the eyes of one of the characters. A flashback can add to the tension of the story by giving the reader new information about the characters or the events taking place.

In "From Mother . . . with Love," Zoa Sherburne uses quite a few flashbacks. All of them involve Minta's memories of her mother. The first one falls early in the story, when Minta goes to the beach with her father. Minta thinks that her father is going to ask her not to go away to school, as he had the year before.

Look at the paragraph on page 37 that begins, "Last year was different." In that flashback, you learn that Minta's mother has had a serious operation. The memory is painful to Minta. As a result of the flashback, however, you learn that Minta had gladly put aside her dream of going to MaryHill so that she could stay with her mother. But now Minta is ready to go away to school.

7. Find two other flashbacks in the story. First describe what you learn from them. Then explain how Minta feels about each memory.

Zoa Sherburne could have written this story in strict chronological order. She could have started with Mrs. Hawley's operation. Then she could have shown the family returning to normal, chasing each other in the winter snow and swimming at the beach in the summer. In that way, she could have included all the events revealed in the flashbacks. However, the story might not have been as interesting. By using flashbacks, the writer added to the tension and heightened interest in the story.

As you read the other stories in this book, look for the elements of plot. Think about how the action in each story fits into the diagram at the beginning of this lesson.

Questions for Thought and Discussion

The questions and activities that follow will help you explore "From Mother . . . with Love" in more depth and at the same time develop your critical thinking skills.

1. **Comparing and Contrasting.** In "The Big Wave," Jiya loses his parents, while in "From Mother . . . with Love," Minta loses her mother. How are Jiya's and Minta's reactions to death similar? How are they different?

2. **Interpreting.** Review Minta's actions at the end of the story. What role does she appear to be playing? Why has she taken on that role? Support your answer with details from the story.

3. **Debating.** Organize a debate about Mr. Hawley's decision to keep his wife's illness a secret. One group should take a position in favor of his decision. The other group should take the opposing position. Each side should prepare arguments—reasons—to support its position. After the debate, students should vote on which set of arguments they found most convincing.

4. **Identifying Alternative Solutions.** Why do you think Minta decided not to tell her father about the Christmas gifts? What might have happened if she had told him about the gifts?
Her mom didn't want her father know.

Writing About Literature

Several suggestions for writing projects are given below. You may be asked to complete one or more of these projects. If you have any questions about how to begin a writing assignment, review Using the Writing Process, beginning on page 337.

1. **Preparing a Logical Argument.** If Minta's mother knew she was dying, why do you think she did not speak about it to her husband and daughter? List the reasons why she may have kept her knowledge secret. Using your list, write a paragraph or two in which you present the possible reasons for her decision, beginning with the most important and working your way to the least important.

2. **Creating Dialogue.** Create a page or two of dialogue between Minta and her father after Minta sits in her mother's chair at the end of the story. The conversation should reveal how each feels about the death of Mrs. Hawley.

3. **Outlining a Plot.** Outline a plot for a short story about the happiest or the saddest time in your life. Begin by listing the five parts of the plot that you studied in this chapter. Then, for each plot part, briefly describe what you would include for your story.

4. **Writing a Eulogy.** Imagine that you were asked to give a eulogy for Minta's mother at her funeral. A eulogy is a speech praising someone who has just died. Your eulogy should be long enough so that you can say something significant in it about Minta's mother.

Chapter 3

Selection *Through the Tunnel*

Doris Lessing

Lesson *Conflict*

About the Selection

What does it feel like to leave childhood and begin to grow up? How do children know that it is time to strike out on their own? How can they become independent of their parents?

Everyone experiences the challenges of growing up. At some point, you begin to make decisions for yourself. Making choices is hard. It involves you in uncertainties about whether or not you can succeed. But making choices can also be very rewarding. As you have seen, Jiya in "The Big Wave" and Minta in "From Mother . . . with Love" each faced a devastating loss and then made important, positive decisions about how they would put their lives back together.

The main character in Doris Lessing's story "Through the Tunnel" is an eleven-year-old boy who is caught up in making important choices for himself. He is struggling toward a goal that will give him a sense of pride and achievement.

The boy's name is Jerry. While Jerry and his mother are on vacation on the French coast, he involves himself in a challenging adventure. Although Jerry loves his mother, he wants to break away from her protectiveness. The adventure offers him that escape.

Jerry's adventure involves a challenge, a test of his physical endurance and of his mental courage. That challenge is posed by the sea. Before Jerry can achieve his goal, he experiences rejection and fear. He also learns patience and persistence. By the end of the story, Jerry has left his childhood behind and acquired a greater sense of himself.

Think about the title of this story, "Through the Tunnel." What images does a tunnel bring to mind? Perhaps you think of a railroad tunnel or a highway tunnel that passes through a mountain.

Some people feel great anxiety when they go through a tunnel. They desperately want to reach the opening at the other end. For the brief time it takes to pass through a tunnel, the person is trapped in a tiny, enclosed world. The tunnel in this story is an underwater cave with openings at both ends. The space inside the underwater tunnel is even more limited than in most tunnels. As you read the story, think about what the tunnel means to Jerry.

Doris Lessing, the author of this short story, has been called one of the most important fiction writers of our time. She has published more than a dozen novels, nine books of short stories, seven plays, and numerous poems and essays. Many of her works of fiction concern the problems of women living on their own.

Lessing was born in Persia (Iran) in 1919. Five years later her father moved the family to a farm in southern Africa. When Lessing was thirty, she moved to England, where she began writing about her experiences in Africa. Her first novel, *The Grass Is Singing,* deals with the relationships between a white farm woman, her husband, and a black servant.

In her later novels, Lessing often explored themes involving the relationships between men and women. She was also concerned with various social issues. Even before the women's movement of the 1960s, Lessing wrote several major novels that focused on women's issues.

Lesson Preview

The lesson that follows "Through the Tunnel" focuses on conflict, an important element of plot in any short story. A conflict can be an argument between two people, a person's battle against society, a contest with nature, or a struggle within a person's mind. Conflict creates tension and excitement. That tension helps to turn a series of related events into a gripping tale.

At first, "Through the Tunnel" may seem to be a simple story. If you look more closely, however, you will see that it has several conflicts. The questions that follow will help you recognize those conflicts. As you read, think about how you would answer these questions.

He has to improve his ability to stay longer under water.

1 What physical conflict does Jerry face in the course of the story? What conflict does Jerry have with another person? How does that person feel about the conflict?

He wanted to join the group of the men

2 Jerry has a conflict within himself. What is it? He wants to become a mature person. He wants to achieve his goal.

3 What is the most exciting moment of the story? How is the excitement related to the conflict in the story? He discover the tunnel successfully.

It means Jerry

4 How are the various conflicts in the story solved? Are they solved all at once, or separately? How do the conflicts in the story cause Jerry to change?

Vocabulary

Here are some difficult words that appear in the selection that follows. Study the words and their definitions, as well as the sentences that show how the words are used. This will help you get the most from your reading.

luminous giving off light; bright. *The metal rooftops were luminous in the bright moonlight.*

buoyant able to float. *Because the cork was buoyant, it bobbed along the surface of the water.*

myriads countless numbers. *Myriads of mosquitoes attacked us each night.*

convulsive moving in a sudden, sharp, twitching way. *After a convulsive start, the old engine ran smoothly.*

Internal conflict – ① depend on mom or independent! ② wants to be like the big boys (man) but still acted like a child. ③ eager to be like a big boy (man). ④ there are some barrier that make it difficult to grow up. ⑤ he determin to do that dangeous adventure.

External conflict – ① stay at safety beach or rocky coast! ② rejected by the big boys. ③ He has to search for the turnnel by himself. (can't see clear, afraid of somethig strange) ④ learn to control his breathing. ⑤ the bleeding nose and physical limited ⑥ struggle with either go through it or not. ⑦ went through the tunnel successfully

Through the Tunnel

DORIS LESSING

Going to the shore on the first morning of the vacation, the young English boy stopped at a turning of the path and looked down at a wild and rocky bay, and then over to the crowded beach he knew so well from other years. His mother walked on in front of him, carrying a bright striped bag in one hand. Her other arm, swinging loose, was very white in the sun. The boy watched that white naked arm, and turned his eyes, which had a frown behind them, towards the bay and back again to his mother. When she felt he was not with her, she swung around. "Oh, there you are, Jerry!" she said. She looked impatient, then smiled. "Why, darling, would you rather not come with me? Would you rather—" She frowned, conscientiously worrying over what amusements he might secretly be longing for, which she had been too busy or too careless to imagine. He was very familiar with that anxious, apologetic smile. Contrition[1] sent him running after her. And

1. contrition: a feeling of remorse.

yet, as he ran, he looked back over his shoulder at the wild bay; and all morning, as he played on the safe beach, he was thinking of it.

Next morning, when it was time for the routine of swimming and sunbathing, his mother said, "Are you tired of the usual beach, Jerry? Would you like to go somewhere else?"

"Oh, no!" he said quickly, smiling at her out of that unfailing impulse of contrition—a sort of chivalry. Yet, walking down the path with her, he blurted out, "I'd like to go and have a look at those rocks down there."

She gave the idea her attention. It was a wild-looking place, and there was no one there; but she said, "Of course, Jerry. When you've had enough, come to the big beach. Or just go straight back to the villa, if you like." She walked away, that bare arm, now slightly reddened from yesterday's sun, swinging. And he almost ran after her again, feeling it unbearable that she should go by herself, but he did not.

She was thinking, Of course, he's old enough to be safe without me. Have I been keeping him too close? He mustn't feel he ought to be with me. I must be careful.

He was an only child, eleven years old. She was a widow. She was determined to be neither possessive nor lacking in devotion. She went worrying off to her beach.

As for Jerry, once he saw that his mother had gained her beach, he began the steep descent to the bay. From where he was, high up among red-brown rocks, it was a scoop of moving bluish green fringed with white. As he went lower, he saw that it spread among small promontories[2] and inlets of rough, sharp rock, and the crisping, lapping surface showed stains of purple and darker blue. Finally, as he ran sliding and scraping down the last few yards, he saw an edge of white surf and the shallow, luminous movement of water over white sand, and beyond that, a solid, heavy blue.

He ran straight into the water and began swimming. He was a good swimmer. He went out fast over the gleaming sand, over a middle region

2. promontories: peaks of high land jutting out into a sea.

where rocks lay like discolored monsters under the surface, and then he was in the real sea—a warm sea where irregular cold currents from the deep water shocked his limbs.

When he was so far out that he could look back not only on the little bay but past the promontory that was between it and the big beach, he floated on the buoyant surface and looked for his mother. There she was, a speck of yellow under an umbrella that looked like a slice of orange peel. He swam back to shore, relieved at being sure she was there, but all at once very lonely.

On the edge of a small cape that marked the side of the bay away from the promontory was a loose scatter of rocks. Above them, some boys were stripping off their clothes. They came running, naked, down to the rocks. The English boy swam towards them, but kept his distance at a stone's throw. They were of that coast; all of them were burned smooth dark brown and speaking a language he did not understand. To be with them, of them, was a craving that filled his whole body. He swam a little closer; they turned and watched him with narrowed, alert dark eyes. Then one smiled and waved. It was enough. In a minute, he had swum in and was on the rocks beside them, smiling with a desperate, nervous supplication.[3] They shouted cheerful greetings at him; and then, as he preserved his nervous, uncomprehending smile, they understood that he was a foreigner strayed from his own beach, and they proceeded to forget him. But he was happy. He was with them.

They began diving again and again from a high point into a well of blue sea between rough, pointed rocks. After they had dived and come up, they swam around, hauled themselves up, and waited their turn to dive again. They were big boys—men, to Jerry. He dived, and they watched him; and when he swam around to take his place, they made way for him. He felt he was accepted and he dived again, carefully, proud of himself.

Soon the biggest of the boys poised himself, shot down into the water, and did not come up. The others stood about, watching. Jerry, after

3. supplication: a humble request.

idly
sleek
*.grave(a). seriously,

waiting for the sleek brown head to appear, let out a yell of warning; they looked at him idly and turned their eyes back towards the water. After a long time, the boy came up on the other side of the big dark rock, letting the air out of his lungs in a sputtering gasp and a shout of triumph. Immediately the rest of them dived in. One moment, the morning seemed full of chattering boys; the next, the air and the surface of the water were empty. But through the heavy blue, dark shapes could be seen moving and groping.

Jerry dived, shot past the school of underwater swimmers, saw a black wall of rock looming at him, touched it, and bobbed up at once to the surface, where the wall was a low barrier he could see across. There was no one visible; under him, in the water, the dim shapes of the swimmers had disappeared. Then one, and then another of the boys came up on the far side of the barrier of rock, and he understood that they had swum through some gap or hole in it. He plunged down again. He could see nothing through the stinging salt water but the blank rock. When he came up the boys were all on the diving rock, preparing to attempt the feat again. And now, in a panic of failure, he yelled up, in English, "Look at me! Look!" and he began splashing and kicking in the water like a foolish dog.

They looked down gravely, frowning. He knew the frown. At moments of failure, when he clowned to claim his mother's attention, it was with just this grave, embarrassed inspection that she rewarded him. Through his hot shame, feeling the pleading grin on his face like a scar that he could never remove, he looked up at the group of big brown boys on the rock and shouted *"Bonjour! Merci! Au revoir! Monsieur, monsieur!"*[4] while he hooked his fingers round his ears and waggled them.

Water surged into his mouth; he choked, sank, came up. The rock, lately weighted with boys, seemed to rear up out of the water as their weight was removed. They were flying down past him now, into the water; the air was full of falling bodies. Then the rock was empty in the

4. ***"Bonjour! Merci! Au revoir! Monsieur, monsieur!":*** These French words mean, "Hello! Thank you! Goodbye! Sir, sir!" They are words that even someone who does not speak French might know.

hot sunlight. He counted one, two, three . . .

At fifty, he was terrified. They must all be drowning beneath him, in the watery caves of the rock! At a hundred, he stared around him in the empty hillside, wondering if he should yell for help. He counted faster, faster, to hurry them up, to bring them to the surface quickly, to drown them quickly—anything rather than the terror of counting on and on into the blue emptiness of the morning. And then, at a hundred and sixty, the water beyond the rock was full of boys blowing like brown whales. They swam back to the shore without a look at him.

He climbed back to the diving rock and sat down, feeling the hot roughness of it under his thighs. The boys were gathering up their bits of clothing and running off along the shore to another promontory. They were leaving to get away from him. He cried openly, fists in his eyes. There was no one to see him, and he cried himself out.

It seemed to him that a long time had passed, and he swam out to where he could see his mother. Yes, she was still there, a yellow spot under an orange umbrella. He swam back to the big rock, climbed up, and dived into the blue pool among the fanged and angry boulders. Down he went, until he touched the wall of rock again. But the salt was so painful in his eyes that he could not see.

He came to the surface, swam to shore and went back to the villa to wait for his mother. Soon she walked slowly up the path, swinging her striped bag, the flushed, naked arm dangling beside her. "I want some swimming goggles," he panted, defiant and beseeching.

She gave him a patient, inquisitive look as she said casually, "Well, of course, darling."

But now, now, now! He must have them this minute, and no other time. He nagged and pestered until she went with him to a shop. As soon as she had bought the goggles, he grabbed them from her hand as if she were going to claim them for herself, and was off, running down the steep path to the bay.

Jerry swam out to the big barrier rock, adjusted the goggles, and dived. The impact of the water broke the rubber-enclosed vacuum, and abstacle (2)

the goggles came loose. He understood that he must swim down to the base of the rock from the surface of the water. He fixed the goggles tight and firm, filled his lungs, and floated, face down, on the water. Now he could see. It was as if he had eyes of a different kind—fish eyes that showed everything clear and delicate and wavering in the bright water.

Under him, six or seven feet down, was a floor of perfectly clean, shining white sand, rippled firm and hard by the tides. Two grayish shapes steered there, like long, rounded pieces of wood or slate. They were fish. He saw them nose towards each other, poise motionless, make a dart forward, swerve off, and come around again. It was like a water dance. A few inches above them the water sparkled as if sequins were dropping through it. Fish again—myriads of minute fish, the length of his fingernail—were drifting through the water, and in a moment he could feel the innumerable tiny touches of them against his limbs. It was like swimming in flaked silver. The great rock the big boys had swum through rose sheer out of the white sand—black, tufted lightly with greenish weed. He could see no gap in it. He swam down to its base.

Again and again he rose, took a big chestful of air, and went down. Again and again he groped over the surface of the rock, feeling it, almost hugging it in the desperate need to find the entrance. And then, once, while he was clinging to the black wall, his knees came up and he shot his feet out forward and they met no obstacle. He had found the hole.

He gained the surface, clambered about the stones that littered the barrier rock until he found a big one, and with this in his arms, let himself down over the side of the rock. He dropped, with the weight, straight to the sandy floor. Clinging tight to the anchor of stone, he lay on his side and looked in under the dark shelf at the place where his feet had gone. He could see the hole. It was an irregular, dark gap; but he could not see deep into it. He let go of his anchor, clung with his hands to the edges of the hole, and tried to push himself in.

He got his head in, found his shoulders jammed, moved them in sidewise, and was inside as far as his waist. He could see nothing ahead. Something soft and clammy touched his mouth; he saw a dark frond moving against the grayish rock, and panic filled him. He thought of octopuses, of clinging weed. He pushed himself out backward and caught a glimpse, as he retreated, of a harmless tentacle of seaweed drifting in the mouth of the tunnel. But it was enough. He reached the sunlight, swam to shore, and lay on the diving rock. He looked down into the blue well of water. He knew he must find his way through that cave, or hole, or tunnel, and out the other side.

First, he thought, he must learn to control his breathing. He let himself down into the water with another big stone in his arms, so that he could lie effortlessly on the bottom of the sea. He counted. One, two, three. He counted steadily. He could hear the movement of blood in his chest. Fifty-one, fifty-two. . . . His chest was hurting. He let go of the rock and went up into the air. He saw that the sun was low. He rushed to the villa and found his mother at her supper. She said only "Did you enjoy yourself?" and he said "Yes."

All night the boy dreamed of the water-filled cave in the rock, and as soon as breakfast was over he went to the bay.

That night, his nose bled badly. For hours he had been underwater, learning to hold his breath, and now he felt weak and dizzy. His mother said, "I shouldn't overdo things, darling, if I were you."

That day and the next, Jerry exercised his lungs as if everything, the whole of his life, all that he would become, depended upon it. Again his nose bled at night, and his mother insisted on his coming with her the next day. It was a torment to him to waste a day of his careful self-training, but he stayed with her on that other beach, which now seemed a place for small children, a place where his mother might lie safe in the sun. It was not his beach.

He did not ask for permission, on the following day, to go to his beach. He went, before his mother could consider the complicated rights and wrongs of the matter. A day's rest, he discovered, had improved his count by ten. The big boys had made the passage while he counted a hundred and sixty. He had been counting fast, in his fright. Probably now, if he tried, he could get through that long tunnel, but he was not going to try yet. A curious, most unchildlike persistence, a controlled impatience, made him wait. In the meantime, he lay underwater on the white sand, littered now by stones he had brought down from the upper air, and studied the entrance to the tunnel. He knew every jut and corner of it, as far as it was possible to see. It was as if he already felt its sharpness about his shoulders.

He sat by the clock in the villa, when his mother was not near, and checked his time. He was incredulous[5] and then proud to find he could hold his breath without strain for two minutes. The words "two minutes," authorized by the clock, brought close the adventure that was so necessary to him.

In another four days, his mother said casually one morning, they must go home. On the day before they left, he would do it. He would do it if it killed him, he said defiantly to himself. But two days before they were to leave—a day of triumph when he increased his count by fifteen—his nose bled so badly that he turned dizzy and had to lie limply over the big rock like a bit of seaweed, watching the thick red blood flow on to the rock and trickle slowly down to the sea. He was frightened. Supposing he turned dizzy in the tunnel? Supposing he died there, trapped? Supposing—his head went around, in the hot sun, and he almost gave up. He thought he would return to the house and lie down, and next summer, perhaps, when he had another year's growth in him—*then* he would go through the hole.

But even after he had made the decision, or thought he had, he found himself sitting up on the rock and looking down into the water; and he knew that now, this moment, when his nose had only just stopped bleeding, when his head was still sore and throbbing—this was the moment when he would try. If he did not do it now, he never would. He was trembling with fear that he would not go; and he was trembling with horror at the long, long tunnel under the rock, under the sea. Even in the open sunlight, the barrier rock seemed very wide and very heavy; tons of rock pressed down on where he would go. If he died there, he

5. **incredulous:** unbelieving.

would lie until one day—perhaps not before next year—those big boys would swim into it and find it blocked.

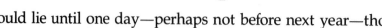

He put on his goggles, fitted them tight, tested the vacuum. His hands were shaking. Then he chose the biggest stone he could carry and slipped over the edge of the rock until half of him was in the cool enclosing water and half in the hot sun. He looked up once at the empty sky, filled his lungs once, twice, and then sank fast to the bottom with the stone. He let it go and began to count. He took the edges of the hole in his hands and drew himself into it, wriggling his shoulders in sidewise as he remembered he must, kicking himself along with his feet.

Soon he was clear inside. He was in a small rock-bound hole filled with yellowish-gray water. The water was pushing him up against the roof. The roof was sharp and pained his back. He pulled himself along with his hands—fast, fast—and used his legs as levers. His head knocked against something; a sharp pain dizzied him. Fifty, fifty-one, fifty-two. . . . He was without light, and the water seemed to press upon him with the weight of rock. Seventy-one, seventy-two . . . There was no strain on his lungs. He felt like an inflated balloon, his lungs were so light and easy, but his head was pulsing.

He was being continually pressed against the sharp roof, which felt slimy as well as sharp. Again he thought of octopuses, and wondered if the tunnel might be filled with weed that could tangle him. He gave himself a panicky, convulsive kick forward, ducked his head, and swam. His feet and hands moved freely, as if in open water. The hole must have widened out. He thought he must be swimming fast, and he was frightened of banging his head if the tunnel narrowed.

A hundred, a hundred and one . . . The water paled. Victory filled him. His lungs were beginning to hurt. A few more strokes and he would be out. He was counting wildly; he said a hundred and fifteen, and then, a long time later, a hundred and fifteen again. The water was a clear jewel-green all around him. Then he saw, above his head, a crack running up through the rock. Sunlight was falling through it, showing the clean, dark rock of the tunnel, a single mussel shell, and darkness ahead.

He was at the end of what he could do. He looked up at the crack as if it were filled with air and not water, as if he could put his mouth to it to draw in air. A hundred and fifteen, he heard himself say inside his head—but he had said that long ago. He must go on into the blackness ahead, or he would drown. His head was swelling, his lungs cracking. A hundred and fifteen, a hundred and fifteen pounded through his head, and he feebly clutched at rocks in the dark, pulling himself forward leaving the brief space of sunlit water behind. He felt he was dying. He was no longer quite conscious. He struggled on in the darkness between lapses into unconsciousness. An immense, swelling pain filled his head, and then the darkness cracked with an explosion of green light. His hands, groping forward, met nothing; and his feet, kicking back, propelled him out into the open sea.

He drifted to the surface, his face turned up to the air. He was gasping like a fish. He felt he would sink now and drown; he could not swim the few feet back to the rock. Then he was clutching it and pulling himself up onto it. He lay face down, gasping. He could see nothing but a red-veined, clotted dark. His eyes must have burst, he thought; they were full of blood. He tore off his goggles and a gout of blood went into the sea. His nose was bleeding, and the blood had filled the goggles.

He scooped up handfuls of water from the cool, salty sea, to splash on his face, and did not know whether it was blood or salt water he tasted After a time, his heart quieted, his eyes cleared, and he sat up. He could see the local boys diving and playing half a mile away. He did not want them. He wanted nothing but to get back home and lie down.

In a short while, Jerry swam to shore and climbed slowly up the path to the villa. He flung himself on his bed and slept, waking at the sound of feet on the path outside. His mother was coming back. He rushed to the bathroom, thinking she must not see his face with bloodstains, or tearstains, on it. He came out of the bathroom and met her as she walked into the villa, smiling, her eyes lighting up.

"Have a nice morning?" she asked, laying her hand on his warm brown shoulder a moment.

"Oh, yes, thank you,'" he said.

"You look a bit pale." And then, sharp and anxious, "How did you bang your head?"

"Oh, just banged it," he told her.

She looked at him closely. He was strained; his eyes were glazed-looking. She was worried. And then she said to herself, Oh, don't fuss! Nothing can happen. He can swim like a fish.

They sat down to lunch together.

"Mummy," he said, "I can stay underwater for two minutes—three minutes, at least." It came bursting out of him.

"Can you, darling?" she said. "Well, I shouldn't overdo it. I don't think you ought to swim any more today."

She was ready for a battle of wills, but he gave in at once. It was no longer of the least importance to go to the bay.

Reviewing the Selection

Answer each of the following questions without looking back at the story.

Recalling Facts

1. The French boys with whom Jerry dives
   - ☐ a. become Jerry's friends.
   - ☑ b. leave Jerry alone after he behaves childishly.
   - ☐ c. teach Jerry how to hold his breath underwater.
   - ☐ d. show Jerry exactly where the tunnel is.

Understanding Main Ideas

2. Jerry's conflict with his mother is the result of his
   - ☐ a. anger at his father's death.
   - ☑ b. mother's protectiveness.
   - ☐ c. desire to impress the French boys.
   - ☐ d. swimming ability.

Placing Events in Order

3. After Jerry finds the underwater tunnel, he
   - ☐ a. swims through it immediately.
   - ☐ b. decides to wait until he is a year older to swim through it.
   - ☐ c. tells his mother about his discovery.
   - ☑ d. practices holding his breath.

Finding Supporting Details

4. The story takes place at a
   - ☑ a. coastal resort.
   - ☐ b. summer camp.
   - ☐ c. lakeside cottage.
   - ☐ d. pool near Jerry's home.

Recognizing Words in Context

5. " 'I want some swimming goggles," he panted, defiant and <u>beseeching</u>." In this context *beseeching* means
   - ☑ a. demanding.
   - ☐ b. angry.
   - ☐ c. pleading.
   - ☐ d. polite.

Interpreting the Selection

Answer each of the following questions. You may look back at the story if necessary.

Making Inferences

6. When Jerry is at the wild bay, he swims out far enough to see his mother at the big beach. He does this because he
   - ☐ a. wants to test his swimming ability.
   - ☑ b. needs to have some contact with his mother.
   - ☐ c. wants to impress her.
   - ☐ d. likes to ride the waves back to shore.

Generalizing

7. Jerry can best be described as a
   - ☐ a. scared young boy.
   - ☐ b. mature young man.
   - ☑ c. boy who is learning about himself.
   - ☐ d. boy who is growing up too fast.

Analyzing Character

8. Which pair of adjectives best describes Jerry's mother?
   - ☑ a. protective and thoughtful
   - ☐ b. possessive and threatening
   - ☐ c. easygoing and secure
   - ☐ d. selfish and indifferent

Comparing

9. At the end of the story, Jerry is
   - ☐ a. less mature than at the beginning.
   - ☐ b. the same as at the beginning.
   - ☑ c. more mature than at the beginning.
   - ☐ d. more confused than at the beginning.

Drawing Conclusions

10. At the end of the story, Jerry has no desire to return to the wild bay because he
   - ☐ a. is tired of it.
   - ☐ b. wants to get back to school.
   - ☐ c. feels it is a place of danger.
   - ☑ d. no longer needs to prove himself.

Conflict

Have you ever had to solve a difficult personal problem? Have you ever competed in a race against other runners? Have you ever had to choose between two or more courses of action? Those situations are all examples of conflict, a struggle between opposing forces.

Everyone experiences conflict at some time. It is an important part of life. Attempting to solve the problems you meet is a challenge that adds interest and excitement to your life. The same is true in literature. The struggles faced by a character in a story make that story more interesting to read.

In literature, you will find two main types of conflict: external and internal. An external conflict is a struggle between a person and an outside force. A war, an athletic contest, and a debate are examples of external conflict. An internal conflict is a struggle that takes place within a person's mind. A person who must make a difficult decision experiences an internal conflict. In Doris Lessing's story "Through the Tunnel," you can find examples of both external and internal conflicts.

External Conflict

You may find several kinds of external conflicts in a short story. One kind is the conflict between two characters. You may have read stories about two men competing for the love of one woman, or two race horses running against each other, or a space explorer battling with an alien. The characters can be humans, animals, or even extraterrestrial beings, but the conflict is the struggle between only one character and another.

A second kind of external conflict is conflict between a person and society. Society can be a group or an institution. You may know of people who have battled to get the local government to take some kind of action, such as putting up a traffic light at a busy intersection. Or sometimes a person is in conflict with society over an idea or a belief. The Italian astronomer Galileo came into conflict with religious authorities because he tried to show that the earth moved around the sun.

A third kind of external conflict is conflict between groups. Such a conflict is the result of differing ideas. During the American Revolution, for example, the colonists fought the British for the right to live according to their own ideas and beliefs, rather than Great Britain's.

A fourth kind of external conflict is conflict between a person and the forces of nature. Have you ever tried to swim against a strong current? Have you walked against a high wind? If you have, then you have experienced a struggle against the forces of nature.

1. Think of the four kinds of external conflict. Then describe a situation illustrating each: (a) a conflict between two people, (b) a conflict between a person and society, (c) a conflict between groups, and (d) a conflict between a person and the forces of nature.

In "Through the Tunnel," two kinds of external conflict are central to the story. The most obvious external conflict is the one between Jerry and nature. It is represented by the challenge of swimming through the underwater tunnel. Jerry feels he must take up the challenge posed by the tunnel. The French boys have met it with apparent ease. He, too, must try it. If he fails, however, the consequence is death. Nature—the ocean—will claim a drowning victim. The life-and-death struggle Jerry faces as he swims through the tunnel creates the most gripping moments of the story.

2. How does Jerry learn about the tunnel? How does he prepare himself to meet the challenge of swimming through it?

The second external conflict is the one between Jerry and his mother. Jerry wants to be independent of his mother, who has been protective of her only child. On the first morning of their vacation, Jerry sees a wild bay and yearns to explore it. Then he sees that his mother wants his company. Her anxiety and concern make Jerry willing to stay with her at their usual beach. Yet the conflict between Jerry's need to be free and his mother's concern for him gives added meaning to the boy's conflict with nature. To assert his independence from his mother, Jerry must swim through the tunnel.

The second day when Jerry's mom agree Jerry can go to the bay, he almost follow his mom, but he wins.

3. Describe one struggle between Jerry and his mother that Jerry wins. Then describe one struggle that his mother wins.

At the first day of their vacation, Jerry is curious about the rocky bay and want to go there, but his mom win.

There is a third external conflict in this story—the almost wordless struggle between Jerry and the French boys. In that struggle, Jerry longs to be a part of the group. Jerry's desire to be included leads him to show off, but his stunts only earn him the French boys' contempt. There seems to be nothing he can do to regain their attention. Yet it is his encounter with the French boys that leads Jerry to set the goal of swimming through the tunnel.

Internal Conflict

Both Jerry and his mother face internal conflicts in the story. Jerry's inner struggle centers both on his feelings toward his mother and on his fear of undertaking the dangerous underwater swim. Jerry loves his mother and likes to be with her, but he sometimes wants to be on his own. Therefore, he has to choose between two courses of action. If he stays with her at the safe beach, he will satisfy his need to be near her, but he will not have any adventures for himself. If he goes to the wild bay and attempts to swim through the tunnel, he will be able to test himself, although it will be at the risk of his life. Both courses of action offer dangers and rewards. Jerry has to keep making a choice between the two.

4. Describe how each of the following passages from the story reveals Jerry's internal conflict:

a. *It was a torment to him to waste a day of his careful self-training, but he stayed with her on that other beach, which now seemed a place for small children, a place where his mother might lie safe in the sun. It was not his beach.*

b. *He thought he would return to the house and lie down, and next summer, perhaps, when he had another year's growth in him*—then *he would go through the hole.*

c. *But even after he had made the decision, or thought he had, he found himself sitting up on the rock and looking down into the water; and he knew that now, this moment, when his nose had only just stopped bleeding, when his head was still sore and throbbing—this was the moment when he would try. If he did not do it now, he never would. He was trembling with fear that he would not go; and he was trembling with horror at the long, long tunnel under the rock, under the sea.*

Jerry's mother also faces an internal conflict. She sees what Jerry wants and tries to put aside her fears. The boy's mother knows that she must give him some freedom. At the same time, she worries about him. In fact, Doris Lessing lets you hear the struggle in the woman's mind.

5. How does Jerry's mother want to behave toward her son? Does she succeed? Explain your answer.

Resolution

The conflicts in this story reach a point where they must be resolved, or concluded. The resolution of a conflict comes when the struggle ends and the outcome becomes clear. When there is more than one conflict in a story, the secondary ones are often cleared up when the main conflict is resolved. For example, in "Through the Tunnel," Jerry triumphs over the forces of nature by swimming through the tunnel. At the same time, his inner conflicts are resolved. He has overcome fear by the successful swim. By asserting his independence, he feels less threatened by his mother's protectiveness.

6. Look back at the story and find the lines that show (a) at what moment Jerry makes the final decision to swim through the tunnel, and (b) at what point his conflict with his mother is resolved.

Jerry's conflict with the French boys is also resolved but in an indirect way. Because he has swum through the tunnel, he no longer feels a need to prove himself to them. In fact, he chooses not to return to the wild bay.

Suspense

Lessing uses the conflicts in "Through the Tunnel" to create a suspenseful story. Suspense is the interest, uncertainty, or excitement you feel while waiting for a conflict to be resolved. Lessing uses several techniques to keep you on edge.

Time Limits. First, she increases the suspense by making you aware of the limited time Jerry has to achieve his goal. He and his mother are on vacation, and you know that their vacation must end. At one point, Jerry's mother tells him that they will go home in four days. At that point, Jerry can hold his breath underwater for only two minutes. If he is to swim through the tunnel, he must be able to hold his breath for almost three minutes. Will he have time to learn to control his breathing? Will he be forced to risk going through the tunnel too soon? Or will he have to give up his goal altogether?

Dangers. Next, Lessing increases the suspense by making you aware of the dangers Jerry faces. You know the dangers of the ocean, the underwater tunnel, and even Jerry's frequent nosebleeds. You also see that Jerry knows and fears those dangers. What if unknown dangers lurk in the tunnel? What if his nosebleeds become serious? What if his fears make him panic during his swim?

Repetition. Third, Lessing heightens the suspense through repetition. As Jerry swims through the tunnel, he counts off the seconds. However, as he nears his time limit, he keeps repeating "a hundred and fifteen."

Soon you realize that Jerry has gone way over his time limit. With each repetition of the count, his chances of drowning increase. Why does he keep repeating "one hundred and fifteen" instead of counting on? How long has he been underwater? Will he survive much longer?

7. Look again at the description of Jerry's swim through the tunnel. Describe two events or two thoughts that go through Jerry's mind that contribute to the suspense. Explain how each increases the suspense.

Once the conflicts are all resolved and Jerry successfully reaches his goal, the suspense is over and you breathe a sigh of relief. Jerry washes the blood off himself and returns to the villa before his mother. When he hears her coming, he rushes to hide any evidence of his ordeal. Yet he cannot hide his bruised head. When she asks him about it, he simply replies, "Oh, just banged it." Then, suddenly, he bursts out with his announcement: "Mummy," he said, "I can stay underwater for two minutes—three minutes, at least."

8. Why do you think Jerry chooses that way to tell his mother of his achievement? How does he respond to her suggestion not to "overdo it"? If you were Jerry, what would you have told your mother?

Questions for Thought and Discussion

The questions and activities that follow will help you explore "Through the Tunnel" in more depth and at the same time develop your critical thinking skills.

1. **Predicting Outcomes.** Given Jerry's achievement, do you think his relationship with his mother will change after they return home from vacation? Explain your answer.
2. **Evaluating.** Do you think that Jerry's mother helped him to become more independent? Find evidence in the story that supports your evaluation.
3. **Analyzing.** Divide the class into small groups. Each group should

draw up a list of qualities that a person needs for success in a career, such as in business or in sports. Then list the qualities that Jerry develops during the story. Compare the two lists. How many qualities for success does Jerry have? Do you think that he is likely to be successful in life? Why or why not?

4. **Interpreting.** Look again at the last sentence of the story: "It was no longer of the least importance to go to the bay." Why was the bay so important to him early in the story? Why is it no longer important to him at the end?

Writing About Literature

Several suggestions for writing projects are given below. You may be asked to complete one or more of these projects. If you have any questions about how to begin a writing assignment, review Using the Writing Process, beginning on page 337.

1. **Summarizing.** Write a summary of the action in "Through the Tunnel." Include only those events that are absolutely necessary for the story's development. Mention details, thoughts, and feelings only when they are needed to explain the events. End your summary with a statement that tells how Jerry changed during the story.

2. **Writing an Autobiographical Sketch.** Think of a time when you faced a conflict and successfully resolved it. The conflict can be an internal or an external one. Write a brief autobiographical sketch in which you describe the conflict and its resolution. Use what you have learned about suspense to make your sketch as interesting as possible.

3. **Taking Another Viewpoint.** During most of this story, you see events through Jerry's eyes. Imagine what the vacation in "Through the Tunnel" was like for Jerry's mother. Write several entries for her diary, expressing what she notices about her son during their vacation. Include her feelings about Jerry and how she sees her role in helping him to grow up.

Chapter 4

Selection *A Mother in Mannville*

MARJORIE KINNAN RAWLINGS

Lesson *Character and Characterization*

About the Selection

Have you ever been given an assignment to write about "The Most Unforgettable Character I've Known" or "The Person Who Changed My Life"? If you have, you were expected to describe a person and explain why he or she made a lasting impression on you. You may have thought of an older person because he or she is someone who has had many experiences in life and who knows a lot about the world. From that person, you may have learned a new way of looking at life or come to understand yourself better.

"A Mother in Mannville," by Marjorie Kinnan Rawlings, is about an unforgettable character. However, the character is not an older man or woman but a twelve-year-old boy. As you will see, there are two main characters in the story—the narrator, who is the person telling the story, and an orphaned boy named Jerry. You don't learn much about the narrator's life except that she is a writer who has rented a cabin in the Carolina mountains because she needs a quiet place to work.

You see the boy largely through the narrator's eyes. In the course of the story, she shows you the boy's many fine qualities. At the same time that the narrator gets to know the boy, the boy appears to develop a fondness for the narrator. He eventually reveals to her something about his loneliness. By the end of the story, you can tell that the narrator will never forget meeting Jerry.

Like the narrator in the story, Marjorie Kinnan Rawlings has spent much of her life in the southeastern United States. She grew up in Washington, D.C., but spent most of her adult life in rural Florida and upstate New York. She began writing short stories as a child. She did not enjoy much success, however, until as an adult she started to write about the people in the tiny village of Cross Creek, Florida, where she lived.

In her books and stories, Rawlings caught the spirit of those rural people. She had studied their mannerisms, speech, and beliefs. Through her characters, she emphasized the qualities of honesty and hard work that were so important in the lives of her rural neighbors.

Among the best-known works of Marjorie Kinnan Rawlings is her novel *The Yearling,* about a boy and his pet fawn. It is based on her Florida experience.

Lesson Preview

The lesson that follows "A Mother in Mannville" focuses on character. The word *character* has two meanings. As you read in Chapter 1, characters are the people, animals, or things that carry out the action of the story. *Character* also refers to their personalities.

One challenge facing a short-story writer is the need to present characters who are interesting and whose emotions and actions are understandable or acceptable. As you will learn in the lesson, Marjorie Kinnan Rawlings uses a number of techniques to show what the two main characters in her story are like.

The questions that follow will help you recognize the ways in which Rawlings creates her characters. As you read, think about how you would answer these questions.

1 What does the author tell you about Jerry's physical appearance?

2 What do you learn about Jerry's character from the way he behaves? What do you learn about him from what he says?

3 What do other people think of Jerry? Are their judgments trustworthy? Why or why not?

4 How would you describe the character of the narrator? How do you learn about her?

5 If you had to choose three words to describe Jerry, what words would you choose? If you had to limit your choice to one word, which would you choose?

Vocabulary

Here are some difficult words that appear in the selection that follows. Study the words and their definitions, as well as the sentences that show how the words are used. This will help you get the most from your reading.

suffused spread over. *The blush of embarrassment suffused her face as she realized her mistake.*

subterfuge a plan used to hide one's true purpose. *The mother realized that the child's complaint of a headache was only a subterfuge to avoid going to school.*

predicated based on certain facts; conditions. *Our decision to cancel the party was predicated on the fact that bad weather had been forecast.*

parturition childbirth. *The expectant mothers took a class so they would know what to expect in parturition.*

abstracted withdrawn; preoccupied; absentminded. *The abstracted professor didn't notice that his students had left the classroom.*

anomalous not following the usual rule; irregular; abnormal. *The ostrich is an anomalous member of the bird family because it can't fly.*

agony n. extreme mental or physical suffering

numb adj without the power to feel or move.

numbness n.

A Mother in Mannville

MARJORIE KINNAN RAWLINGS

The orphanage is high in the Carolina mountains. Sometimes in winter the snowdrifts are so deep that the institution is cut off from the village below, from all the world. Fog hides the mountain peaks, the snow swirls down the valleys, and a wind blows so bitterly that the orphanage boys who take the milk twice daily to the baby cottage reach the door with fingers stiff in an agony of numbness.

"Or when we carry trays from the cookhouse for the ones that are sick," Jerry said, "we get our faces frostbit, because we can't put our hands over them. I have gloves," he added. "Some of the boys don't have any."

He liked the late spring, he said. The rhododendron was in bloom, a carpet of color, across the mountainsides, soft as the May winds that stirred the hemlocks. He called it laurel.

"It's pretty when the laurel blooms," he said. "Some of it's pink and some of it's white."

I was there in the autumn. I wanted quiet, isolation, to do some troublesome writing. I wanted mountain air to blow out the malaria[1] from too long a time in the subtropics. I was homesick, too, for the flaming of maples in October, and for corn shocks[2] and pumpkins and black-walnut trees and the lift of hills. I found them all, living in a cabin that belonged to the orphanage, half a mile beyond the orphanage farm. When I took the cabin, I asked for a boy or man to come and chop wood for the fireplace. The first few days were warm, I found what wood I needed about the cabin, no one came, and I forgot the order.

I looked up from my typewriter one late afternoon, a little startled. A boy stood at the door, and my pointer dog, my companion, was at his side and had not barked to warn me. The boy was probably twelve years old, but undersized. He wore overalls and a torn shirt, and was barefooted.

He said, "I can chop some wood today."

I said, "But I have a boy coming from the orphanage."

"I'm the boy."

"You? But you're small."

"Size don't matter, chopping wood," he said. "Some of the big boys don't chop good. I've been chopping wood at the orphanage a long time."

I visualized mangled and inadequate branches for my fires. I was well into my work and not inclined to conversation. I was a little blunt.

"Very well. There's the ax. Go ahead and see what you can do."

I went back to work, closing the door. At first the sound of the boy dragging brush annoyed me. Then he began to chop. The blows were rhythmic and steady, and shortly I had forgotten him, the sound no more of an interruption than a consistent rain. I suppose an hour and a half passed, for when I stopped and stretched, and heard the boy's steps on the cabin stoop, the sun was dropping behind the farthest mountain, and the valleys were purple with something deeper than the asters.

The boy said, "I have to go to supper now. I can come again tomorrow evening."

---

1. **malaria:** a disease that gives a person frequent chills and fever.
2. **corn shocks:** bundles of corn stalks stacked to dry.

splendid (adj) - magnificent; display splendour.
texture n - way a surface, substance of fibric looks or feels to the touch.
intergrity (n) - quality of being honest and morally upright.

I said, "I'll pay you now for what you've done," thinking I should probably have to insist on an older boy. "Ten cents an hour?"

"Anything is all right."

We went together back of the cabin. An astonishing amount of solid wood had been cut. There were cherry logs and heavy roots of rhododendron, and blocks from the waste pine and oak left from the building of the cabin.

"But you've done as much as a man," I said, "This is a splendid pile."

I looked at him, actually, for the first time. His hair was the color of the corn shocks and his eyes, very direct, were like the mountain sky when rain is pending—gray, with a shadowing of that miraculous blue. As I spoke, a light came over him, as though the setting sun had touched him with the same suffused glory with which it touched the mountains. I gave him a quarter.

"You may come tomorrow," I said, "and thank you very much."

He looked at me, and at the coin, and seemed to want to speak, but could not, and turned away.

"I'll split kindling tomorrow," he said over his thin ragged shoulder. "You'll need kindling and medium wood and logs and backlogs."

At daylight I was half wakened by the sound of chopping. Again it was so even in texture that I went back to sleep. When I left my bed in the cool morning, the boy had come and gone, and a stack of kindling was neat against the cabin wall. He came again after school in the afternoon and worked until time to return to the orphanage. His name was Jerry; he was twelve years old, and he had been at the orphanage since he was four. I could picture him at four, with the same grave gray-blue eyes and the same—independence? No, the word that comes to me is "integrity."

The word means something very special to me, and the quality for which I use it is a rare one. My father had it—there is another of whom I am almost sure—but almost no man of my acquaintance possesses it with the clarity, the purity, the simplicity of a mountain stream. But the boy Jerry had it. It is bedded on courage, but it is more than brave. It is honest, but it is more than honesty. The ax handle broke one day. Jerry said the woodshop at the orphanage would repair it. I brought money to pay for the job and he refused it.

" I'll pay for it," he said. "I broke it. I brought the ax down careless."

"But no one hits accurately every time," I told him. "The fault was in the wood of the handle. I'll see the man from whom I bought it."

It was only then that he would take the money. He was standing back of his own carelessness. He was a free-will agent and he chose to do careful work, and if he failed, he took the responsibility without subterfuge.

And he did for me the unnecessary thing, the gracious thing, that we find done only by the great of heart. Things no training can teach, for they are done on the instant, with no predicated experience. He found a cubbyhole beside the fireplace that I had not noticed. There, of his own accord, he put kindling and "medium" wood, so that I might always have dry fire material ready in case of sudden wet weather. A stone was loose in the rough walk to the cabin. He dug a deeper hole and steadied it, although he came, himself, by a short cut over the bank. I found that when I tried to return his thoughtfulness with such things as candy and apples, he was wordless. "Thank you" was, perhaps, an expression for which he had had no use, for his courtesy was instinctive. He only looked at the gift and at me, and a curtain lifted, so that I saw deep into the clear well of his eyes, and gratitude was there, and affection, soft over the firm granite of his character.

He made simple excuses to come and sit with me. I could no more have turned him away than if he had been physically hungry. I suggested once that the best time for us to visit was just before supper, when I left off my writing. After that, he waited always until my typewriter had been some time quiet. One day I worked until nearly dark. I went outside the cabin, having forgotten him. I saw him going up over the hill in the twilight toward the orphanage. When I sat down on my stoop, a place was warm from his body where he had been sitting.

He became intimate, of course, with my pointer, Pat. There is a strange communion[3] between a boy and a dog. Perhaps they possess the same singleness of spirit, the same kind of wisdom. It is difficult to explain, but it exists. When I went across the state for a week end, I left the dog in Jerry's charge. I gave him the dog whistle and the key to the cabin, and left sufficient food. He was to come two or three times a day and let out the dog, and feed and exercise him. I should return Sunday night, and Jerry would take out the dog for the last time Sunday afternoon and then leave the key under an agreed hiding place.

My return was belated and fog filled the mountain passes so treacherously that I dared not drive at night. The fog held the next morning, and it was Monday noon before I reached the cabin. The dog had been fed and cared for that morning. Jerry came early in the afternoon, anxious.

"The superintendent said nobody would drive in the fog," he said. "I came just before bedtime last night and you hadn't come. So I brought Pat some of my breakfast this morning. I wouldn't have let anything happen to him."

"I was sure of that. I didn't worry."

"When I heard about the fog, I thought you'd know."

He was needed for work at the orphanage and he had to return at once. I gave him a dollar in payment, and he looked at it and went away. But that night he came in the darkness and knocked at the door.

"Come in, Jerry," I said, "if you're allowed to be away this late."

"I told maybe a story," he said. "I told them I thought you would want to see me."

"That's true," I assured him, and I saw his relief. "I want to hear about how you managed with the dog."

He sat by the fire with me, with no other light, and told me of their two days together. The dog lay close to him, and found a comfort there that I did not have for him. And it seemed to me that being with my dog, and caring for him, had brought the boy and me, too, together, so that he felt that he belonged to me as well as to the animal.

3. **communion:** a deep understanding.

"He stayed right with me," he told me, "except when he ran in the laurel. He likes the laurel. I took him up over the hill and we both ran fast. There was a place where the grass was high and I lay down in it and hid. I could hear Pat hunting for me. He found my trail and he barked. When he found me, he acted crazy, and he ran around and around me, in circles."

We watched the flames.

"That's an apple log," he said. "It burns the prettiest of any wood."

We were very close.

He was suddenly impelled to speak of things he had not spoken of before, nor had I cared to ask him.

"You look a little bit like my mother," he said. "Especially in the dark, by the fire."

"But you were only four, Jerry, when you came here. You have remembered how she looked, all these years?"

"My mother lives in Mannville," he said.

For a moment, finding that he had a mother shocked me as greatly as anything in my life has ever done, and I did not know why it disturbed me. Then I understood my distress. I was filled with a passionate resentment that any woman should go away and leave her son. A fresh anger added itself. A son like this one—The orphanage was a wholesome place, the executives were kind, good people, the food was more than adequate, the boys were healthy, a ragged shirt was no hardship, nor the doing of clean labor. Granted, perhaps, that the boy felt no lack, what blood fed the bowels[4] of a woman who did not yearn over this child's lean body that had come in parturition out of her own? At four he would have looked the same as now. Nothing, I thought, nothing in life could change those eyes. His quality must be apparent to an idiot, a fool. I burned with questions I could not ask. In any, I was afraid, there would be pain.

"Have you seen her, Jerry—lately?"

4. **bowels:** the part deep inside a person that used to be thought of as the source of kindness and compassion.

"I see her every summer. She sends for me."

I wanted to cry out, "Why are you not with her? How can she let you go away again?"

He said, "She comes up here from Mannville whenever she can. She doesn't have a job now."

His face shone in the firelight.

"She wanted to give me a puppy, but they can't let any one boy keep a puppy. You remember the suit I had on last Sunday?" He was plainly proud. "She sent me that for Christmas. The Christmas before that"—he drew a long breath, savoring the memory—"she sent me a pair of skates."

"Roller skates?"

My mind was busy, making pictures of her, trying to understand her. She had not, then, entirely deserted or forgotten him. But why, then—I thought, "I must not condemn her without knowing."

"Roller skates. I let the other boys use them. They're always borrowing them. But they're careful of them."

What circumstance other than poverty——

"I'm going to take the dollar you gave me for taking care of Pat," he said, "and buy her a pair of gloves."

I could only say, "That will be nice. Do you know her size?"

"I think it's 8½," he said.

He looked at my hands.

"Do you wear 8½?" he asked.

"No. I wear a smaller size, a 6."

"Oh! Then I guess her hands are bigger than yours."

I hated her. Poverty or no, there was other food than bread, and the soul could starve as quickly as the body. He was taking his dollar to buy gloves for her big stupid hands, and she lived away from him, in Mannville, and contented herself with sending him skates.

"She likes white gloves," he said. "Do you think I can get them for a dollar?"

"I think so," I said.

I decided that I should not leave the mountains without seeing her and knowing for myself why she had done this thing.

The human mind scatters its interests as though made of thistle-down,[5] and every wind stirs and moves it. I finished my work. It did not please me, and I gave my thoughts to another field. I should need some Mexican material.

I made arrangements to close my Florida place. Mexico immediately, and doing the writing there, if conditions were favorable. Then, Alaska with my brother. After that, heaven knew what or where.

I did not take time to go to Mannville to see Jerry's mother, nor even to talk with the orphanage officials about her. I was a trifle abstracted about the boy, because of my work and plans. And after my first fury at her—we did not speak of her again—his having a mother, any sort at all, not far away, in Mannville, relieved me of the ache I had had about him. He did not question the anomalous relation. He was not lonely. It was none of my concern.

He came every day and cut my wood and did small helpful favors and stayed to talk. The days had become cold, and often I let him come inside the cabin. He would lie on the floor in front of the fire, with one arm across the pointer, and they would both doze and wait quietly for me. Other days they ran with a common ecstasy through the laurel, and since the asters were now gone, he brought me back vermilion[6] maple leaves, and chestnut boughs dripping with imperial yellow. I was ready to go.

I said to him, "You have been my good friend, Jerry. I shall often think of you and miss you. Pat will miss you too. I am leaving tomorrow."

He did not answer. When he went away, I remember that a new moon hung over the mountains, and I watched him go in silence up the hill. I expected him the next day, but he did not come. The details of packing my personal belongings, loading my car, arranging the bed over

5. **thistledown:** the light, feathery seeds of the thistle plant.
6. **vermilion:** bright red or scarlet.

the seat, where the dog would ride, occupied me until late in the day. I closed the cabin and started the car, noticing that the sun was in the west and I should do well to be out of the mountains by nightfall. I stopped by the orphanage and left the cabin key and money for my light bill with Miss Clark.

"And will you call Jerry for me to say good-by to him?"

"I don't know where he is," she said. "I'm afraid he's not well. He didn't eat his dinner this noon. One of the other boys saw him going over the hill into the laurel. He was supposed to fire the boiler this afternoon. It's not like him; he's unusually reliable."

I was almost relieved, for I knew I should never see him again, and it would be easier not to say good-by to him.

I said, "I wanted to talk with you about his mother—why he's here—but I'm in more of a hurry than I expected to be. It's out of the question for me to see her now too. But here's some money I'd like to leave with you to buy things for him at Christmas and on his birthday. It will be better than for me to try to send him things. I could so easily duplicate—skates, for instance."

She blinked her honest spinster's eyes.

"There's not much use for skates here," she said.

Her stupidity annoyed me.

"What I mean," I said, "is that I don't want to duplicate things his mother sends him. I might have chosen skates if I didn't know she had already given them to him."

She stared at me.

"I don't understand," she said. "He has no mother. He has no skates."

Reviewing the Selection

Answer each of the following questions without looking back at the story.

Recalling Facts

1. When does this story take place?
   - ☐ a. midsummer
   - ☑ b. autumn
   - ☐ c. midwinter
   - ☐ d. early spring

Understanding Main Ideas

2. "A Mother in Mannville" is about
   - ☐ a. an orphan's love for his dog.
   - ☐ b. a woman adopting a son.
   - ☑ c. a lonely boy's need for a mother.
   - ☐ d. the problems of living in an orphanage.

Placing Events in Order

3. "You look a little bit like my mother," Jerry tells the narrator. When does that dialogue occur?
   - ☐ a. before Jerry breaks the ax
   - ☐ b. on the day Jerry fixes the stone walk
   - ☐ c. on the day the narrator leaves for Mexico
   - ☑ d. after the narrator returns from a weekend trip

Finding Supporting Details

4. When Jerry first came to the writer's cabin, the woman's dog, Pat,
   - ☐ a. barked to warn her.
   - ☐ b. jumped up on Jerry.
   - ☑ c. stood quietly by Jerry's side.
   - ☐ d. slept soundly in front of the fire.

Recognizing Words in Context

5. "I visualized the mangled and inadequate branches for my fires." In this context *visualized* means
   - ☐ a. pictured.
   - ☐ b. disliked.
   - ☑ c. split.
   - ☐ d. burned.

Interpreting the Selection

Answer each of the following questions. You may look back at the story if necessary.

Making Inferences

6. Jerry probably says that the narrator looks like his mother because he
   - ☐ a. has a picture of his mother.
   - ☐ b. has been told his mother is a writer.
   - ☑ c. wants to believe that his mother is like the narrator.
   - ☐ d. wants the narrator to adopt him.

Generalizing

7. What does the narrator feel toward Jerry?
   - ☐ a. She is often angry with him.
   - ☑ b. She is impressed by his honesty and discipline.
   - ☐ c. She wishes he would leave her alone.
   - ☐ d. She is happy that his mother sends him nice presents.

Analyzing Character

8. What adjective can be used to describe both Jerry and the narrator?
   - ☐ a. fun loving
   - ☐ b. hardworking
   - ☐ c. short-tempered
   - ☐ d. talkative

Comparing

9. At the end of the story, the writer tells Jerry that she is leaving. You can tell that
   - ☐ a. Jerry was sadder than the writer about the parting.
   - ☐ b. the writer was sadder than Jerry about the parting.
   - ☐ c. Jerry felt worse about not seeing the dog again than about not seeing the woman.
   - ☐ d. neither Jerry nor the writer cared much about the separation.

Drawing Conclusions

10. From the information in the story, you can conclude that Jerry's mother
    - ☐ a. remarried and had other children.
    - ☐ b. was not a good mother.
    - ☐ c. died when Jerry was an infant.
    - ☐ d. did not come to visit him.

Character and Characterization

As you have seen, character has two meanings: It refers to the people, animals, or things that are active in a story, as well as to the personalities of those individuals. How does a writer reveal what his or her characters are like? In this lesson, you will study characterization—the methods by which a writer develops a character's personality.

Think of how you get to know the people who become your friends. You look at them to see their expressions. You watch what they do, listen to what they say, and learn what they think. From those observations, you form an opinion about them. If someone asks you what a friend of yours is like, you might answer with one or two words, such as lively, kind, fun loving, or sensitive.

You can use the same powers of observation to learn about a character in a short story. An author develops a character in a number of ways. The five basic methods of characterization are (1) describing the character's physical appearance, (2) showing the character's actions, (3) revealing the character's thoughts and words, (4) showing what other characters think and say about the character, and (5) telling the reader directly what the writer thinks of the character.

As you have seen, "A Mother in Mannville" has two main characters:

the narrator and Jerry. In the story, your attention focuses on the character of Jerry, although you also learn something about the narrator's feelings and her responses to Jerry. A brief review of the story will show how Marjorie Kinnan Rawlings uses the five basic methods of characterization.

The Character's Physical Appearance

When you meet someone for the first time, you probably notice the person's physical appearance right away. Is the person a man or a woman, a boy or a girl, young or old, tall or short? You might look at his or her clothes, coloring, hair style, or any number of other external features. You might even start to make judgments based on your observations. Later, as you get to know the person, your opinions may change.

You will find that in short stories some writers give detailed physical descriptions of their characters, while others do not. Early in "A Mother in Mannville," Marjorie Kinnan Rawlings begins to describe Jerry, but she gives only a few details, as seen through the narrator's eyes: "The boy was probably twelve years old, but undersized. He wore overalls and a torn shirt, and was barefooted."

She think Jerry is too small to chop woods for her. Propably she thinks Jery is too young to work too.

1. What is the narrator's first reaction to Jerry's physical appearance? Why does she respond to him in that way?

She doesn't like Jerry to work for her. She is somehow look down on him for what he wear and his barefooted

Later, the narrator gives us a few more details about Jerry's appearance: "His hair was the color of the corn shocks and his eyes, very direct, were like the mountain sky when rain is pending—gray, with a shadowing of that miraculous blue." We get the feeling that as the narrator gets to know Jerry better she views him in a more favorable light.

In the first description, the narrator states bluntly that Jerry was "undersized," wore "a torn shirt," and was "barefooted." In the second, she uses figurative language to describe the boy. Figurative language involves using words and phrases in unusual ways to create strong, vivid images, to focus attention on certain ideas, or to compare dissimilar things. When words and phrases are used figuratively, they have meanings other than their usual meanings.

Suffuse (v). (of color, moisture) spread throughout or over from within.
☆ reluctant (a) – to do : unwilling, disinclined

In the passage describing Jerry's hair and eyes, the narrator uses a figure of speech, which is a specific kind of figurative language, called a simile. A simile is a direct comparison between unlike things using the word *like, as,* or *resembles* to connect them. A commonly-heard simile is, "We ate like pigs." In that simile the manners of humans are compared to those of pigs. As with other kinds of figurative language, similes offer vivid new ways of looking at things.

A second figure of speech that uses comparison is a metaphor. A metaphor is an implied comparison between unlike things. A writer will often use a metaphor in order to give you an unusual way of looking at one of the things. A metaphor is a comparison that suggests one thing *is* another. You may have heard this common metaphor, "He is a bear in the morning." The metaphor suggests that the man has the same traits as the bear. You know that the man is surly, mean, and generally ill tempered.

hair was very direct
(1) His eyes were like the mountain sky when rain is pending.

2. Reread the second description of Jerry (page 92). What simile or similes are used in that passage? Does the writer use any metaphors there? How does the writer's use of figurative language show Jerry in a favorable way?

△ She use the color of the corn shocks to describe his hair with a shawdoing of that miraculous blue. She also use the light of the setting sun to imply the boy's personality – glory come through him!

The Character's Actions

You have probably heard the old saying "Actions speak louder than words." Think about how that saying applies to a character in a story. A writer can *tell* you what the character is like, or can *show* you the character in action. Showing the way a person acts gives a clearer, stronger indication of his or her character because you can then see the character for yourself and make your own judgments. When you are simply told what a character is like, you have no detailed images of the character's actions to explore, and you are forced to depend on someone else's judgment.

In "A Mother in Mannville," you can learn a lot about Jerry through his actions. When Jerry first appears at the cabin, the narrator doubts that he can chop the wood she needs. She reluctantly agrees to let him try: "Go ahead and see what you can do." The boy chops wood steadily for about an hour and a half. Through his action he shows that he is disciplined and persistent. The next day, he returns at dawn and cuts the kindling that the narrator will need for a good fire. His actions show that Jerry is determined to finish any job that he starts. He is a hard worker.

As the story unfolds, the author reveals more about Jerry's character through his actions. The boy shows himself to be thoughtful, responsible, intelligent, and honest.

He do some unnecessary things.

3. Skim the story. In your own words, summarize two actions that reveal Jerry's thoughtfulness. He offer to split kindling and other good firewoods and arranges them neat against the cabin wall. He come, finish his work and leave without weak up the author for money
② When the author go out on weeken, and return late, he offer his own breaskfast to feed the dog.

The Character's Thoughts and Words

To know what a character thinks, the story must be written so that you can see into his or her mind. "A Mother in Mannville" is written from the narrator's point of view—you see everything through her eyes. You know what she thinks because she tells you. For example, she tells you what Jerry does and says, as well as what she thinks of him. However, she cannot know Jerry's thoughts. To understand his thoughts, you must infer them from his words and actions.

Think about the scene in which Jerry visits the narrator on the night she returns from a weekend away.

> "Come in, Jerry," I said, "if you're allowed to be away this late."
>
> "I told maybe a story," he said. "I told them I thought you would want to see me."
>
> "That's true," I assured him, and I saw his relief.

Jerry's words reveal that his conscience is bothering him about the "story" he told the people at the orphanage. When the narrator backs up his story, he is greatly relieved.

Jerry is a person of few words. All he says when the narrator offers to pay him for his work is, "Anything is all right." When he breaks the ax, he doesn't give endless excuses. He simply says, "I brought the ax down careless." His words show him as a soft-spoken, honest, innocent country boy who makes few demands on other people.

Sometimes, a writer lets you know how a character's words sound by giving a dialogue tag, such as "he said *softly*" or "she added *jokingly*." Rawlings, however, uses few dialogue tags. Instead, she lets the mood—the general feeling or atmosphere—of a scene tell you how the character's words probably sound. The night of the narrator's return, she and Jerry watch the fire together: " 'That's an apple log,' he said. 'It burns the prettiest of any wood.' "

4. Reread that scene in the story. What mood has the author established in it? How do you think Jerry's words about the apple log sound?

5. Look at the passage in which the following lines appear: " 'You look a little bit like my mother,' he said. 'Especially in the dark, by the fire.' " What dialogue tag would you put with "he said"? Explain your choice.

The narrator is the other main character in "A Mother in Mannville." You can learn something about her personality from her thoughts and words. At first, you see her as impatient with the small boy who has come to chop wood. Then you see her as a sympathetic character—someone who cares about Jerry.

6. Find several passages in which the narrator shows through her thoughts what she is like. Describe two traits of the narrator and how she reveals them in her thoughts.

What Others Think and Say About a Character

A fourth method of characterization is showing what others think of or say about a character. In this story, much of what we learn about Jerry comes from the narrator. Early on, the narrator reveals what she thinks of Jerry. She tells what she imagines Jerry was like when he first entered the orphanage: "I could picture him at four, with the same grave gray-blue eyes and the same—independence? No, the word that comes to me is 'integrity.' "

7. Look at the paragraph on pages 92–93 in which the narrator discusses exactly what she means by integrity. What words does she associate with integrity? How does she show us Jerry's integrity?

Jerry himself doesn't say very much. He doesn't show his feelings openly. He never puts his arms around the woman and never says thank you outright. When the woman gives him gifts such as candy and apples, Jerry's response is silence.

> He only looked at the gift and at me, and a curtain lifted, so that I saw deep into the clear well of his eyes, and gratitude was there, and affection, soft over the firm granite of his character.

Through those words, the narrator reveals that the boy was capable of gratitude and affection even though he did not show such feelings openly. You, however, must decide whether her thoughts and judgments about the boy are accurate. You can do that by weighing what she says against what you know about Jerry from his own words and actions.

8. Do the narrator's thoughts about Jerry seem accurate? Why or why not?

The Writer's Direct Statements

The fifth and most direct way in which a writer develops a character is by stating outright what the person is like. However, few writers of fiction step into their stories to give their opinions of their characters. Instead, writers of fiction generally speak through other voices, and they do not necessarily think in the same ways as their narrators or characters. In "A Mother in Mannville" Marjorie Kinnan Rawlings does not make any direct statements. Instead, she speaks through the narrator.

Character and Plot

In some short stories, writers develop their characters quite fully at the beginning. The rest of the story is then devoted to the plot. In "A Mother in Mannville," Jerry's character is developed slowly, through each incident in the plot. You continue to learn about him up to the last line of the story. As the story unfolds, you become aware of the many sides of Jerry's character.

Through the various methods of characterization, Rawlings shows Jerry to be an honest, hardworking, responsible, reliable person. He is unusually mature in certain ways. He is silent but still shows affection behind his quiet manner. At the end of the story, however, you get a new insight into Jerry's character—he has lied to the narrator about his mother. Was his lying deliberate, or was it simply a lonely child's fantasy? What motives, or reasons, might the boy have had for inventing the story about his mother, the presents she gave him, and his visits with her? If the author has developed the boy's character well, you should be able to suggest answers to those questions.

9. In a paragraph or two, explain why you think Jerry told the narrator the stories about his mother. Use what you know about the boy's character to support your opinion.

Questions for Thought and Discussion

The questions and activities that follow will help you explore "A Mother in Mannville" in more depth and at the same time develop your critical thinking skills.

1. **Drawing Conclusions.** You know from the story that Jerry entered the orphanage at age four. He is now twelve. Why do you suppose that Jerry has been in the orphanage so long? What do you think he will be like as an adult?

2. **Evaluating.** The narrator is greatly impressed by Jerry's integrity. Do you think her opinion of Jerry changed after she found out the truth about his mother? What stumbling blocks stand in the way of someone—especially a young person—maintaining complete integrity?

3. **Analyzing Character.** At the end of the story, you meet Miss Clark from the orphanage. Which of the five methods of characterization

does Rawlings use to present Miss Clark? What kind of person do you think she is? Give reasons for your answer.

4. **Drawing a Plot Diagram.** The plot diagram you studied in Chapter 2 (page 53) can be adapted to other stories. Remember that sometimes the exposition and rising action are short and the story reaches its climax quickly. In other instances, the rising action and the falling action are gradual. Draw a plot diagram for "A Mother in Mannville," and label the five parts on your diagram.

Writing About Literature

Several suggestions for writing projects are given below. You may be asked to complete one or more of these projects. If you have any questions about how to begin a writing assignment, review Using the Writing Process, beginning on page 337.

1. **Writing About an Unforgettable Person.** Write a brief description of an unforgettable person. The person may be someone real whom you've known or someone you've imagined. Use at least three of the methods of characterization discussed in the chapter.

2. **Using a Point of View.** Imagine that you are Jerry on the day the narrator leaves the cabin for good. Write a diary entry explaining what you did and how you felt on that day.

3. **Explaining a Decision.** The narrator must have debated whether or not to return at a later time to visit Jerry. Imagine that you are the narrator. Decide whether or not you will visit Jerry. Then write a letter to him explaining your decision. Whatever decision you make, try to make your letter sound like one that the narrator would have written.

4. **Using Figurative Language.** In a few paragraphs, describe a person, place, or event using both kinds of figurative language—metaphor and simile—that you learned about in this chapter.

UNIT TWO

The World of Fantasy and Imagination

The Pit and the Pendulum
EDGAR ALLAN POE

Setting and Mood

The Secret Life of Walter Mitty
JAMES THURBER

Humor and Satire

Of Missing Persons
JACK FINNEY

Point of View

The Rule of Names
URSULA LE GUIN

Foreshadowing and Suspense

Science fiction
fantasy — put someone unreal situation

The stories in Unit One all take place in the real world. They are stories with recognizable settings, characters, and plots. By contrast, the stories in Unit Two take you into a variety of unusual worlds—a world of extraordinary, nightmarish terror, a world of daydreams, a world in which ordinary people can travel through space to another planet, and the world of magicians and dragons.

Imagination is a powerful tool. A skilled writer can use his or her imagination to create startling and intriguing tales that offer you new possibilities for thought.

Writers have invented many types of stories. You have already read stories of realistic fiction. In addition, there are detective stories, mystery stories, westerns, historical fiction, fantasy, and science fiction. The last two fascinate many readers because they explore fanciful, often bizarre, ideas.

A fantasy is an imagined reality. Fantasy may include magic, ghosts, demons, imaginary beasts, or other supernatural powers. It may take place in the past, present, or future. Many fantasies are set in other worlds; some, however, are set on earth with real characters drawn into unusual circumstances. Science fiction is a special kind of fantasy in which technology, machines, robots, computers, or other scientific inventions play a major role in taking you to extraordinary worlds.

As you will see in the stories that follow, writers use a variety of imaginative devices to reveal the thoughts and feelings of their characters and to create whole new worlds. Authors use their imaginations to create new events and characters; you use your imagination to suspend your disbelief and experience the author's work. At the same time writers build their stories around the same basic elements—setting, plot, character, theme—that you read about in Unit One.

Chapter 5

Selection *The Pit and the Pendulum*

EDGAR ALLAN POE

Lesson *Setting and Mood*

About the Selection

Try to remember your worst nightmare. What was the most unforgettable feeling in that nightmare? Was it fear? Suffering? Anger? Terror? For many people, terror is the worst part of a nightmare—terror that propels the body into wide-eyed, heart-pounding wakefulness. The feeling hangs on until you can shake the cobwebs out of your head and realize that you were just dreaming.

Even when you are fully awake, you hold onto the feelings of the experience. You can still feel your skin crawling. It takes time for the fear to wear off completely and for you to shake off the sense of danger.

The main character in "The Pit and the Pendulum" suffers through a "living nightmare." That expression refers to a dreadful ordeal in real life. Early in the story you learn that the main character is a prisoner of the Inquisition. For hundreds of years the name of the Inquisition brought images of persecution and imprisonment to the minds of Europeans.

In 1231 religious authorities set up a special court, called the Inquisition, to fight heresy—any teachings with which the authorities disagreed. Over the centuries, the Inquisition became an instrument of power in the hands of the clergy and state. It was used to force people to be loyal and obedient to the clergy and the government.

In 1478 the rulers of Spain created the Spanish Inquisition. The Spanish Inquisition used torture, imprisonment, and death to enforce uniform beliefs among the Spanish people. Under the leadership of

Tomás de Torquemada, the Spanish Inquisition convicted many people and burned them at the stake.

Fear of the Inquisition was widespread in Spain. People never knew when they might be called before it—perhaps because an enemy had denounced them. The accused were arrested and were tortured until they confessed. Tens of thousands suffered the cruelty of the Inquisition. The Spanish Inquisition remained a threat for over 350 years.

Edgar Allan Poe, the author of "The Pit and the Pendulum," used the Inquisition as the background for his story of terror and doom. You don't know why the main character, whose name you never learn, is a prisoner of the Inquisition, or why he has been arrested. You only witness his terror as he narrowly escapes death time after time. His end is inevitable. He is a doomed man in the face of an all-powerful force, the dreaded Inquisition.

Poe is a master of the suspense story. In the mid-1800s, he pioneered the development of two other types of stories—the detective story and science fiction. Poe is also among the best-known American poets. "The Raven" is perhaps his most famous poem.

Poe's life has fascinated biographers, as well as the readers of his strange and often bizarre stories. He was born in Boston in 1809. At the age of three, after his father deserted the family and his mother died, Poe became an orphan. He was raised by John and Frances Allan of Richmond, Virginia. Although the Allans helped him to get an education, Edgar and his foster father quarreled. Eventually, the ties between Poe and the Allans were broken.

In 1836 Poe married his thirteen-year-old cousin, Virginia Clemm. By then, he had already embarked on a writing career. He had had some success as a writer and editor but had never earned very much. In 1837 he and Virginia moved to New York City. Over the next ten years, Poe produced many stories and poems. But although he wrote constantly, the family lived in near poverty. His wife developed tuberculosis and died in 1847. Poe was desperately unhappy without her. His last years were grim. Critics blamed his troubles on his heavy drinking.

In 1849 Poe became engaged to a woman he had known since childhood. A short time before the wedding date, however, he was found lying on a street in Baltimore in a coma. He died without ever regaining consciousness. Poe was only forty years old.

Poe's stories often expose the dark side of human nature. They are strange tales of bizarre happenings. Many were collected in a book called *Tales of the Grotesque and Arabesque,* which Poe published in 1840. In "The Tell-Tale Heart," one of his best-known stories, Poe explores the psychology of a man who murders a neighbor and then feels compelled to confess his deed. Several stories feature characters who are buried alive. Being buried alive was one of Poe's greatest dreads.

Lesson Preview

The lesson that follows "The Pit and the Pendulum" focuses on setting and mood. As you have read, setting is the time and place of a story, and mood is the general feeling or atmosphere that the writer creates in a story.

Edgar Allan Poe is a master of description. Through various methods, he reveals the setting and draws you into the story. In "The Pit and the Pendulum" Poe's descriptions are so vivid that they force you to experience the narrator's terror.

The story is quite long. Poe goes into great detail as he slowly reveals the state of mind and the emotions of the narrator. Those details build the sense of terror and doom. The questions that follow will help you see how Poe uses setting and develops the mood in the story. As you read, think about how you would answer these questions.

1 Where does the story take place? How do you learn this?

2 Can you figure out when the story takes place? Why or why not?

3 How much time passes from the beginning to the end of the story?

4 What is the overall feeling of the story? Does that feeling change as the story unfolds? If so, how does it change?

5 What do you feel at the end of the story? Why?

Vocabulary

Here are some difficult words that appear in the selection that follows. Study the words and their definitions, as well as the sentences that show how the words are used. This will help you get the most from your reading.

locution style of speech; form of expression. *The locution of the people from the hill area is quite different from the speech of the people in the valley.*

imperceptible so small or slight that it is not noticed. *The differences between the two kittens were so imperceptible that we couldn't tell which one we had decided to take with us.*

interminableness endlessness. *The interminableness of the debate left most of the audience tired and bored.*

insuperable unable to be overcome. *The fact that the two tourists spoke different languages created an insuperable barrier to conversation.*

avidity great eagerness or greed. *When the starving refugees reached the camp, they ate the food with avidity.*

sunder break or tear apart. *For a moment, the flash of lightning seemed to sunder the sky.*

conjecture a guess. *Scientists' theories of why the dinosaurs died are based mainly on conjecture.*

demoniac fiendish; of or like demons. *Torturing people to make them confess to witchcraft was a demoniac custom which lasted for centuries.*

obtuse an angle of more than 90 degrees. *The shape of a diamond has two acute angles and two obtuse angles.*

seared burned or scorched. *Last summer's fires seared the dry grasslands.*

discordant not in harmony; clashing. *The discordant sounds of the sirens disturbed the stillness of the night.*

The Pit and the Pendulum

EDGAR ALLAN POE

Impia tortorum longos hic turba furores
Here the impious mob, unsated, nourished
Sanguinis innocui, non satiata, aluit.
The torturers' long orgies of shedding innocent blood.
Sospite nunc patria, fracto nunc funeris antro,
Now that the country is safe, now that the funeral tumbril is shattered,
Mors ubi dira fuit vita salusque patent.
Where there was horrible death, life and health are seen.

[Quatrain composed for the gates of a market to be erected upon the site of the Jacobin Club House at Paris.]

I was sick—sick unto death with that long agony; and when they at length unbound me, and I was permitted to sit, I felt that my senses were leaving me. The sentence—the dread sentence of death—was the last of distinct accentuation which reached my ears. After that, the sound of the inquisitorial voices seemed merged in one dreamy indeterminate hum. It conveyed to my soul the idea of *revolution*—perhaps from its association in fancy with the burr of a mill-wheel. This only for a brief period; for presently I heard no more. Yet, for a while, I saw; but with how terrible an exaggeration! I saw the lips of the black-robed judges. They appeared to me white—whiter than the sheet upon which I trace these words—and thin even to grotesqueness;

thin with the intensity of their expression of firmness—of immovable resolution—of stern contempt of human torture. I saw that the decrees of what to me was Fate, were still issuing from those lips. I saw them writhe with a deadly locution. I saw them fashion the syllables of my name; and I shuddered because no sound succeeded. I saw, too, for a few moments of delirious horror, the soft and nearly imperceptible waving of the sable draperies which enwrapped the walls of the apartment. And then my vision fell upon the seven tall candles upon the table. At first they wore the aspect of charity, and seemed white slender angels who would save me; but then, all at once, there came a most deadly nausea over my spirit, and I felt every fiber in my frame thrill as if I had touched the wire of a galvanic battery, while the angel forms became meaningless specters, with heads of flame, and I saw that from them there would be no help. And then there stole into my fancy, like a rich musical note, the thought of what sweet rest there must be in the grave. The thought came gently and stealthily, and it seemed long before it attained full appreciation; but just as my spirit came at length properly to feel and entertain it, the figures of the judges vanished, as if magically, from before me; the tall candles sank into nothingness; their flames went out utterly; the blackness of darkness supervened; all sensations appeared swallowed up in a mad rushing descent as of the soul into Hades. Then silence, and stillness, and night were the universe.

I had swooned; but still will not say that all of consciousness was lost. What of it there remained I will not attempt to define, or even to describe; yet all was not lost. In the deepest slumber—no! In delirium—no! In a swoon[1]—no! In death—no! even in the grave all *is not* lost. Else there is no immortality for man. Arousing from the most profound of slumbers, we break the gossamer web of *some* dream. Yet in a second afterward, (so frail may that web have been) we remember not that we have dreamed. In the return to life from the swoon there are two stages; first, that of the sense of mental or spiritual; secondly, that of the sense of physical, existence. It seems probable that if, upon reaching the second

1. swoon: a faint.

stage, we could recall the impressions of the first, we should find these impressions eloquent in memories of the gulf beyond. And that gulf is—what? How at least shall we distinguish its shadows from those of the tomb? But if the impressions of what I have termed the first stage, are not, at will, recalled, yet, after long interval, do they not come unbidden, while we marvel whence they come? He who has never swooned, is not he who finds strange palaces and wildly familiar faces in coals that glow; is not he who beholds floating in mid-air the sad visions that the many may not view; is not he who ponders over the perfume of some novel flower—is not he whose brain grows bewildered with the meaning of some musical cadence which has never before arrested his attention.

Amid frequent and thoughtful endeavors to remember; amid earnest struggles to regather some token of the state of seeming nothingness into which my soul had lapsed, there have been moments when I have dreamed of success; there have been brief, very brief periods when I have conjured up remembrances which the lucid reason of a later epoch assures me could have had reference only to that condition of seeming unconsciousness. These shadows of memory tell, indistinctly, of tall figures that lifted and bore me in silence down—down—still down—till a hideous dizziness oppressed me at the mere idea of the interminableness of the descent. They tell also of a vague horror at my heart, on account of that heart's unnatural stillness. Then comes a sense of sudden motionlessness throughout all things; as if those who bore me (a ghastly train!) had outrun, in their descent, the limits of the limitless, and paused from the wearisomeness of their toil. After this I call to mind flatness and dampness; and that all is *madness*—the madness of a memory which busies itself among forbidden things.

Very suddenly there came back to my soul motion and sound—the tumultuous motion of the heart, and, in my ears, the sound of its beating. Then a pause in which all is blank. Then again sound, and motion, and touch—a tingling sensation pervading my frame. Then the mere consciousness of existence, without thought—a condition which lasted long. Then, very suddenly, *thought*, and shuddering terror, and earnest endeavor to comprehend my true state. Then a strong desire to lapse into insensibility.[2] Then a rushing revival of soul and a successful effort to move. And now a full memory of the trial, of the judges, of the sable draperies, of the sentence, of the sickness, of the swoon. Then entire forgetfulness of all that followed; of all that a later day and much earnestness of endeavor have enabled me vaguely to recall.

So far, I had not opened my eyes. I felt that I lay upon my back, unbound. I reached out my hand, and it fell heavily upon something damp and hard. There I suffered it to remain for many minutes, while I strove to imagine where and *what* I could be. I longed, yet dared not to employ my vision. I dreaded the first glance at objects around me. It was not that I feared to look upon things horrible, but that I grew aghast lest there should be *nothing* to see. At length, with a wild desperation at heart, I quickly unclosed my eyes. My worst thoughts, then, were confirmed. The blackness of eternal night encompassed me. I struggled for breath. The intensity of the darkness seemed to oppress and stifle me. The atmosphere was intolerably close. I still lay quietly, and made effort to exercise my reason. I brought to mind the inquisitorial proceedings, and attempted from that point to deduce my real condition. The sentence had passed; and it appeared to me that a very long interval of time had since elapsed. Yet not for a moment did I suppose myself actually dead. Such a supposition, notwithstanding what we read in fiction, is altogether inconsistent with real existence;—but where and in what state was I? The condemned to death, I knew, perished usually at the *autos-da-fé,*[3] and one of these had been held on the very night of the day of my trial. Had I been remanded to my dungeon, to await the next sacrifice, which would not take place for many months? This I at once saw could not be. Victims had been in immediate demand. Moreover, my dungeon, as well as all the condemned cells at Toledo, had stone floors, and light was not altogether excluded.

A fearful idea now suddenly drove the blood in torrents upon my

2. insensibility: unconsciousness.

3. *autos-da-fe*: the public burnings of those condemned as heretics by the Inquisition.

heart, and for a brief period, I once more relapsed into insensibility. Upon recovering, I at once started to my feet, trembling convulsively in every fiber. I thrust my arms wildly above and around me in all directions. I felt nothing; yet dreaded to move a step, lest I should be impeded[4] by the walls of the *tomb.* Perspiration burst from every pore and stood in cold big beads on my forehead. The agony of suspense grew at length intolerable, and I cautiously moved forward, with my arms extended, and my eyes straining from their sockets, in the hope of catching some faint ray of light. I proceeded for many paces; but still all was blackness and vacancy. I breathed more freely. It seemed evident that mine was not, at least, the most hideous of fates.

And now, as I still continued to step cautiously onward, there came thronging upon my recollection a thousand vague rumors of the horrors of Toledo. Of the dungeons there had been strange things narrated—fables I had always deemed them—but yet strange, and too ghastly to repeat, save in a whisper. Was I left to perish of starvation in the subterranean world of darkness; or what fate, perhaps even more fearful, awaited me? That the result would be death, and a death of more than customary bitterness, I knew too well the character of my judges to doubt. The mode and the hour were all that occupied or distracted me.

My outstretched hands at length encountered some solid obstruction. It was a wall, seemingly of stone masonry—very smooth, slimy, and cold. I followed it up! stepping with all the careful distrust with which certain antique narratives had inspired me. This process, however, afforded me no means of ascertaining the dimensions of my dungeon; as I might make its circuit, and return to the point whence I set out, without being aware of the fact; so perfectly uniform seemed the wall. I therefore sought the knife which had been in my pocket, when led into the inquisitorial chamber; but it was gone; my clothes had been exchanged for a wrapper of coarse serge.[5] I had thought of forcing the blade in some minute crevice of the masonry, so as to identify my point of departure.

4. impeded: blocked.
5. serge: a strong fabric made of wool.

The difficulty, nevertheless, was but trivial; although, in the disorder of my fancy, it seemed at first insuperable. I tore a part of the hem from the robe and placed the fragment at full length, and at right angles to the wall. In groping my way around the prison I could not fail to encounter this rag upon completing the circuit. So, at least I thought: but I had not counted upon the extent of the dungeon, or upon my own weakness. The ground was moist and slippery. I staggered onward for some time, when I stumbled and fell. My excessive fatigue induced me to remain prostrate; and sleep soon overtook me as I lay.

Upon awakening, and stretching forth an arm, I found beside me a loaf and a pitcher with water. I was too much exhausted to reflect upon this circumstance, but ate and drank with avidity. Shortly afterward, I resumed my tour around the prison, and with much toil, came at last upon the fragment of the serge. Up to the period when I fell I had counted fifty-two paces, and upon resuming my walk, I counted forty-eight more; —when I arrived at the rag. There were in all, then, a hundred paces; and, admitting two paces to the yard, I presumed the dungeon to be fifty yards in circuit. I had met, however, with many angles in the wall, and thus I could form no guess at the shape of the vault; for vault I could not help supposing it to be.

I had little object—certainly no hope—in these researches; but a vague curiosity prompted me to continue them. Quitting the wall, I resolved to cross the area of the enclosure. At first I proceeded with extreme caution, for the floor, although seemingly of solid material, was treacherous with slime. At length, however, I took courage, and did not hesitate to step firmly; endeavoring to cross in as direct a line as possible. I had advanced some ten or twelve paces in this manner, when the remnant of the torn hem of my robe became entangled between my legs. I stepped on it, and fell violently on my face.

In the confusion attending my fall, I did not immediately apprehend a somewhat startling circumstance, which yet, in a few seconds afterward, and while I still lay prostrate, arrested my attention. It was this— my chin rested upon the floor of the prison, but my lips and the upper portion of my head, although seemingly at a less elevation than the chin, touched nothing. At the same time my forehead seemed bathed in a clammy vapor, and the peculiar smell of decayed fungus[6] arose to my nostrils. I put forward my arm, and shuddered to find that I had fallen at the very brink of a circular pit, whose extent, of course, I had no means of ascertaining at the moment. Groping about the masonry just below the margin, I succeeded in dislodging a small fragment, and let it fall into the abyss.[7] For many seconds I hearkened to its reverberations[8] as it dashed against the sides of the chasm in its descent; at length there was a sullen plunge into water, succeeded by loud echoes. At the same moment there came a sound resembling the quick opening, and as rapid closing of a door overhead, while a faint gleam of light flashed suddenly through the gloom, and as suddenly faded away.

I saw clearly the doom which had been prepared for me, and congratulated myself upon the timely accident by which I had escaped. Another step before my fall, and the world had seen me no more. And the death just avoided, was of that very character which I had regarded as fabulous and frivolous in the tales respecting the Inquisition. To the victims of its tyranny, there was the choice of death with its direst physical agonies, or death with its most hideous moral horrors. I had been reserved for the latter. By long suffering my nerves had been unstrung, until I trembled at the sound of my own voice, and had become in every respect a fitting subject for the species of torture which awaited me.

Shaking in every limb, I groped my way back to the wall; resolving there to perish rather than risk the terrors of the wells, of which my imagination now pictured many in various positions about the dungeon. In other conditions of mind I might have had courage to end my misery at once by a plunge into one of these abysses; but now I was the veriest of cowards. Neither could I forget what I had read of these pits—that the *sudden* extinction of life formed no part of their most horrible plan.

6. **fungus:** mold or mildew.
7. **abyss:** a bottomless pit.
8. **reverberations:** echoes.

Agitation of spirit kept me awake for many long hours; but at length I again slumbered. Upon arousing, I found by my side as before, a loaf and a pitcher of water. A burning thirst consumed me, and I emptied the vessel at a draught.[9] It must have been drugged; for scarcely had I drunk, before I became irresistibly drowsy. A deep sleep fell upon me—a sleep like that of death. How long it lasted of course, I know not; but when, once again, I unclosed my eyes, the objects around me were visible. By a wild sulphurous luster,[10] the origin of which I could not at first determine, I was enabled to see the extent and aspect of the prison.

In its size I had been greatly mistaken. The whole circuit of its walls did not exceed twenty-five yards. For some minutes this fact occasioned me a world of vain trouble; vain indeed! for what could be of less importance, under the terrible circumstances which environed me, than the mere dimensions of my dungeon? But my soul took a wild interest in trifles, and I busied myself in endeavors to account for the error I had committed in my measurement. The truth at length flashed upon me. In my first attempt at exploration I had counted fifty-two paces, up to the period when I fell; I must then have been within a pace or two of the fragments of serge; in fact, I had nearly performed the circuit of the vault. I then slept, and upon awaking, I must have returned upon my steps—thus supposing the circuit nearly double what it actually was. My confusion of mind prevented me from observing that I began my tour with the wall to the left, and ended it with the wall to the right.

I had been deceived, too, in respect to the shape of the enclosure. In feeling my way around I had found many angles, and thus deduced an idea of great irregularity; so potent is the effect of total darkness upon one arousing from lethargy or sleep! The angles were simply those of a few slight depressions, or niches, at odd intervals. The general shape of the prison was square. What I had taken for masonry seemed now to be iron, or some other metal, in huge plates, whose sutures or joints occasioned the depression. The entire surface of this metallic enclosure

9. at a draught: at a single drink.
10. sulphurous luster: a greenish-yellow light.

was rudely daubed[11] in all the hideous and repulsive devices to which the charnel superstitions[12] of the monks has given rise. The figures of fiends in aspects of menace, with skeleton forms, and other more really fearful images, overspread and disfigured the walls. I observed that the outlines of these monstrosities were sufficiently distinct, but that the colors seemed faded and blurred, as if from the effects of a damp atmosphere. I now noticed the floor, too, which was of stone. In the center yawned the circular pit from whose jaws I had escaped; but it was the only one in the dungeon.

All this I saw distinctly and by much effort: for my personal condition had been greatly changed during slumber. I now lay upon my back, and at full length, on a species of low framework of wood. To this I was securely bound by a long strap resembling a surcingle.[13] It passed in many convolutions about my limbs and body, leaving at liberty only my head, and my left arm to such extent that I could, by dint of much exertion, supply myself with food from an earthen dish which lay by my side on the floor. I saw, to my horror, that the pitcher had been removed. I say to my horror; for I was consumed with intolerable thirst. This thirst it appeared to be the design of my persecutors to stimulate: for the food in the dish was meat pungently seasoned.

Looking upward I surveyed the ceiling of my prison. It was some thirty or forty feet overhead, and constructed much as the side walls. In one of its panels a very singular figure riveted my whole attention. It was the painted figure of Time as he is commonly represented, save that, in lieu of a scythe,[14] he held what, at a casual glance, I supposed to be the pictured image of a huge pendulum such as we see on antique clocks. There was something, however, in the appearance of this machine which caused me to regard it more attentively. While I gazed directly upward at it (for its position was immediately over my own) I fancied that I saw

11. **daubed:** crudely applied paint.
12. **charnel superstitions:** the ignorant beliefs about the dead.
13. **surcingle:** a strap passed around a horse's body to hold a saddle in place.
14. **in lieu of a scythe:** in place of a scythe, a tool with a long, single-edged blade and curved handle that is used for cutting long grass. A scythe is often shown as a symbol of time.

it in motion. In an instant afterward the fancy was confirmed. Its sweep was brief, and of course slow. I watched it for some minutes, somewhat in fear, but more in wonder. Wearied at length with observing its dull movement, I turned my eyes upon the other objects in the cell.

A slight noise attracted my notice, and, looking to the floor, I saw several enormous rats traversing[15] it. They had issued from the well, which lay just within view to my right. Even then, while I gazed, they came up in troops, hurriedly, with ravenous[16] eyes, allured by the scent of the meat. From this it required much effort and attention to scare them away.

It might have been half an hour, perhaps even an hour, (for I could take but imperfect note of time) before I again cast my eyes upward. What I then saw confounded and amazed me. The sweep of the pendulum had increased in extent by nearly a yard. As a natural consequence, its velocity was also much greater. But what mainly disturbed me was the idea that it had perceptibly *descended.* I now observed—with what horror it is needless to say—that its nether extremity was formed of a crescent of glittering steel, about a foot in length from horn to horn; the horns upward, and the under edge evidently as keen as that of a razor. Like a razor also, it seemed massy and heavy, tapering from the edge into a solid and broad structure above. It was appended to a weighty rod of brass, and the whole *hissed* as it swung through the air.

I could no longer doubt the doom prepared for me by monkish ingenuity in torture. My cognizance of the pit had become known to the inquisitorial agents—*the pit* whose horrors had been destined for so bold a recusant as myself—*the pit,* typical of hell, and regarded by rumor as the Ultima Thule[17] of all their punishments. The plunge into this pit I had avoided by the merest of accidents, and I knew that surprise, or entrapment into torment, formed an important portion of all the grotesquerie of these dungeon deaths. Having failed to fall, it was no part of the demon plan to hurl me into the abyss; and thus (there being no

15. traversing: crossing.
16. ravenous: extremely hungry.
17. Ultima Thule: the last extremity.

alternative) a different and a milder destruction awaited me. Milder! I half smiled in my agony as I thought of such application of such a term.

What boots it to tell of the long, long hours of horror more than mortal, during which I counted the rushing vibrations of the steel! Inch by inch—line by line—with a descent only appreciable at intervals that seemed ages—down and still down it came! Days passed—it might have been that many days passed—ere it swept so closely over me as to fan me with its acrid breath. The odor of the sharp steel forced itself into my nostrils. I prayed—I wearied heaven with my prayer for its more speedy descent. I grew frantically mad, and struggled to force myself upward against the sweep of the fearful scimitar.[18] And then I fell suddenly calm, and lay smiling at the glittering death, as a child at some rare bauble.

There was another interval of utter insensibility; it was brief; for, upon again lapsing into life there had been no perceptible descent in the pendulum. But it might have been long; for I knew there were demons who took note of my swoon, and who could have arrested the vibration at pleasure. Upon my recovery, too, I felt very—oh, inexpressibly sick and weak, as if through long inanition.[19] Even amid the agonies of that period, the human nature craved food. With painful effort I outstretched my left arm as far as my bonds permitted, and took possession of the small remnant which had been spared me by the rats. As I put a portion of it within my lips, there rushed to my mind a half formed thought of joy—of hope. Yet what business had *I* with hope? It was, as I say, a half formed thought —man has many such which are never completed. I felt that it was of joy—of hope; but I felt also that it had perished in its formation. In vain I struggled to perfect—to regain it. Long suffering had nearly annihilated all my ordinary powers of mind. I was an imbecile—an idiot.

The vibration of the pendulum was at right angles to my length. I saw that the crescent was designed to cross the region of the heart. It would fray the serge of my robe—it would return and repeat its operations—

18. scimitar: a short, curved sword.
19. inanition: weakness from lack of food and water.

again—and again. Notwithstanding its terrifically wide sweep (some thirty feet or more) and the hissing vigor of its descent, sufficient to sunder these very walls of iron, still the fraying of my robe would be all that, for several minutes, it would accomplish. And at this thought I paused. I dared not go farther than this reflection. I dwelt upon it with a pertinacity[20] of attention—as if, in so dwelling, I could arrest *here* the descent of the steel. I forced myself to ponder upon the sound of the crescent as it should pass across the garment—upon the peculiar thrilling sensation which the friction of cloth produces on the nerves. I pondered upon all this frivolity until my teeth were on edge.

Down—steadily down it crept. I took a frenzied pleasure in contrasting its downward with its lateral velocity.[21] To the right—to the left—far and wide—with the shriek of a damned spirit; to my heart with the stealthy pace of the tiger! I alternately laughed and howled as the one or the other idea grew predominant.

Down—certainly, relentlessly down! It vibrated within three inches of my bosom! I struggled violently, furiously, to free my left arm. This was free only from the elbow to the hand. I could reach the latter, from the platter beside me, to my mouth, with great effort, but no farther. Could I have broken the fastenings above the elbow, I would have seized and attempted to arrest the pendulum. I might as well have attempted to arrest an avalanche!

Down—still unceasingly—still inevitably down! I gasped and struggled at each vibration. I shrunk convulsively at its every sweep. My eyes followed its outward or upward whirls with the eagerness of the most unmeaning despair; they closed themselves spasmodically at the descent, although death would have been a relief, oh! how unspeakable! Still I quivered in every nerve to think how slight a sinking of the machinery would precipitate that keen, glistening axe upon my bosom. It was *hope* that prompted the nerve to quiver—the frame to shrink. It

20. pertinacity: stubborn persistence.
21. lateral velocity: the speed in moving sideways.

was *hope*—the hope that triumphs on the rack—that whispers to the death-condemned even in the dungeons of the Inquisition.

I saw that some ten or twelve vibrations would bring the steel in actual contact with my robe, and with this observation there suddenly came over my spirit all the keen, collected calmness of despair. For the first time during many hours—or perhaps days—I *thought.* It now occurred to me that the bandage, or surcingle, which enveloped me, was *unique.* I was tied by no separate cord. The first stroke of the razor-like crescent athwart any portion of the band, would so detach it that it might be unwound from my person by means of my left hand. But how fearful, in that case, the proximity of the steel! The result of the slightest struggle how deadly! Was it likely, moreover, that the minions[22] of the torturer had not foreseen and provided for this possibility! Was it probable that the bandage crossed my bosom in the track of the pendulum? Dreading to find my faint, and, as it seemed, my last hope frustrated, I so far elevated my head as to obtain a distinct view of my breast. The surcingle enveloped my limbs and body close in all directions—*save in the path of the destroying crescent.*

Scarcely had I dropped my head back into its original position, when there flashed upon my mind what I cannot better describe than as the unformed half of that idea of deliverance to which I have previously alluded, and of which a moiety[23] only floated indeterminately through my brain when I raised food to my burning lips. The whole thought was now present —feeble, scarcely sane, scarcely definite,—but still entire. I proceeded at once, with the nervous energy of despair, to attempt its execution.

For many hours the immediate vicinity of the low framework upon which I lay, had been literally swarming with rats. They were wild, bold, ravenous; their red eyes glaring upon me as if they waited but for motionlessness on my part to make me their prey. "To what food," I thought, "have they been accustomed in the well?"

22. minions: faithful, slavish followers.
23. moiety: half, or part.

They had devoured, in spite of all my efforts to prevent them, all but a small remnant of the contents of the dish. I had fallen into an habitual seesaw, or wave of the hand about the platter: and, at length, the unconscious uniformity of the movement deprived it of effect. In their voracity the vermin frequently fastened their sharp fangs into my fingers. With the particles of the oily and spicy viand[24] which now remained, I thoroughly rubbed the bandage wherever I could reach it; then, raising my hand from the floor, I lay breathlessly still.

At first the ravenous animals were startled and terrified at the change—at the cessation of movement. They shrank alarmedly back; many sought the well. But this was only for a moment. I had not counted in vain upon their voracity. Observing that I remained without motion, one or two of the boldest leaped upon the frame-work, and smelt at the surcingle. This seemed the signal for a general rush. Forth from the well they hurried in fresh troops. They clung to the wood—they overran it, and leaped in hundreds upon my person. The measured movement of the pendulum disturbed them not at all. Avoiding its strokes they busied themselves with the anointed bandage. They pressed—they swarmed upon me in ever accumulating heaps. They writhed upon my throat; their cold lips sought my own; I was half stifled by their thronging pressure; disgust, for which the world has no name, swelled my bosom, and chilled, with a heavy clamminess, my heart. Yet one minute, and I felt that the struggle would be over. Plainly I perceived the loosening of the bandage. I knew that in more than one place it must be already severed. With a more than human resolution I lay *still.*

Nor had I erred in my calculations—nor had I endured in vain. I at length felt that I was *free.* The surcingle hung in ribands[25] from my body. But the stroke of the pendulum already pressed upon my bosom. It had divided the serge of the robe. It had cut through the linen beneath. Twice again it swung, and a sharp sense of pain shot through every nerve. But the moment of escape had arrived. At a wave of my hand my deliverers

24. viand: food.
25. ribands: ribbons.

hurried tumultuously away. With a steady movement—cautious, sidelong, shrinking, and slow—I slid from the embrace of the bandage and beyond the reach of the scimitar. For the moment, at least, *I was free.*

Free!—and in the grasp of the Inquisition! I had scarcely stepped from my wooden bed of horror upon the stone floor of the prison, when the motion of the hellish machine ceased and I beheld it drawn up, by some invisible force, through the ceiling. This was a lesson which I took desperately to heart. My every motion was undoubtedly watched. Free!—I had but escaped death in one form of agony, to be delivered unto worse than death in some other. With that thought I rolled my eyes nervously around the barriers of iron that hemmed me in. Something unusual—some change which at first I could not appreciate distinctly—it was obvious, had taken place in the apartment. For many minutes in a dreamy and trembling abstraction, I busied myself in vain, unconnected conjecture. During this period, I became aware, for the first time, of the origin of the sulphurous light which illuminated the cell. It proceeded from a fissure,[26] about half an inch in width, extending entirely around the prison at the base of the walls, which thus appeared, and were, completely separated from the floor. I endeavored, but of course in vain, to look through the aperture.

As I arose from the attempt, the mystery of the alteration in the chamber broke at once upon my understanding. I have observed that, although the outlines of the figures upon the walls were sufficiently distinct, yet the colors seemed blurred and indefinite. These colors had now assumed, and were momentarily assuming, a startling and most intense brilliancy, that gave to the spectral and fiendish portraitures an aspect that might have thrilled even firmer nerves than my own. Demon eyes, of a wild and ghastly vivacity, glared upon me in a thousand directions, where none had been visible before, and gleamed with the lurid luster of a fire that I could not force my imagination to regard as unreal.

Unreal!—Even while I breathed there came to my nostrils the breath

26. fissure: a long, narrow, deep crack.

of the vapor of heated iron! A suffocating odor pervaded[27] the prison! A deeper glow settled each moment in the eyes that glared at my agonies! A richer tint of crimson diffused itself over the pictured horrors of blood. I panted! I gasped for breath! There could be no doubt of the design of my tormentors—oh! most unrelenting! oh! most demoniac of men! I shrank from the glowing metal to the center of the cell. Amid the thought of the fiery destruction that impended, the idea of the coolness of the well came over my soul like balm.[28] I rushed to its deadly brink. I threw my straining vision below. The glare from the enkindled roof illumined its inmost recesses. Yet, for a wild moment, did my spirit refuse to comprehend the meaning of what I saw. At length it forced—it wrestled its way into my soul—it burned itself in upon my shuddering reason.—Oh! for a voice to speak!—oh! horror!—oh! any horror but this! With a shriek, I rushed from the margin, and buried my face in my hands—weeping bitterly.

The heat rapidly increased, and once again I looked up, shuddering as with a fit of the ague.[29] There had been a second change in the cell—and now the change was obviously in the *form.* As before, it was in vain that I, at first, endeavored to appreciate or understand what was taking place. But not long was I left in doubt. The Inquisitorial vengeance had been hurried by my two-fold escape, and there was to be no more dallying with the King of Terrors. The room had been square. I saw that two of its iron angles were now acute—two, consequently, obtuse. The fearful difference quickly increased with a low rumbling or moaning sound. In an instant the apartment had shifted its form into that of a lozenge.[30] But the alteration stopped not here—I neither hoped nor desired it to stop. I could have clasped the red walls to my bosom as a garment of eternal peace. "Death," I said, "any death but that of the pit!" Fool! might I have not known that *into the pit* it was the object of the

27. pervaded: spread throughout.
28. balm: a soothing, healing substance.
29. ague: a fever marked by shivering and chills.
30. lozenge: a diamond-shaped figure.

burning iron to urge me? Could I resist its glow? or, if even that, could I withstand its pressure? And now, flatter and flatter grew the lozenge, with a rapidity that left me no time for contemplation. Its center, and of course, its greatest width, came just over the yawning gulf. I shrank back—but the closing walls pressed me resistlessly onward. At length for my seared and writhing body there was no longer an inch of foothold on the firm floor of the prison. I struggled no more, but the agony of my soul found vent in one loud, long, and final scream of despair. I felt that I tottered upon the brink—I averted my eyes—

There was a discordant hum of human voices! There was a loud blast of many trumpets! There was a harsh grating as of a thousand thunders! The fiery walls rushed back! An outstretched arm caught my own as I fell, fainting, into the abyss. It was that of General Lasalle. The French army had entered Toledo. The Inquisition was in the hands of its enemies.

1. It is fast action.

2. Plant

3. Before this paragraphy we read faster because it doesn't have any long vowl words.

4.

Internal conflict: fighting to stay alive, try to survive.

External conflict: The torture.

Reviewing the Selection

Answer each of the following questions without looking back at the story.

Recalling Facts

1. When the prisoner first feels his way around the walls of the dungeon, he thinks that his cell is
   - ☑ a. larger than it really is.
   - ☐ b. smaller than it really is.
   - ☐ c. made of wood.
   - ☐ d. made of heated iron.

Understanding Main Ideas

2. In "The Pit and the Pendulum" the narrator is
   - ☒ a. suffering from a nightmare.
   - ☐ b. awaiting execution for murder.
   - ☑ c. describing the tortures he underwent in prison.
   - ☐ d. planning how he can take revenge on the Inquisition.

Placing Events in Order

3. The final danger that the narrator faces is being
   - ☑ a. forced into the pit by the moving walls.
   - ☐ b. eaten alive by the starving rats.
   - ☐ c. cut in half by the pendulum.
   - ☐ d. shot by the French soldiers.

Finding Supporting Details

4. The prisoner gets the rats to chew through his bonds by
   - ☑ a. lying perfectly still.
   - ☐ b. rubbing the bandages with meat.
   - ☐ c. holding their tails.
   - ☐ d. waving his free hand.

Recognizing Words in Context

5. "Long suffering had nearly annihilated all my ordinary powers of mind." In this context *annihilated* means
   - ☐ a. sharpened.
   - ☐ b. helped.
   - ☐ c. dulled.
   - ☑ d. destroyed.

Interpreting the Selection

Answer each of the following questions. You may look back at the story if necessary.

Making Inferences

6. Why does the pendulum descend so slowly?
   - ☐ a. It is tied to a clock that times its movements.
   - ☐ b. It is too heavy for the machinery to move it faster.
   - ☑ c. The jailers want the prisoner to die a slow death.
   - ☐ d. The French army is invading Toledo.

Generalizing

7. The narrator knows that all his efforts to save himself are likely to be in vain because
   - ☐ a. the food he ate contained a slow-working poison.
   - ☐ b. he will be burned at the next *auto-da-fé.*
   - ☐ c. the Inquisition will not free him until he confesses.
   - ☑ d. the Inquisition has condemned him to death.

Analyzing Character

8. Which of the following words best describes the prisoner's behavior?
   - ☐ a. self-destructive
   - ☐ b. cowardly
   - ☐ c. aggressive
   - ☑ d. clever

Comparing

9. When the prisoner realizes that the pendulum is descending, he refers to it as "a milder destruction." To him, it is "milder" than
   - ☐ a. being burned at the stake.
   - ☐ b. being tortured on the rack.
   - ☑ c. falling into the pit.
   - ☐ d. being crushed by the burning walls.

Drawing Conclusions

10. What conclusion can you draw from the last scene, in which the prisoner is rescued?
    - ☐ a. The French have not heard of the Spanish Inquisition.
    - ☐ b. The prisoner is a French noble.
    - ☐ c. The prisoner is a Spanish general.
    - ☑ d. The French are at war with the Spanish.

Setting and Mood

As you have seen, setting is the place and time of the action in a story. In some stories, the author briefly describes the setting at the beginning of the story and then focuses on the characters or the plot. In others, the author sprinkles details about the setting throughout the story. Adding more information about the setting may be necessary if the action shifts from one place to another.

Writers use details about the setting to create a particular mood. The feeling, or atmosphere, of "The Pit and the Pendulum" is one of terror and horror. As you will learn in this lesson, setting greatly influences that mood.

Details of Place

How does a writer establish the setting of a story? Sometimes, a writer gives a few factual details, such as, "My story begins in Chicago in 1983." Other writers use a range of details to describe the place where the action occurs. By giving vivid details, they create a clear picture of the setting. Through details, you can sense what the place is like. In "The Pit and the Pendulum" Poe describes the setting so that you can experience it with all five senses: sight, sound, touch, taste, and smell.

The story takes place in a dungeon, yet Poe doesn't simply state that fact and tell you about the dungeon. He forces you to struggle along with the prisoner, learning with him what the place is like. Sharing the prisoner's terrifying experience as he explores the dungeon builds the suspense that you feel while reading the story.

When the story begins, the prisoner is only semi-conscious. He is confused and disoriented. He slowly recalls his trial and remembers the sensations he has recently experienced. Gradually, the prisoner comes to full consciousness.

> So far, I had not opened my eyes. I felt that I lay upon my back, unbound. I reached out my hand, and it fell heavily upon something damp and hard. There I suffered it to remain for many minutes, while I strove to imagine where and *what* I could be. I longed, yet dared not to employ my vision . . . . At length, with a wild desperation at heart, I quickly unclosed my eyes. My worst thoughts, then, were confirmed. The blackness of eternal night encompassed me. I struggled for breath. The intensity of the darkness seemed to oppress and stifle me. The atmosphere was intolerably close.

That passage is the first description you have of the setting. Notice the details that Poe includes: The prisoner touches "something damp and hard." When he opens his eyes, he sees the darkness of the dungeon and suffers a sense of suffocation.

1. Skim the story to find other passages in which Poe describes the setting. Then write one detail about the setting that affects each of the senses—sight, sound, touch, taste, and smell.

The dungeon is central to Poe's story. The plot that unfolds could take place in no other setting. To give you a true sense of the dungeon, Poe has the prisoner explore and report on every inch of the walls and floor. Even though that exploration yields a false picture of what the dungeon is like, you are made to share the prisoner's perception of the place, with all its horrible and confusing details. Poe puts you in the dungeon, too.

2. Describe in your own words, or sketch the cell as the prisoner first perceived it. How does his knowledge of the dungeon change?

Details of Time

Time is the other element of setting. *When* does a particular story take place? The answer can be general, such as "in the present," or it can be specific: "Friday, October 17, 1886."

Often, a short-story writer does not state the time of the action. You have to infer the time from the details in the story, such as the clothing, the way of speaking, or the technology. After reading the first few paragraphs of "The Pit and the Pendulum," you can tell that the story is set in the past.

3. What is the first clue you get that the story takes place in the past? List two other details in the story that support that conclusion.

Two other questions about time are important—how much time passes between the beginning and the end of the story, and how much time passes between the individual events in the story? You need to have some idea of the answers to those questions in order to understand the prisoner's state of mind as the story unfolds.

Writers signal the passage of time with phrases such as *then, next, an hour later,* or *the next day.* In "The Pit and the Pendulum," however, you don't really know how much time passes. Poe uses phrases such as *at length, for some time,* and *for many long hours* to indicate the passage of time. His vagueness is purposeful. The prisoner himself doesn't know how long he has been there. He cannot keep track of time in the ordinary way because he has no watch or clock, and he cannot see daylight. Then, too, the prisoner is unconscious or sleeping for long periods. Like the prisoner, you are left confused and uncertain about time.

On the other hand, Poe sometimes shows time moving swiftly, with phrases such as *in a few seconds* or *for a wild moment.* Those phrases hurry the story along. They signal that actions will quickly follow one another.

4. Make your own estimate as to how much time passes between the beginning and the end of the story. Give reasons for your estimate.

Creating the Mood

Poe's setting contributes greatly to the mood, or feeling, of the story. As the story begins, the main character tells of his weariness after the many horrors of his recent trial. You hear his recollection of strange and frightening experiences. When Poe describes the setting in the passage quoted earlier, you start to share the prisoner's feelings.

The darkness, dampness, and suffocating atmosphere create a sense of oppression and dread. As the prisoner lies in the impenetrable darkness and thinks about his situation, his feeling of dread increases. At first, he fears that he is in a tomb. Caught up in an agony of fear, he starts to explore his imagined tomb—the dungeon.

5. Find the paragraph on page 123 that begins, "My outstretched hands at length encountered some solid obstruction." Review the prisoner's exploration of his dungeon. What mood does the author create for you? How does the mood change as the prisoner completes his exploration? Why does it change?

After the prisoner discovers the pit in the middle of his cell, he sleeps, wakes, and then drinks the drugged water. When he wakes again, the cell is lighted. For the first time he sees where he is. You, too, learn the exact appearance of the cell. Ordinarily, light helps to chase away fears. When you can see what is going on, you don't have to be afraid of unknown dangers hidden by darkness. In this story the opposite is true.

First, the light is no ordinary light—it is "a wild sulphurous luster" whose source is unknown. The eerie luster provides just enough light for the prisoner to see the size of his cell. It reveals other horrors besides the pit. On the walls the prisoner sees fiendish figures and "other more really fearful images." The most fearful discovery is yet to come. When he awakes he sees the pendulum hanging from the ceiling, and he soon realizes that the pendulum is descending on him. What horror that sight brings! Bound to a wooden frame beneath the gradually descending blade, the prisoner lies helpless.

6. Review the scene in which the prisoner is lying on his back watching the pendulum descend. What changes in mood does Poe create during that episode? Why do those changes occur?

Mood and Suspense

The mood in this story is closely related to suspense. As you read in Chapter 3, suspense is the excitement, uncertainty, or tension that you feel while waiting for the outcome of the story. Suspense makes you want to know what will happen next.

In this story Poe uses the most fearsome kind of suspense. The prisoner is literally fighting for his life. The Inquisition is all-powerful, and he is a helpless prisoner in its hands. Will he survive the awful tortures his jailers have invented? How can he escape his fate? Those questions force you to read on to find out whether he can save himself from what seems to be certain death.

Poe builds the suspense through a series of unexpected or unusual happenings. First, the prisoner is saved from the abyss when he accidentally trips and falls. However, that fortunate escape from death is only temporary. The prisoner faces death a second time when he is bound to a frame beneath the descending pendulum. The suspense increases as the prisoner first discovers his danger and then realizes how helpless he is. Like him, you can see no way of escape.

Then, as the pendulum swings closer to his chest, the prisoner cleverly discovers a way to get free of his bonds. Another lucky escape. Or is it? "Free!—I had but escaped death in one form of agony, to be delivered unto worse than death in some other," the prisoner realizes.

The new threat generates still greater suspense, as the prisoner realizes that the heated iron walls of the dungeon are closing in on him.

Before long, the walls will force him into the horrible pit. Once again, you can see no way for the man to escape.

7. Make a list of the tortures that the prisoner suffers in the dungeon. During which of the tortures did you feel the most suspense? Why?

The Surprise Ending

Just as the suspense reaches a new peak, with the prisoner tottering on the brink of the most awful death, Poe creates a surprise ending to the story. A surprise ending is an unexpected twist that concludes a story.

The surprise ending in "The Pit and the Pendulum" is delivered in one short paragraph. In it, you learn how the prisoner escapes from his torturers. The surprise twist comes at the moment of highest suspense. Neither you nor the prisoner has any idea that his rescue from death is possible. Although the prisoner does not say so, he probably feels great relief at his rescue. Certainly you, the reader, breathe freely again after the tension and uncertainty of the last few pages.

Yet the surprise ending raises several unanswered questions. Who is General Lasalle? How does the prisoner know him? Did Lasalle know that the prisoner was about to be killed? Why are the French entering Toledo? Poe offers no answer to those questions, just as he has left you uncertain all along about who the prisoner is and why he has been condemned by the Inquisition. By leaving those questions unanswered, he continues the story's suspense and uncertainties beyond its last lines.

8. Reread the last paragraph of "The Pit and the Pendulum." Then compare its sentences and language to any other paragraph in the story. How are they different from the rest of the story? Why do you think Poe wrote the last paragraph in this way?

Questions for Thought and Discussion

The questions and activities that follow will help you explore "The Pit and the Pendulum" in more depth and at the same time develop your critical thinking skills.

1. **Analyzing Character.** Divide the class into small groups. Each group should discuss what they can learn about the prisoner from his actions and his thoughts. Have the group try to imagine the reasons why he finds himself in his present situation. How might his character have led him into trouble with the Inquisition? Finally, share your group's ideas with the rest of the class.

2. **Comparing.** Which form of death does the prisoner think is worse—the pit or the pendulum? Why does he dread one more than the other?

3. **Identifying Conflict.** In Chapter 3 you learned about the different kinds of conflict. What is the main conflict in this story? Is it an internal or an external conflict? What other examples of conflict do you find in "The Pit and the Pendulum"?

4. **Distinguishing Reality and Fantasy.** Do you think this story could actually have taken place? Explain your answer.

Writing About Literature

Several suggestions for writing projects are given below. You may be asked to complete one or more of these projects. If you have any questions about how to begin a writing assignment, review Using the Writing Process, beginning on page 337.

1. **Creating a Mood.** Write two or three paragraphs describing an experience, place, or event, in which you create a specific mood. First, choose the mood you want to establish—for instance, peaceful, frightening, or despairing. Then, use description, narration, or dialogue to build the mood. Finally, read your paragraphs to the class and see if the other students can identify the mood.

2. **Describing a Place.** Choose a place that you know well and for which you have a special feeling. Make a list of details you have observed about the place. Include details that affect all five senses. Then write a brief description of the place, using the details on your list.

3. **Creating Dialogue.** Imagine the conversation that might have taken place between General Lasalle and the prisoner at the end of the story. Write a page of dialogue between the prisoner and his rescuer. Use what you have learned about the prisoner in the story to help you write his part of the dialogue in such a way that it sounds like something he might have said.

4. **Writing About a Personal Experience.** Describe a terrifying ordeal that you or someone you know has experienced. Try to establish the setting and mood of your story as clearly as possible. You might create the setting and mood by giving many details, or you might use Poe's techniques and have your readers discover facts and information along with your character.

PUPPY

Chapter 6

Selection *The Secret Life of Walter Mitty*

JAMES THURBER

Lesson *Humor and Satire*

About the Selection

What is a daydream? A dictionary definition is, "pleasant, dreamy thinking or wishing." Yet a daydream can be a lot more than that. For many people, it is an escape from a harsh, dull, or unhappy life. For some, it is a way of setting goals for the future.

You have probably heard people say, "I always dreamed of doing this (or seeing that)." Olympic gold medalists, for example—or any other prize winners—might use such words to describe their pleasure at achieving their goals. Did they actually daydream about their successes? Did they picture themselves walking up to accept their awards, with a large audience applauding? Perhaps they did.

Very few people go through life without thinking dreamily about "what life would be like if . . . ." Most of us imagine what it would be like to be stronger, older, smarter, richer, braver, or otherwise different from what we are now. Such daydreams as those are sometimes called fantasies. Both words refer to unreal situations created by our imaginations. Whether or not a fantasy is turned into reality depends both on the dream and on the dreamer.

The main character in James Thurber's "The Secret Life of Walter Mitty" is a man who plunges into one daydream after another. In fact, his daydreams take up most of the story. Real events, as we know them, seem incidental to Walter Mitty's life, which is lived in his daydreams.

Mitty's daydreams are unlikely stories, but we can't help smiling at the situations in which he mentally puts himself. Perhaps we can see a bit of ourselves in the wild flights of his imagination.

The author, James Thurber, has cleverly used humor to portray a gentle man whose greatest pleasure in life is escaping into his daydreams. Yet there is a sadness mixed in with the humor. Like many daydreamers, Walter Mitty will never be able to make his dreams come true. His "secret life" will always exist only in his imagination.

James Thurber is counted among the best American humorists. He is also well-known for his cartoons and the cartoonlike drawings with which he illustrated his stories and books. Thurber's favorite fictional subjects were timid, dissatisfied men who had a hard time coping with the complexities of modern life. In many of his stories, Thurber showed those men at the mercy of domineering wives. Like Walter Mitty in the story you are about to read, they sought to escape from their troubles at home or on the job.

Thurber began his career as a reporter. He worked first in Columbus, Ohio, before moving on to Chicago and later to New York. Through a friend, the well-known writer E. B. White, Thurber got a job at *The New Yorker* magazine. The managing editor of the magazine, Harold Ross, hired Thurber as an editor. Thurber was not happy with editorial work; he wanted to write. After a few months at the magazine, Thurber was pleased to be "demoted" to a job as a writer.

Thurber wrote many short stories, essays and plays, as well as books for children. In his work he often poked fun at people and at human weaknesses in general. The humor in his stories brought chuckles from people who recognized their own behavior in the actions and words of Thurber's characters. Several Thurber stories, including "The Secret Life of Walter Mitty," were made into movies.

Thurber poked fun at himself, too, especially at his own poor eyesight. As a result of a childhood accident, he lost the sight in one eye. Later, he had problems with the other eye and became almost blind. Although he had to give up his illustrating, he continued to write.

Lesson Preview

The lesson that follows "The Secret Life of Walter Mitty" focuses on humor and the techniques that Thurber used to create humor in the story. A major source of humor lies in the striking contrast between Walter Mitty's real-life situation and his heroic fantasies. Thurber also creates humor through dialogue and his use of language.

The questions that follow will help you to identify the elements of humor in the story. As you read, think about how you would answer these questions.

1 What is the major difference between Walter Mitty's daydreams and his everyday life?

2 What kind of person is Mitty in his daydreams? In real life?

3 In Mitty's daydreams, what do other people think of him? What do people think of Mitty in real life?

4 What actions or events trigger Mitty's escape into daydreams? What brings him back to reality?

5 Are Mitty's daydreams humorous? Why or why not? How does the dialogue in the daydreams contribute to the humor of the story.

6 How does Thurber use the humorous situations in the story to make a serious point?

Vocabulary

Here are some difficult words that appear in the selection that follows. Study the words and their definitions, as well as the sentences that show how the words are used. This will help you get the most from your reading.

turret a low, towerlike structure on a warship or tank. *The gunners took their position in the turret after enemy planes were sighted.*

distraught extremely troubled with doubt or mental conflict. *While distraught family and friends waited, rescue workers continued to search for survivors of the mine accident.*

haggard having a wild, worn look from worry, sleeplessness, or illness. *The climbers returned home looking hungry and haggard.*

insinuatingly gradually causing doubt or distrust by subtle hints or suggestions. *"Unfortunately, Reynolds is late—again," the manager remarked insinuatingly.*

cur a mongrel; a person who is mean and cowardly. *The more we heard of his cowardly behavior, the more we thought him a spineless cur.*

inscrutable not easily understood; mysterious; baffling. *"You may think we have no clues to this inscrutable mystery," said the detective, "but I can solve the case!"*

The Secret Life of Walter Mitty

James Thurber

"We're going through!" The Commander's voice was like thin ice breaking. He wore his full-dress uniform, with the heavily braided white cap pulled down rakishly over one cold gray eye. "We can't make it, sir. It's spoiling for a hurricane, if you ask me." "I'm not asking you, Lieutenant Berg," said the Commander. "Throw on the power lights! Rev her up to 8,500! We're going through!" The pounding of the cylinders increased: ta-pocketa-pocketa-pocketa-*pocketa-pocketa.* The Commander stared at the ice forming on the pilot window. He walked over and twisted a row of complicated dials. "Switch on No. 8 auxiliary!" he shouted. "Switch on No. 8 auxiliary!" repeated Lieutenant Berg. "Full strength in No. 3 turret!" shouted the Commander. "Full strength in No. 3 turret!" The crew, bending to their various tasks in the huge, hurtling eight-engined Navy hydroplane, looked at each other and grinned. "The Old Man'll get us through," they said to one another. "The Old Man ain't afraid of Hell!" . . .

"Not so fast! You're driving too fast!" said Mrs. Mitty. "What are you driving so fast for?"

"Hmm?" said Walter Mitty. He looked at his wife, in the seat beside him, with shocked astonishment. She seemed grossly unfamiliar, like a strange woman who had yelled at him in a crowd. "You were up to fifty-five," she said. "You know I don't like to go more than forty. You were up to fifty-five." Walter Mitty drove on toward Waterbury in silence, the roaring of the SN202 through the worst storm in twenty years of Navy flying fading in the remote, intimate airways of his mind. "You're tensed up again," said Mrs. Mitty. "It's one of your days. I wish you'd let Dr. Renshaw look you over."

Walter Mitty stopped the car in front of the building where his wife went to have her hair done. "Remember to get those overshoes while I'm having my hair done," she said. "I don't need overshoes," said Mitty. She put her mirror back into her bag. "We've been through all that," she said, getting out of the car. "You're not a young man any longer." He raced the engine a little. "Why don't you wear your gloves? Have you lost your gloves?" Walter Mitty reached in a pocket and brought out the gloves. He put them on, but after she had turned and gone into the building and he had driven on to a red light, he took them off again. "Pick it up, brother!" snapped a cop as the light changed, and Mitty hastily pulled on his gloves and lurched ahead. He drove around the streets aimlessly for a time, and then he drove past the hospital on his way to the parking lot.

. . . "It's the millionaire banker, Wellington McMillan," said the pretty nurse. "Yes?" said Walter Mitty, removing his gloves slowly. "Who has the case?" "Dr. Renshaw and Dr. Benbow, but there are two specialists here, Dr. Remington from New York and Dr. Pritchard-Mitford from London. He flew over." A door opened down a long, cool corridor and Dr. Renshaw came out. He looked distraught and haggard. "Hello, Mitty," he said. "We're having the devil's own time with McMillan, the millionaire banker and close personal friend of Roosevelt. Obstreosis of the ductal tract. Tertiary. Wish you'd take a look at him." "Glad to," said Mitty.

In the operating room there were whispered introductions: "Dr. Remington, Dr. Mitty. Dr. Pritchard-Mitford, Dr. Mitty." "I've read your book on streptothricosis," said Pritchard-Mitford, shaking hands. "A brilliant performance, sir." "Thank you," said Walter Mitty. "Didn't know you were in the States, Mitty," grumbled Remington. "Coals to Newcastle,[1] bringing Mitford and me up here for a tertiary." "You are very kind," said Mitty. A huge, complicated machine, connected to the operating table, with many tubes and wires, began at this moment to go pocketa-pocketa-pocketa. "The new anesthetizer[2] is giving way!" shouted an intern. "There is no one in the East who knows how to fix it!" "Quiet man!" said Mitty, in a low, cool voice. He sprang to the machine, which was now going pocketa-pocketa-queep-pocketa-queep. He began fingering delicately a row of glistening dials. "Give me a fountain pen!" he snapped. Someone handed him a fountain pen. He pulled a faulty piston out of the machine and inserted the pen in its place. "That will hold for ten minutes," he said. "Get on with the operation." A nurse hurried over and whispered to Renshaw, and Mitty saw the man turn pale. "Coreopsis has set in," said Renshaw nervously. "If you would take over, Mitty?" Mitty looked at him and at the craven figure of Benbow, who drank, and at the grave, uncertain faces of the two great specialists. "If you wish," he said. They slipped a white gown on him; he adjusted a mask and drew on thin gloves; nurses handed him shining . . .

"Back it up, Mac! Look out for that Buick!" Walter Mitty jammed on the brakes. "Wrong lane, Mac," said the parking-lot attendant, looking at Mitty closely. "Gee. Yeh," muttered Mitty. He began cautiously to back out of the lane marked "Exit Only." "Leave her sit there," said the attendant. "I'll put her away." Mitty got out of the car. "Hey, better leave the key." "Oh," said Mitty, handing the man the ignition key. The attendant vaulted

1. **"Bringing coals to Newcastle":** an old expression that means doing something unnecessarily. Newcastle is a city in northern England that was a center of coal mining.
2. **anesthetizer:** a machine used to make a patient unconscious during surgery.

into the car, backed it up with insolent skill, and put it where it belonged.

They're so damn cocky, thought Walter Mitty, walking along Main Street; they think they know everything. Once he had tried to take his chains off, outside New Milford, and he had got them wound around the axles. A man had had to come out in a wrecking car and unwind them, a young, grinning garageman. Since then Mrs. Mitty always made him drive to a garage to have the chains taken off. The next time, he thought, I'll wear my right arm in a sling; they won't grin at me then. I'll have my right arm in a sling and they'll see I couldn't possibly take the chains off myself. He kicked at the slush on the sidewalk. "Overshoes," he said to himself, and he began looking for a shoe store.

When he came out into the street again, with the overshoes in a box under his arm, Walter Mitty began to wonder what the other thing was his wife had told him to get. She had told him, twice, before they set out from their house for Waterbury. In a way he hated these weekly trips to town—he was always getting something wrong. Kleenex, he thought, Squibb's, razor blades? No. Toothpaste, toothbrush, bicarbonate, carborundum, initiative and referendum?[3] He gave it up. But she would remember it. "Where's the what's-its-name?" she would ask. "Don't tell me you forgot the what's-its-name?" A newsboy went by shouting something about the Waterbury trial.

. . . "Perhaps this will refresh your memory." The District Attorney suddenly thrust a heavy automatic at the quiet figure on the witness stand. "Have you ever seen this before?" Walter Mitty took the gun and examined it expertly. "This is my Webley-Vickers 50.80," he said calmly. An excited buzz ran around the courtroom. The Judge rapped for order. "You are a crack shot with any sort of firearms, I believe?" said the District Attorney, insinuatingly. "Objection!" shouted Mitty's attorney. "We have shown that the defendant could not have fired the shot. We

3. **bicarbonate, carborundum, initiative and referendum:** a series of unrelated words running through Mitty's mind. Bicarbonate refers to bicarbonate of soda, or baking soda. Carborundum is a hard substance used for grinding. Initiative and referendum refer to various political actions taken by voters.

have shown that he wore his right arm in a sling on the night of the fourteenth of July." Walter Mitty raised his hand briefly and the bickering attorneys were stilled. "With any known make of gun," he said evenly, "I could have killed Gregory Fitzhurst at three hundred feet *with my left hand.*" Pandemonium[4] broke loose in the courtroom. A woman's scream rose above the bedlam and suddenly a lovely, dark-haired girl was in Walter Mitty's arms. The District Attorney struck at her savagely. Without rising from his chair, Mitty let the man have it on the point of the chin. "You miserable cur!" . . .

"Puppy biscuit," said Walter Mitty. He stopped walking and the buildings of Waterbury rose up out of the misty courtroom and surrounded him again. A woman who was passing laughed. "He said 'Puppy biscuit,' " she said to her companion. "That man said 'Puppy biscuit' to himself." Walter Mitty hurried on. He went into an A & P, not the first one he came to but a smaller one farther up the street. "I want some biscuit for small, young dogs," he said to the clerk. "Any special brand, sir?" The greatest pistol shot in the world thought a moment. "It says 'Puppies Bark for It' on the box," said Walter Mitty.

His wife would be through at the hairdresser's in fifteen minutes, Mitty saw in looking at his watch, unless they had trouble drying it; sometimes they had trouble drying it. She didn't like to get to the hotel first; she would want him to be there waiting for her as usual. He found a big leather chair in the lobby, facing a window, and he put the overshoes and the puppy biscuit on the floor beside it. He picked up an old copy of *Liberty* and sank down into the chair. "Can Germany Conquer the World Through the Air?" Walter Mitty looked at the pictures of bombing planes and of ruined streets.

. . . "The cannonading has got the wind up in young Raleigh, sir," said the sergeant. Captain Mitty looked up at him through tousled hair. "Get him to bed," he said wearily, "with the others. I'll fly alone." "But you can't, sir," said the sergeant anxiously. "It takes two men to handle

4. pandemonium: wild disorder.

that bomber and the Archies are pounding hell out of the air. Von Richtman's circus is between here and Saulier." "Somebody's got to get that ammunition dump," said Mitty. "I'm going over. Spot of brandy?" He poured a drink for the sergeant and one for himself. War thundered and whined around the dugout and battered at the door. There was a rending of wood and splinters flew through the room. "A bit of a near thing," said "Captain Mitty carelessly. "The box barrage[5] is closing in," said the sergeant. "We only live once, Sergeant," said Mitty, with his faint, fleeting smile. "Or do we?" He poured another brandy and tossed it off. "I never see a man could hold his brandy like you, sir," said the sergeant. "Begging your pardon, sir." Captain Mitty stood up and strapped on his huge Webley-Vickers automatic. "It's forty kilometers through hell, sir," said the sergeant. Mitty finished one last brandy. "After all," he said softly, "what isn't?" The pounding of the cannon increased; there was the rat-tat-tatting of machine guns, and from somewhere came the menacing pocketa-pocketa-pocketa of the new flame throwers. Walter Mitty walked to the door of the dugout humming "Auprès de Ma Blonde."[6] He turned and waved to the sergeant. "Cheerio!" he said. . . .

Something struck his shoulder. "I've been looking all over this hotel for you," said Mrs. Mitty. "Why do you have to hide in this old chair? How did you expect me to find you?" "Things close in," said Walter Mitty vaguely. "What?" Mrs. Mitty said. "Did you get the what's-its-name? The puppy biscuit? What's in that box?" "Overshoes," said Mitty. "Couldn't you have put them on in the store?" "I was thinking," said Walter Mitty. "Does it ever occur to you that I am sometimes thinking?" She looked at him. "I'm going to take your temperature when I get you home," she said.

They went out through the revolving doors that made a faintly derisive whistling sound when you pushed them. It was two blocks to the parking lot. At the drug store on the corner she said, "Wait here for me.

5. **box barrage:** heavy shelling by large guns that bombards a box, or square, of land.

6. **"Auprès de Ma Blonde":** title of a popular French song in World War I. The title can be translated as "Close to My Blonde Girlfriend."

I forgot something. I won't be a minute." She was more than a minute. Walter Mitty lighted a cigarette. It began to rain, rain with sleet in it. He stood up against the wall of the drug store, smoking. . . . He put his shoulders back and his heels together. "To hell with the handkerchief," said Walter Mitty scornfully. He took one last drag on his cigarette and snapped it away. Then, with that faint, fleeting smile playing about his lips, he faced the firing squad; erect and motionless, proud and disdainful, Walter Mitty the Undefeated, inscrutable to the last.

Reviewing the Selection

Answer each of the following questions without looking back at the story.

Recalling Facts

1. Walter Mitty and his wife are driving to Waterbury to
   - ☐ a. attend the theater.
   - ☐ b. stay at a hotel.
   - ☐ c. buy a new car.
   - ☐ d. do their weekly errands.

Understanding Main Ideas

2. In all of Mitty's daydreams, he
   - ☐ a. is a retired Navy pilot.
   - ☐ b. shows his easygoing nature.
   - ☐ c. is fearless and strong.
   - ☐ d. shares jokes with his colleagues.

Placing Events in Order

3. Mitty's first fantasy in the story is about
   - ☐ a. saving the life of a millionaire banker.
   - ☐ b. standing before a firing squad.
   - ☐ c. facing a district attorney.
   - ☐ d. commanding a hydroplane.

Finding Supporting Details

4. What detail in the story shows that Mrs. Mitty is not content with her husband?
   - ☐ a. She allows him to daydream.
   - ☐ b. She goes to the hairdresser once a week.
   - ☐ c. She criticizes him all the time.
   - ☐ d. She wants him to be at the hotel before her.

Recognizing Words in Context

5. "A woman's scream rose above the bedlam and suddenly a lovely, dark-haired girl was in Walter Mitty's arms." In this context *bedlam* means
   - ☐ a. noisy confusion.
   - ☐ b. sudden hush.
   - ☐ c. crowd.
   - ☐ d. ceiling.

Interpreting the Selection

Answer each of the following questions. You may look back at the story if necessary.

Making Inferences

6. Why do you think Mitty has never revealed his secret life to anyone?
   - ☐ a. He doesn't want anyone to know what he is thinking.
   - ☐ b. He quickly forgets his daydreams.
   - ☐ c. He wants to live up to his dreams before telling anyone.
   - ☐ d. He is completely caught up in his own world.

Generalizing

7. Walter Mitty's daydreams can be said to provide a way for Mitty to
   - ☐ a. escape his dull, unhappy life.
   - ☐ b. take revenge on other people.
   - ☐ c. punish his wife.
   - ☐ d. make up for the fact that he has no children.

Analyzing Character

8. To his wife, Mitty seems to be
   - ☐ a. lonely and depressed.
   - ☐ b. tense and thoughtless.
   - ☐ c. kind and considerate.
   - ☐ d. strong and brave.

Comparing

9. How does Mitty's life compare to his daydreams?
   - ☐ a. His life is sometimes just like his daydreams.
   - ☐ b. His life is dull compared to his daydreams.
   - ☐ c. He once did all the things that he now daydreams about.
   - ☐ d. He cannot decide if he prefers his life or his daydreams.

Drawing Conclusions

10. In the future, Mitty is likely to
    - ☐ a. continue daydreaming as he has always done.
    - ☐ b. tell his wife about his daydreams to stop her complaints.
    - ☐ c. tell Dr. Renshaw about his daydreams to get help.
    - ☐ d. stop daydreaming because he has a puppy to love.

Humor and Satire

In literature, humor is whatever is funny or amusing in a situation. Humor takes many forms, and everyone has his or her own idea of what is funny. A familiar kind of humor is a joke—something that is said or done on purpose to get a laugh. Another kind of humor is slapstick, which depends on fast, foolish action to make people laugh. Humor can be light and gentle, or it can be sarcastic and mocking.

In literature, an important kind of humor is satire. Satire is a kind of writing in which certain ideas, customs, or human weaknesses are ridiculed. Often, a writer satirizes behavior or ideas by using exaggeration. In "The Secret Life of Walter Mitty" Thurber uses satire to reveal the foolishness of a person who uses daydreams of being a great hero to escape a boring, uneventful life.

Satire can be gentle or harsh. The satire in this story could be called gentle, for you feel some sympathy toward Walter Mitty. At the same time, you laugh at the extreme situations he imagines in his daydreams.

In "The Secret Life of Walter Mitty," Thurber creates humor in several ways. He establishes humor in the situations Mitty dreams up and in the personalities Mitty adopts. Thurber further develops the humor of the story through his use of language. In this lesson you will explore examples of Thurber's humor.

Humor and Situation

One way a writer creates humor is by setting up an amusing situation. Often, the humor of a situation is ironic. Irony is a contrast between appearance and reality, or between what is expected and what actually happens.

In "The Secret Life of Walter Mitty" you see almost right away the irony, or contrast, between Mitty's dreamworld and his real life. In the first line of the story you are thrust into the middle of one of Mitty's fantasies, although you don't know at first that it is a daydream. The situation is tense. A high-ranking naval officer is dealing with a major crisis—or so it seems.

Suddenly the daydream is cut short. " 'Not so fast! You're driving too fast!' said Mrs. Mitty." At first, those words seem to be part of the commander's crisis, but then you realize that Mrs. Mitty is part of another world, the real world in which Mitty lives.

1. Look at the first three paragraphs of the story. Describe the contrast between Mitty's situation in the daydream and his situation in real life. What is amusing about the contrast?

Mitty barely emerges from his first daydream before he plunges into another one. This time he is a well-known surgeon who arrives at the hospital just in time to save the life of a millionaire banker. The situation has been suggested to Mitty's fanciful mind by three events: his wife has urged him to "let Dr. Renshaw look you over," she has suggested he wear his gloves, and Mitty has just driven by a hospital.

As the daydream builds to a climax, Mitty is once again dragged back to reality. The parking lot attendant barks out a series of commands: " 'Back it up, Mac! Look out for that Buick!' " A moment before, Mitty was the highly respected Dr. Mitty. Quick-witted, he had just fixed the faulty "anesthetizer" with his fountain pen and was about to save the patient from "coreopsis." Now, he is "Mac," just another clumsy driver to the parking lot attendant.

2. Summarize Mitty's three other daydreams. Explain what triggers each daydream and how each ends. In each, how does the contrast between Mitty's real life and his fantasy life add to the humor of the situation?

Humor and Character

Thurber creates humor through his characters. In Chapter 4 you learned about the different ways in which an author develops his or her characters. In "The Secret Life of Walter Mitty" Thurber reveals his main character mostly through Mitty's own thoughts. Occasionally, you see Mitty through his actions or through what others say about him.

Mitty's thoughts—his daydreams—are humorous because they are so unlikely. They stand in such sharp contrast to what he is really like. In his daydreams Mitty is a capable naval commander, a talented doctor, a daring defendant in a murder trial, a reckless World War I pilot, and a courageous condemned man facing a firing squad.

Those characters are unreal not only because they are figments of Mitty's imagination but also because each is a stereotype. In literature, a stereotype is a character who matches a fixed idea held by a number of people. A stereotype conforms to a certain pattern and lacks individuality. The naval commander, for example, fits the stereotype of a strong, fearless military officer who commands the respect and confidence of his men—" 'The Old Man'll get us through . . . The Old Man ain't afraid of Hell!' "

3. The characters that Mitty becomes in his daydreams are like standard heroic figures in old movies. Choose two of Mitty's characters and explain how each fits the popular stereotype of what that kind of person is like.

In real life Walter Mitty is meek and mild-mannered. Almost without resistance, he accepts his wife's complaints about his driving and her reminders to wear his gloves. Yet Mitty is not totally passive.

> "You're not a young man any longer." He raced the engine a little. "Why don't you wear your gloves? Have you lost your gloves?" Walter Mitty reached in a pocket and brought out the gloves. He put them on, but after she had turned and gone into the building and he had driven on to a red light, he took them off again.

4. What does the passage just quoted tell you about how Mrs. Mitty behaves toward her husband and how Walter Mitty behaves toward his wife? How does that brief glimpse into those two characters add humor to the story?

Humor and Dialogue

Thurber is a master of humorous dialogue. In "The Secret Life of Walter Mitty" much of the dialogue takes place between Mitty's fanciful characters and their colleagues. Although the humor lies in the situations, the dialogue brings them to life. Sometimes, the dialogue heightens the irony. At other times, the humor lies in the way the characters speak to one another. They may use very stilted, or formal, language, for example.

5. Look at the following passages from the story. What is humorous about each of the conversations?

a. *In the operating room there were whispered introductions: "Dr. Remington, Dr. Mitty. Dr. Pritchard-Mitford, Dr. Mitty." "I've read your book on streptothricosis," said Pritchard-Mitford, shaking hands. "A brilliant performance, sir." Thank you," said Walter Mitty.*

b. *"I want some biscuit for small, young dogs," he said to the clerk. "Any special brand, sir?" The greatest pistol shot in the world thought a moment. "It says 'Puppies Bark for It' on the box," said Walter Mitty.*

c. *"But you can't, sir," said the sergeant anxiously. "It takes two men to handle that bomber and the Archies are pounding hell out of the air. Von Richtman's circus is between here and Saulier." "Somebody's got to get that ammunition dump," said Mitty. "I'm going over. Spot of brandy?"*

Humor and Language

Thurber adds to the humor of the story through his use of language. He plays with language, creating special sound effects, stringing unusual words together, and inventing words. For example, in Walter Mitty's first daydream, the pounding cylinders in the hydroplane's engine produced the following sound: "ta-pocketa-pocketa-pocketa-*pocketa-pocketa.*" By italicizing the last two *pocketas,* he shows how hard the cylinders were working.

6. Skim the story. Where else does Thurber use the same sound effects? What do they signify in the other situations? Why do you think Mitty keeps hearing the same sound in his different daydreams?

Like all good writers, Thurber chooses his words carefully. At times, he puts oddly contrasting words together. In the third paragraph, as Mrs. Mitty is scolding her husband for driving too fast, Walter Mitty's hydroplane daydream is "fading in the remote, intimate airways of his mind." The words *remote* and *intimate,* describing the "airways of his mind," seem to contradict each other. How can something be remote and intimate at the same time? But they describe Mitty's situation perfectly. The "airways of his mind" are far away from reality. At the same time, they are essential to Mitty and familiar only to him.

7. Look at the last line of the paragraph in which the parking lot attendant tells Mitty to leave the key to his car: "The attendant vaulted into the car, backed it up with insolent skill, and put it where it belonged." Why do you think Thurber put the words ***insolent*** *and* ***skill*** *together?*

Thurber uses language to create humor by stringing words together when Mitty tries to remember what his wife told him to buy. "Kleenex, he thought, Squibb's, razor blades? No. Toothpaste, toothbrush, bicarbonate, carborundum, initiative and referendum?" Those words are all real words, but the last three don't belong on a shopping list.

In fact, Thurber is having fun. He is creating a pattern of sounds that has a rhythm and that almost rhymes. He is mocking Mitty. At the same time, Mitty seems to be like any of us when we are wracking our brains to remember something. People often try to recall a forgotten item by association. They try out sounds or ideas that might bring it back to mind.

8. In the end, what association helps Mitty remember what he is supposed to buy? Why is that association funny?

Jargon. Another technique of humor that Thurber uses is to make fun of the jargon, or special words and phrases, used by people in certain kinds of work. Jargon can have a particular meaning to one group but little or no meaning to people outside of that group. Still, we smile at it because we recognize it as jargon.

If you look closely at the jargon in this story, you see that most of it is gibberish, or nonsense. Walter Mitty has made up his own jargon. He has the people in his daydreams speak the way he imagines they should talk. The jargon sounds realistic, but it makes no sense.

9. Look at Mitty's daydream in the hospital. List two examples of his invented jargon in that scene. Why is that use of jargon amusing?

Use of Clichés. Thurber also uses language to add humor through the clichés spoken by the characters in Mitty's dreams. A cliché is an expression or idea that has become stale from overuse. "Tried and true," for example, is a cliché. Think about the daydream that centers around Captain Mitty, the World War I pilot. Some clichés in that daydream are British, since Captain Mitty is a British flying ace.

10. What are two clichés in that daydream?

Often humor contains a note of sadness, as it does in this story, because the humorist is making fun of human weaknesses. In "The Secret Life of Walter Mitty" Thurber shows a need shared by most people—the need to daydream. Like Mitty, most people have unfulfilled dreams. People can recognize part of themselves in Walter Mitty. Mitty's need to escape from a boring, unhappy life through his heroic daydreams is both funny and sad. In many ways, we can't help but sympathize with him.

11. Skim the story to find the passage that you find most amusing. Summarize the passage? Then explain why you find it funny. Does it also contain a serious or sad note? If so, explain.

Questions for Thought and Discussion

The questions and activities that follow will help you explore "The Secret Life of Walter Mitty" in more depth and at the same time develop your critical thinking skills.

1. **Evaluating Character.** Mrs. Mitty is usually discussed as a nagging, complaining wife. Do you think that is a fair portrait of her? Why or why not? Base your answer on what James Thurber shows you about her character.

2. **Organizing a Debate.** Divide the class in half. Each half should take a different position on this question: Is daydreaming good or bad? Each group should develop arguments to support its position and reasons why the opposing position is wrong. After the debate, vote on which set of arguments the class found most convincing.

3. **Identifying Setting.** What is the setting of "The Secret Life of Walter Mitty"? How important is the setting to the story?

4. **Analyzing Outcomes.** In this story you see Walter Mitty as a middle-aged man. What do you think he was like as a boy? What do you think he will be like as an old man? Suggest several reasons why he has become the kind of person he is.

Writing About Literature

Several suggestions for writing projects are given below. You may be asked to complete one or more of these projects. If you have any questions about how to begin a writing assignment, review Using the Writing Process. beginning on page 337.

1. **Creating Humorous Dialogue.** Create humorous dialogue between two or more people. You might want to try some of Thurber's techniques of humor, such as using jargon and clichés to satirize something or someone. Or, you can use other techniques to make the

conversation entertaining. You might, for example, create a misunderstanding between two speakers, and then have them say unexpected, comical things based on that misunderstanding.

2. **Explaining a Daydream.** Many sleep dreams are triggered by events that people have actually experienced. In daydreams, however, the events and roles played by people are greatly changed, as you have seen in Walter Mitty's daydreams. Write several paragraphs in which you explain a recent daydream or a dream you had while sleeping. Try to find the roots of the dream or daydream in recent experiences.

3. **Taking Another Point of View.** Write a brief description of Walter Mitty as he might be seen by another person. You could show him from the point of view of his wife, the parking lot attendant, Dr. Renshaw, or the clerk in the A & P. Use your imagination to show how the other person might see Mitty, but base your description on Mitty's character in the story.

Chapter 7

Selection *Of Missing Persons*

JACK FINNEY

Lesson *Point of View*

About the Selection

What would you do if you had the chance to move to a place where you would have no troubles? What would you say to living in a world where anger, suspicion, and fear did not exist? Would you jump at the opportunity to travel to such a place?

The only hitch to the offer is that you could never come back to visit your family or friends. Would you still accept the offer?

Those are questions that Charley Ewell, the main character in "Of Missing Persons," must answer for himself. Ewell is a young man who is tired and discontented with the routines of his life. He lives in New York City. His job is uninteresting. He is lonely and bored. Moreover, he dislikes the frantic pace of city life. Suddenly, he has the chance to "get away from it all." He can travel to the planet Verna, where everyone is relaxed and happy. On Verna, people like their work, and there is no malice.

The world of Verna seems too good to be true, and Charley is greatly attracted to it. He must quickly decide whether he can leave behind everything he has known in order to go there. Once he makes his decision to leave, he must hold onto his dream so that he can actually reach Verna. Yet Verna is an imaginary world. How is it possible for an ordinary man like Charley Ewell to reach such a distant place? Can he achieve his dream?

Jack Finney, the author of this story, has a highly inventive imagination. Most of his stories are fantasies or science fiction. Fantasy and science fiction go beyond reality and require you to suspend disbelief; that is, you must be willing to accept certain ideas or situations that the writer has invented, even though they may seem unbelievable. Finney tells his stories so realistically that you almost believe they are true.

Finney is best known for his science fiction. He won popular acclaim for his first novel, *The Body Snatchers,* which was published in 1955. The novel is about aliens who occupy the bodies of human beings. It was made into a popular movie, *The Invasion of the Body Snatchers,* that has become a classic among science fiction films.

In his stories and novels Finney blends fantasy, humor, and nostalgia, which is a longing for the past. His works often deal with escape from a harsh, confusing world to a simpler, more easygoing time and place. In his novel *Time and Again* Finney recounts the story of an illustrator, Si Morely, who leaves his apartment one night and finds himself in the winter of 1822. The movement through "holes" in the fabric of time often occurs in Finney's short stories, too.

Jack Finney has also written nonfiction. In *Forgotten News: The Crime of the Century and Other Lost Stories,* he brings to life mysterious and almost forgotten stories that once made the headlines. Each of the stories is true. Finney reexamines the facts, trying to solve the mysteries.

Lesson Preview

The lesson that follows "Of Missing Persons" focuses on point of view, or the vantage point, from which the story is told. Some stories are told in the first person: the person telling the story speaks of himself or herself as "I" or "me." Other stories are told in the third person: the person telling the story refers to the characters as "she" or "he." In the lesson you will learn other ways to describe the point of view of a story.

"Of Missing Persons" is longer than most of the other stories in this book. However, it moves quickly because you, like Charley Ewell, are caught up in the fantasy of Verna. The questions that follow will help you understand point of view and its effect on the story. As you read, think about how you would answer these questions.

1 Who is telling the story? Is it the same person throughout? How can you tell?

2 Does the person telling the story know everything that is going on, or does he know only certain things?

3 What do you learn about the main character in the story? How do you learn about him?

4 What is fantastic, or unreal, about the story? Is the story believable? Why or why not?

Vocabulary

Here are some difficult words that appear in the selection that follows. Study the words and their definitions, as well as the sentences that show how the words are used. This will help you get the most from your reading.

wryly in an ironic, bitter, or disgusted manner. *The editors of the magazine decided not to publish the wryly humorous article because they felt it was too caustic and bitter.*

balmy mild; soothing; gentle. *We knew that spring had finally arrived because the air was warm and balmy.*

drudgery dull, tiresome work. *Even though she constantly complained about the drudgery of Latin homework, she was happy to see the high grade on her test.*

evolved developed or worked out gradually; unfolded. *The colonists' ideas of independence evolved into the Constitution.*

lumber to move in a heavy clumsy way. *The old elephant could only lumber across the plain, while the younger ones moved more swiftly.*

gullible easily cheated or deceived. *You must think that I'm gullible if you assumed that I would buy the used car without looking it over first!*

Of Missing Persons

JACK FINNEY

Walk in as though it were an ordinary travel bureau, the stranger I'd met at a bar had told me. *Ask a few ordinary questions—about a trip you're planning, a vacation, anything like that. Then hint about The Folder a little, but whatever you do, don't mention it directly; wait till he brings it up himself. And if he doesn't, you might as well forget it. If you can. Because you'll never see it; you're not the type, that's all. And if you ask about it, he'll just look at you as though he doesn't know what you're talking about.*

I rehearsed it all in my mind, over and over, but what seems possible at night over a beer isn't easy to believe on a raw, rainy day, and I felt like a fool, searching the store fronts for the street number I'd memorized. It was noon hour, West 42nd Street, New York, rainy and windy; and like half the men around me, I walked with a hand on my hatbrim, wearing an old trench coat, head bent into the slanting rain, and the world was real and drab, and this was hopeless.

Anyway, I couldn't help thinking, who am I to see The Folder, even if there is one? Name? I said to myself, as though I were already being asked. It's Charley Ewell, and I'm a young guy who works in a bank; a teller. I don't like the job; I don't make much money, and I never will. I've lived in New York for over three years and haven't many friends. What the hell, there's really nothing to say—I see more movies than I want to, read too many books, and I'm sick of meals alone in restaurants. I have ordinary abilities, looks and thoughts. Does that suit you; do I qualify?

Now I spotted it, the address in the two-hundred block, an old, pseudo-modernized[1] office building, tired, outdated, refusing to admit it but unable to hide it. New York is full of them west of Fifth.

I pushed through the brass-framed glass doors into the tiny lobby, paved with freshly mopped, permanently dirty tile. The green-painted walls were lumpy from old plaster repairs; in a chrome frame hung a little wall directory—white celluloid[2] easily-changed letters on a black felt background. There were some twenty-odd names, and I found "Acme Travel Bureau" second on the list, between "A-1 Mimeo" and "Ajax Magic Supplies." I pressed the bell beside the old-style open-grille elevator door; it rang high up in the shaft. There was a long pause, then a thump, and the heavy chains began rattling slowly down toward me, and I almost turned and left—this was insane.

But upstairs the Acme office had divorced itself from the atmosphere of the building. I pushed open the pebble-glass door, walked in, and the big square room was bright and clean, fluorescent-lighted. Beside the wide double windows, behind a counter, stood a tall, gray-haired, grave-looking man, a telephone at his ear. He glanced up, nodded to beckon me in, and I felt my heart pumping—he fitted the description exactly. "Yes, United Air Lines," he was saying into the phone. "Flight"—he glanced at a paper on the glass-topped counter—"seven-o-three, and I suggest you check in forty minutes early."

Standing before him now, I waited, leaning on the counter, glancing

1. **pseudo-modernized:** falsely updated.
2. **celluloid:** a plastic made from nitrate and camphor, used to make toys and novelties.

around; he was the man, all right, and yet this was just an ordinary travel agency: big bright posters on the walls, metal floor racks full of folders, printed schedules under the glass on the counter. This is just what it looks like and nothing else, I thought, and again I felt like a fool.

"Can I help you?" Behind the counter the tall gray-haired man was smiling at me, replacing the phone, and suddenly I was terribly nervous.

"Yes." I stalled for time, unbuttoning my raincoat. Then I looked up at him again and said, "I'd like to—get away." You fool, that's too fast! I told myself. Don't rush it! I watched in a kind of panic to see what effect my answer had had, but he didn't flick an eyelash.

"Well, there are a lot of places to go," he said politely. From under the counter he brought out a long, slim folder and laid it on the glass, turning it right side up for me. "Fly to Buenos Aires—Another World!" it said in a double row of pale green letters across the top.

I looked at it long enough to be polite. It showed a big silvery plane banking over a harbor at night, a moon shining on the water, mountains in the background. Then I just shook my head; I was afraid to talk, afraid I'd say the wrong thing.

"Something quieter, maybe?" He brought out another folder: thick old tree trunks, rising way up out of sight, sunbeams slanting down through them—"The Virgin Forests of Maine, via Boston and Maine Railroad." "Or"—he laid a third folder on the glass—"Bermuda is nice just now." This one said, "Bermuda, Old World in the New."

I decided to risk it. "No," I said, and shook my head. "What I'm really looking for is a permanent place. A new place to live and settle down in." I stared directly into his eyes. "For the rest of my life." Then my nerve failed me, and I tried to think of a way to backtrack.

But he only smiled pleasantly and said, "I don't know why we can't advise you on that." He leaned forward on the counter, resting on his forearms, hands clasped; he had all the time in the world for me, his posture conveyed. "What are you looking for; what do you want?"

I held my breath, then said it. "Escape."

"From what?"

"Well——" Now I hesitated; I'd never put it into words before. "From New York, I'd say. And cities in general. From worry. And fear. And the things I read in my newspapers. From loneliness." And then I couldn't stop, though I knew I was talking too much, the words spilling out. "From never doing what I really want to do or having much fun. From selling my days just to stay alive. From life itself—the way it is today, at least." I looked straight at him and said softly, "From the world."

Now he was frankly staring, his eyes studying my face intently with no pretense of doing anything else, and I knew that in a moment he'd shake his head and say, "Mister, you better get to a doctor." But he didn't. He continued to stare, his eyes examining my forehead now. He was a big man, his gray hair crisp and curling, his lined face very intelligent, very kind; he looked the way ministers should look; he looked the way all fathers should look.

He lowered his gaze to look into my eyes and beyond them; he studied my mouth, my chin, the line of my jaw, and I had the sudden conviction that without any difficulty he was learning a great deal about me, more than I knew myself. Suddenly he smiled and placed both elbows on the counter, one hand grasping the other fist and gently massaging it. "Do you like people? Tell the truth, because I'll know if you aren't."

"Yes. It isn't easy for me to relax though, and be myself, and make friends."

He nodded gravely, accepting that. "Would you say you're a reasonably decent kind of man?"

"I guess so; I think so." I shrugged.

"Why?"

I smiled wryly; this was hard to answer. "Well—at least when I'm not, I'm usually sorry about it."

He grinned at that, and considered it for a moment or so. Then he smiled— deprecatingly,[3] as though he were about to tell a little joke that wasn't too good. "You know," he said casually, "we occasionally get people in here who seem to be looking for pretty much what you are.

3. **deprecatingly:** as if apologizing.

So just as a sort of little joke——"

I couldn't breathe. This was what I'd been told he would say if he thought I might do.

"——we've worked up a little folder. We've even had it printed. Simply for our own amusement, you understand. And for occasional clients like you. So I'll have to ask you to look at it here if you're interested. It's not the sort of thing we'd care to have generally known."

I could barely whisper, "I'm interested."

He fumbled under the counter, then brought out a long, thin folder, the same size and shape as the others, and slid it over the glass toward me.

I looked at it, pulling it closer with a finger tip, almost afraid to touch it. The cover was dark blue, the shade of a night sky, and across the top in white letters it said, "Visit Enchanting Verna!" The blue cover was sprinkled with white dots—stars—and in the lower left corner was a globe, the world, half surrounded by clouds. At the upper right, just under the word "Verna," was a star larger and brighter than the others; rays shot out from it, like those from a star on a Christmas card. Across the bottom of the cover it said, "Romantic Verna, where life is the way it *should* be." There was a little arrow beside the legend, meaning Turn the page.

I turned, and the folder was like most travel folders inside—there were pictures and text, only these were about "Verna" instead of Paris, or Rome, or the Bahamas. And it was beautifully printed; the pictures looked real. What I mean is, you've seen color stereopticon[4] pictures? Well, that's what these were like, only better, far better. In one picture you could see dew glistening on grass, and it looked wet. In another, a tree trunk seemed to curve out of the page, in perfect detail, and it was a shock to touch it and feel smooth paper instead of the rough actuality of bark. Miniature human faces, in a third picture, seemed about to speak, the lips moist and alive, the eyeballs shining, the actual texture of skin right there on paper; and it seemed impossible, as you

4. stereopticon: a type of slide projector that produces realistic images.

stared, that the people wouldn't move and speak.

I studied a large picture spreading across the upper half of two open pages. It seemed to have been taken from the top of a hill; you saw the land dropping away at your feet far down into a valley, then rising up again, way over on the other side. The slopes of both hills were covered with forest, and the color was beautiful, perfect; there were miles of green, majestic trees, and you knew as you looked that this forest was virgin, almost untouched. Curving through the floor of the valley, far below, ran a stream, blue from the sky in most places; here and there, where the current broke around massive boulders, the water was foaming white; and again it seemed that if you'd only look closely enough you'd be certain to see that stream move and shine in the sun. In clearings beside the stream there were shake-roofed cabins, some of logs, some of brick or adobe. The caption under the picture simply said, "The Colony."

"Fun fooling around with a thing like that," the man behind the counter murmured, nodding at the folder in my hands. "Relieves the monotony. Attractive-looking place, isn't it?"

I could only nod dumbly, lowering my eyes to the picture again because that picture told you even more than just what you saw. I don't know how you knew this, but you realized, staring at that forest-covered valley, that this was very much the way America once looked when it was new. And you knew this was only part of a whole land of unspoiled, unharmed forests, where every stream ran pure; you were seeing what people, the last of them dead over a century ago, had once looked at in Kentucky and Wisconsin, and the old Northwest. And you knew that if you could breathe in that air you'd feel it flow into your lungs sweeter than it's been anywhere on earth for a hundred and fifty years.

Under that picture was another, of six or eight people on a beach —the shore of a lake, maybe, or the river in the picture above. Two children were squatting on their haunches, dabbling in the water's edge, and in the foreground a half circle of adults were sitting, kneeling, or squatting in comfortable balance on the yellow sand. They were talking, several were smoking, and most of them held half-filled coffee cups; the sun was bright, you knew the air was balmy and that it was morning, just after breakfast. They were smiling, one woman talking, the others listening. One man had half risen from his squatting position to skip a stone out onto the surface of the water.

You knew this: that they were spending twenty minutes or so down on that beach after breakfast before going to work, and you knew they were friends and that they did this every day. You knew—I tell you, you *knew*—that they liked their work, all of them, whatever it was; that there was no forced hurry or pressure about it. And that—well, that's all, I guess; you just knew that every day after breakfast these families spent a leisurely half hour sitting and talking, there in the morning sun, down on that wonderful beach.

I'd never seen anything like their faces before. They were ordinary enough in looks, the people in that picture—pleasant, more or less familiar types. Some were young, in their twenties; others were in their thirties; one man and woman seemed around fifty. But the faces of the youngest couple were completely unlined, and it occurred to me then that they had been born there, and that it was a place where no one worried or was ever afraid. The others, the older ones, there were lines in their foreheads, grooves around their mouths, but you felt that the lines were no longer deepening, that they were healed and untroubled scars. And in the faces of the oldest couple was a look of—I'd say it was a look of permanent *relief*. Not one of those faces bore a trace of malice; these people were *happy*. But even more than that, you knew they'd *been* happy, day after day after day for a long, long time, and that they always would be, and they knew it.

I wanted to join them. The most desperate longing roared up in me from the bottom of my soul to *be* there—on the beach, after breakfast, with those people in the sunny morning—and I could hardly stand it. I looked up at the man behind the counter and managed to smile. "This is—very interesting."

"Yes." He smiled back, then shook his head in amusement. "We've had customers so interested, so carried away, that they didn't want to talk about anything else." He laughed. "They actually wanted to know rates, details, everything."

I nodded to show I understood and agreed with them. "And I suppose you've worked out a whole story to go with this?" I glanced at the folder in my hands.

"Oh, yes. What would you like to know?"

"These people," I said softly, and touched the picture of the group on the beach. "What do they do?"

"They work; everyone does." He took a pipe from his pocket. "They simply live their lives doing what they like. Some study. We have, according to our little story," he added, and smiled, "a very fine library. Some of our people farm, some write, some make things with their hands. Most of them raise children, and—well, they work at whatever it is they really want to do."

"And if there isn't anything they really want to do?"

He shook his head. "There is always something, for everyone, that he really wants to do. It's just that here there is so rarely time to find out what it is." He brought out a tobacco pouch and, leaning on the counter, began filling his pipe, his eyes level with mine, looking at me gravely. "Life is simple there, and it's serene. In some ways, the good ways, it's like the early pioneering communities here in your country, but without the drudgery that killed people young. There is electricity. There are washing machines, vacuum cleaners, plumbing, modern bathrooms, and modern medicine, very modern. But there are no radios, television, telephones, or automobiles. Distances are small, and people live and work in small communities. They raise or make most of the things they use. Every man builds his own house, with all the help he needs from his neighbors. Their recreation is their own, and there is a great deal of it, but there is no recreation for sale, nothing you buy a ticket to. They have dances, card parties, weddings, christenings, birthday celebrations, harvest parties. There are swimming and sports of all kinds. There is conversation, a lot of it, plenty of joking and laughter. There is a great deal of visiting and sharing of meals, and each day is well filled and well spent. There are no pressures, economic or social, and life holds few threats. Every man, woman and child is a happy person." After a moment he smiled. "I'm repeating the text, of course, in our little joke." He nodded at the folder.

"Of course," I murmured, and looked down at the folder again, turning a page. "Homes in The Colony," said a caption, and there, true and real, were a dozen or so pictures of the interiors of what must have been the cabins I'd seen in the first photograph, or others like them. There were living rooms, kitchens, dens, patios. Many of the homes seemed to be furnished in a kind of Early American style, except that it looked—authentic, as though those rocking chairs, cupboards, tables and hooked rugs had been made by the people themselves, taking their time and making them well and beautifully. Others of the interiors seemed modern in style; one showed a definite Oriental influence.

All of them had, plainly and unmistakably, one quality in common: You knew as you looked at them that these rooms were *home,* really home, to the people who lived in them. On the wall of one living room, over the stone fireplace, hung a hand-stitched motto; it said, "There Is No Place Like Home," but the words didn't seem quaint or amusing, they didn't seem old-fashioned, resurrected or copied from a past that was gone. They seemed real; they belonged; those words were nothing more or less than a simple expression of true feeling and fact.

"Who are you?" I lifted my head from the folder to stare into the man's eyes.

He lighted his pipe, taking his time, sucking the match flame down into the bowl, eyes glancing up at me. "It's in the text," he said then, "on the back page. We—that is to say, the people of Verna, the original inhabitants—are people like yourself. Verna is a planet of air, sun, land and sea, like this one. And of the same approximate temperature. So life evolved there, of course, just about as it has here, though rather earlier;

and we are people like you. There are trivial anatomical differences,[5] but nothing important. We read and enjoy your James Thurber, John Clayton, Rabelais, Allen Marple, Hemingway, Grimm, Mark Twain, Alan Nelson. We like your chocolate, which we didn't have, and a great deal of your music. And you'd like many of the things we have. Our thoughts, though, and the great aims and directions of our history and development have been—drastically different from yours." He smiled and blew out a puff of smoke. "Amusing fantasy, isn't it?"

"Yes," I knew I sounded abrupt, and I hadn't stopped to smile; the words were spilling out. "And where is Verna?"

"Light years away, by your measurements."

I was suddenly irritated, I didn't know why. "A little hard to get to, then, wouldn't it be?"

For a moment he looked at me; then he turned to the window beside him. "Come here," he said, and I walked around the counter to stand beside him. "There, off to the left"—he put a hand on my shoulder and pointed with his pipe stem—"are two apartment buildings, built back to back. The entrance to one is on Fifth Avenue, the entrance to the other on Sixth. See them? In the middle of the block; you can just see their roofs."

I nodded, and he said, "A man and his wife live on the fourteenth floor of one of those buildings. A wall of their living room is the back wall of the building. They have friends on the fourteenth floor of the other building, and a wall of *their* living room is the back wall of *their* building. These two couples live, in other words, within two feet of one another, since the back building walls actually touch."

The big man smiled. "But when the Robinsons want to visit the Bradens, they walk from their living room to the front door. Then they walk down a long hall to the elevators. They ride fourteen floors down; then, in the street, they must walk around to the next block. And the city blocks there are long; in bad weather they have sometimes actually taken a cab. They walk into the other building, they go on through the

5. **trivial anatomical differences:** slight differences in the structure of the body.

lobby, ride up fourteen floors, walk down a hall, ring a bell, and are finally admitted into their friends' living room—only two feet from their own."

The big man turned back to the counter, and I walked around to the other side again. "All I can tell you," he said then, "is that the way the Robinsons travel is like space travel, the actual physical crossing of those enormous distances." He shrugged. "But if they could only step through those two feet of wall without harming themselves or the wall—well, that is how we 'travel.' We don't cross space, we avoid it." He smiled. "Draw a breath here—and exhale it on Verna."

I said softly, "And that's how they arrived, isn't it? The people in the picture. You took them there." He nodded, and I said. "Why?"

He shrugged. "If you saw a neighbor's house on fire, would you rescue his family if you could? As many as you could, at least?"

"Yes."

"Well—so would we."

"You think it's that bad, then? With us?"

"How does it look to you?"

I thought about the headlines in my morning paper, that morning and every morning. "Not so good."

He just nodded and said, "We can't take you all, can't even take very many. So we've been selecting a few."

"For how long?"

"A long time." He smiled. "One of us was a member of Lincoln's cabinet. But it was not until just before your First World War that we felt we could see what was coming; until then we'd been merely observers. We opened our first agency in Mexico City in nineteen thirteen. Now we have branches in every major city.

"Nineteen thirteen," I murmured, as something caught in my memory. "Mexico. Listen! Did——"

"Yes." He smiled, anticipating my question. "Ambrose Bierce[6] joined us that year, or the next. He lived until nineteen thirty-one, a very old

6. **Ambrose Bierce:** an American journalist and short-story writer. In 1913, at the age of 71, he disappeared in Mexico while reporting on the Mexican Revolution.

man, and wrote four more books, which we have." He turned back a page in the folder and pointed to the cabin in the first large photograph. "That was his home."

"And what about Judge Crater?"

"Crater?"

"Another famous disappearance; he was a New York judge who simply disappeared some years ago."

"I don't know. We had a judge, I remember, from New York City, some twenty-odd years ago, but I can't recall his name."

"I leaned across the counter toward him, my face, very close to his, and I nodded. "I like your little joke," I said. "I like it very much, more than I can possibly tell you." Very softly I added, "When does it stop being a joke?"

For a moment he studied me; then he spoke. "Now. If you want it to."

You've got to decide on the spot, the middle-aged man at the Lexington Avenue bar had told me, *because you'll never get another chance. I know; I've tried.* Now I stood there thinking; there were people I'd hate never to see again, and a girl I was just getting to know, and this was the world I'd been born in. Then I thought about leaving that room, going back to my job, then back to my room at night. And finally I thought of the deep green valley in the picture and the little yellow beach in the morning sun. "I'll go," I whispered. "If you'll have me."

He studied my face. "Be sure," he said sharply. "Be certain. We want no one there who won't be happy, and if you have any least doubt, we'd prefer that——"

"I'm sure," I said.

After a moment the gray-haired man slid open a draw under the counter and brought out a little rectangle of yellow cardboard. One side was printed, and through the printing ran a band of light green; it looked like a railroad ticket to White Plains or somewhere. The printing said, "Good, when validated, for ONE TRIP TO VERNA. Nontransferable. One way only."

"Ah—how much?" I said, reaching for my wallet, wondering if he wanted me to pay.

He glanced at my hand on my hip pocket. "All you've got. Including your small change." He smiled. "You won't need it any more, and we can use your currency for operating expenses. Light bills, rent, and so on."

"I don't have much."

"That doesn't matter." From under the counter he brought out a heavy stamping machine, the kind you see in railroad ticket offices. "We once sold a ticket for thirty-seven hundred dollars. And we sold another just like it for six cents." He slid the ticket into the machine, struck the lever with his fist, then handed the ticket to me. On the back, now, was a freshly printed rectangle of purple ink, and within it the words, "Good this day only," followed by the date. I put two five-dollar bills, a one, and seventeen cents in change on the counter. "Take the ticket to the Acme Depot," the gray-haired man said, and, leaning across the counter, began giving me directions for getting there.

It's a tiny hole in the wall, the Acme Depot; you may have seen it—just a little store front on one of the narrow streets west of Broadway. On the window is painted, not very well, "Acme." Inside, the walls and ceiling, under layers of old paint, are covered with the kind of stamped tin you see in old buildings. There's a worn wooden counter and a few battered chrome and imitation red leather chairs. There are scores of places like the Acme Depot in that area—little theater-ticket agencies, obscure busline offices, employment agencies. You could pass this one a thousand times and never really see it; and if you live in New York, you probably have.

Behind the counter, when I arrived, stood a shirt-sleeved man, smoking a cigar stump and working on some papers; four or five people silently waited in the chairs. The man at the counter glanced up as I stepped in, looked down at my hand for my ticket, and when I showed it, nodded at the last vacant chair, and I sat down.

There was a girl beside me, hands folded on her purse. She was pleasant-looking, rather pretty; I thought she might have been a stenographer. Across the narrow little office sat a young Negro in work clothes, his wife beside him holding their little girl in her lap. And there was a man of around fifty, his face averted from the rest of us, staring out into the rain at passing pedestrians. He was expensively dressed and wore a gray Homburg;[7] he could have been the vice-president of a large bank, I thought, and I wondered what his ticket had cost.

Maybe twenty minutes passed, the man behind the counter working on some papers; then a small battered old bus pulled up at the curb outside, and I heard the hand brake set. The bus was a shabby thing, bought third- or fourthhand and painted red and white over the old paint, the fenders lumpy from countless pounded-out dents, the tire treads worn almost smooth. On the side, in red letters, it said "Acme," and the driver wore a leather jacket and the kind of worn cloth cap that cab drivers wear. It was precisely the sort of obscure little bus you see around there, ridden always by shabby, tired, silent people, going no one knows where.

It took nearly two hours for the little bus to work south through the traffic, toward the tip of Manhattan, and we all sat, each wrapped in his own silence and thoughts, staring out the rain-spattered windows; the little girl was asleep. Through the streaking glass beside me I watched drenched people huddled at city bus stops, and saw them rap angrily on the closed doors of buses jammed to capacity, and saw the strained, harassed faces of the drivers. At Fourteenth Street I saw a speeding cab splash a sheet of street-dirty water on a man at the curb, and saw the man's mouth writhe as he cursed. Often our bus stood motionless, the traffic light red, as throngs flowed out into the street from the curb, threading their way around us and the other waiting cars. I saw hundreds of faces, and not once did I see anyone smile.

7. **Homburg:** a felt hat with a soft, dented crown and a partially rolled brim, often worn by business executives in the 1920s and 1930s.

I dozed; then we were on a glistening black highway somewhere on Long Island. I slept again, and awakened in darkness as we jolted off the highway onto a muddy double-rut road, and I caught a glimpse of a farmhouse, the windows dark. Then the bus slowed, lurched once, and stopped. The hand brake set, the motor died, and we were parked beside what looked like a barn.

It *was* a barn. . . . The driver walked up to it, pulled the big sliding wood door open, its wheels creaking on the rusted old trolley overhead, and stood holding it open as we filed in. Then he released it, stepping inside with us, and the big door slid closed of its own weight. The barn was damp, old, the walls no longer plumb, and it smelled of cattle; there was nothing inside on the packed-dirt floor but a bench of unpainted pine, and the driver indicated it with the beam of a flashlight. "Sit here, please," he said quietly. "Get your tickets ready." Then he moved down the line, punching each of our tickets, and on the floor I caught a momentary glimpse, in the shifting beam of his light, of tiny mounds of countless more round bits of cardboard, like little drifts of yellow confetti. Then he was at the door again, sliding it open just enough to pass through, and for a moment we saw him silhouetted against the night sky. "Good luck," he said. "Just wait where you are." He released the door; it slid closed, snipping off the wavering beam of his flashlight; and a moment later we heard the motor start and the bus lumber away in low gear.

The dark barn was silent now, except for our breathing. Time ticked away, and I felt an urge, presently, to speak to whoever was next to me. But I didn't quite know what to say, and I began to feel embarrassed, a little foolish, and very aware that I was simply sitting in an old and deserted barn. The seconds passed, and I moved my feet restlessly; presently I realized that I was getting cold and chilled. Then suddenly I knew—and my face flushed in violent anger and a terrible shame. We'd been tricked! Bilked out of our money by our pathetic will to believe an absurd and fantastic fable and left, now, to sit there as long as we pleased, until we came to our senses finally, like countless others before us, and made our way home as best we could. It was suddenly impossible to understand or even remember how I could have been so gullible, and I was on my feet, stumbling through the dark across the uneven floor, with some notion of getting to a phone and the police. The big barn door was heavier than I'd thought, but I slid it back, took a running step through it, then turned to shout back to the others to come along.

You have seen how very much you can observe in the fractional instant of a lightning flash—an entire landscape sometimes, every detail etched on your memory, to be seen and studied in your mind for long moments afterward. As I turned back toward the opened door the inside of that barn came alight. Through every wide crack of its walls and ceiling and through the big dust-coated windows in its side streamed the light of an intensely brilliant blue and sunny sky, and the air pulling into my lungs as I opened my mouth to shout was sweeter than any I had ever tasted in my life. Dimly, through a wide, dust-smeared window of that barn, I looked—for less than the blink of an eye—down into a deep majestic V of forest-covered slope, and I saw, tumbling through it, far below, a tiny stream, blue from the sky, and at that stream's edge between two low roofs a yellow patch of sun-drenched beach. And then, that picture engraved on my mind forever, the heavy door slid shut, my fingernails rasping along the splintery wood in a desperate effort to stop it—and I was standing alone in a cold and rain-swept night.

It took four or five seconds, no longer, fumbling at that door, to heave it open again. But it was four or five seconds too long. The barn was empty, dark. There was nothing inside but a worn pine bench—and, in the flicker of the lighted match in my hand, tiny drifts of what looked like damp confetti on the floor. As my mind had known even as my hands scratched at the outside of that door, there was no one inside now; and I knew where they were—knew they were walking, laughing aloud in a sudden wonderful and eager ecstasy, down into that forest-green valley, toward home.

I work in a bank, in a job I don't like; and I ride to and from it in the subway, reading the daily papers, the news they contain. I live in a rented room, and in the battered dresser under a pile of my folded handkerchiefs is a little rectangle of yellow cardboard. Printed on its face are the words, "Good, when validated, for one trip to Verna," and stamped on the back is a date. But the date is gone, long since, the ticket void, punched in a pattern of tiny holes.

I've been back to the Acme Travel Bureau. The first time the tall gray-haired man walked up to me and laid two five-dollar bills, a one, and seventeen cents in change before me. "You left this on the counter last time you were here," he said gravely. Looking me squarely in the eyes, he added bleakly, "I don't know why." Then some customers came in, he turned to greet them, and there was nothing for me to do but leave.

Walk in as though it were the ordinary agency it seems—you can find it, somewhere, in any city you try! Ask a few ordinary questions—about a trip you're planning, a vacation, anything you like. Then hint about The Folder a little, but don't mention it directly. Give him time to size you up and offer it himself. And if he does, if you're the type, if you can believe—*then make up your mind and stick to it! Because you won't ever get a second chance. I know, because I've tried. And tried. And tried.*

Reviewing the Selection

Answer each of the following questions without looking back at the story.

Recalling Facts

1. Verna is different from Earth in that
   - ☐ a. its people come from another world.
   - ☐ b. everyone lives in log cabins there.
   - ☐ c. life is simple and serene there.
   - ☐ d. the people there are all young.

Understanding Main Ideas

2. To Charley Ewell, Verna represents a place where
   - ☐ a. people will leave him alone.
   - ☐ b. he can find a better life.
   - ☐ c. no one has to work.
   - ☐ d. people live forever.

Placing Events in Order

3. Which of the following events in the story occurs last?
   - ☐ a. Charley first visits the Acme Travel Bureau.
   - ☐ b. Charley speaks with a stranger in a bar.
   - ☐ c. Charley takes a bus ride to Long Island.
   - ☐ d. Charley gives the man in the travel bureau all his money.

Finding Supporting Details

4. What is one reason why Charley Ewell is ready to go to Verna?
   - ☐ a. He has lost his job at the bank.
   - ☐ b. He has always dreamed of space travel.
   - ☐ c. He is lonely and has few friends in the city.
   - ☐ d. The stranger in the bar promises that Charley will be a successful man on Verna.

Recognizing Words in Context

5. " 'Fun fooling around with a thing like that,' the man behind the counter murmured, nodding at the folder in my hands. 'Relieves the monotony.' " In this context *monotony* means
   - ☐ a. surprise.
   - ☐ b. excitement.
   - ☐ c. boredom.
   - ☑ d. unhappiness.

Interpreting the Selection

Answer each of the following questions. You may look back at the story if necessary.

Making Inferences

6. The other people in the barn are probably there because they
   - ☑ a. are unhappy with their lives.
   - ☐ b. have read about Verna in the newspaper.
   - ☐ c. have lost their homes in disasters.
   - ☐ d. are anxious to get their money's worth for their tickets.

Generalizing

7. Charley's dream
   - ☐ a. is shared by many people.
   - ☐ b. has no purpose.
   - ☑ c. can be realized anywhere.
   - ☐ d. is opposed by newspaper reporters.

Analyzing Character

8. At the last moment, why does Charley miss going to Verna?
   - ☑ a. He gives in to the suspicious side of his nature.
   - ☐ b. He makes the other passengers angry.
   - ☐ c. He refuses to follow orders to remain silent.
   - ☐ d. He is frightened in the enclosed space of the barn.

Comparing

9. How is Charley Ewell different from the other people in the barn?
   - ☐ a. He is smarter.
   - ☐ b. He has taken the travel agent's joke seriously.
   - ☐ c. He is lonelier.
   - ☑ d. He has less faith in the dream.

Drawing Conclusions

10. At the end of the story, Charley has kept his ticket to Verna because he wants to
    - ☐ a. have proof that the Acme Travel Bureau is a fraud.
    - ☐ b. get his $11.17 back.
    - ☐ c. show others that they can travel to Verna.
    - ☑ d. remind himself of what might have been.

Point of View

When an author writes a short story, one of the first decisions he or she must make is who will tell, or narrate, the story. The narrator is either a character within the story, or someone who is outside the story and relates the events and actions to the reader. The author always gives the narrator a point of view, or vantage point from which he or she tells the story.

Points of view are divided into two main groups: first-person point of view and third-person point of view. In the first-person point of view the narrator is a character in the story who tells the story as he or she experiences or understands it. First-person point of view is easy to identify by the use of first-person pronouns: *I, we, me, us, my,* and *our.* For example, a story that begins, "*I* struggled with *my* conscience, but in the end, *I* agreed to the plan," is told from the first-person point of view.

In the third-person point of view the narrator is not one of the characters in the story. The narrator stands outside of the story and refers to the characters as *he, she, his, her,* or *they.* A story in which a narrator says, "*He* struggled with *his* conscience, but in the end, *he* agreed to the plan," is told from the third-person point of view.

In the lesson you will study the point of view that Jack Finney uses to tell his story "Of Missing Persons," and you will analyze the effect that point of view has on other elements in the story.

First-Person Point of View

If you look at the opening paragraphs of Finney's story, you can see right away that it is told from the first-person point of view. "*Walk in as though it were an ordinary travel bureau,* the stranger I'd met at a bar had told me." You don't know who "me" is, but the narrator is clearly speaking of himself or herself in the first person. In the second and third paragraphs, you learn that the "I" is a New Yorker named Charley Ewell.

Jack Finney has chosen to use a first-person narrator in order to give the story a sense of intimacy and immediacy. From the outset, you feel as though Charley Ewell is speaking directly to you. He seems to be telling you his story in a very personal way.

1. Imagine that Finney wrote the story from the third-person point of view. Reread the first three paragraphs with "he" and "him" replacing "I" and "me." Explain how that change—using the third-person point of view—affects those paragraphs.

In the first-person point of view the narrator may have information about or insights into the other characters or events in the story, but the narrator can relate those observations only from his or her point of view. For example, in "Of Missing Persons" Charley gives you his interpretation of the events, but you have to decide for yourself whether his ideas and impressions are correct.

Third-Person Point of View

If the author decides to use the third-person point of view, he or she can choose several ways to tell the story. When the author uses the omniscient point of view, the narrator is all-knowing; he or she enters into the minds of all the characters and tells you all their secret thoughts and emotions. Nothing escapes the narrator's understanding. He or she not only describes the events, but also explains what they mean. When the author decides to use the selective or limited omniscient point of view, the narrator's insight is limited to the minds of only a few of the characters, or even to one of the characters. If the writer chooses an objective point of view, the narrator does not comment on or interpret any of the characters or their actions. This point of view is often called "the camera" or "fly-on-the-wall" because the narrator records only what can be seen or overheard.

Think about Charley Ewell's meeting with the man behind the counter at the Acme Travel Bureau. Charley is unsure of what to say to get the man to show him "The Folder." You know exactly how Charley feels because he tells you—"I felt like a fool," "I watched in a kind of panic," "My nerve failed me." But you don't know what the tall gray-haired man is thinking or feeling. You only know how Charley sees him.

2. Find a place in the story in which Charley tries to figure out the man's reaction to him. Summarize the scene. Then explain how the scene might be different if the author used (a) an omniscient point of view and (b) an objective point of view.

Point of View and Character

A story told from the first-person point of view lets you observe the character of the narrator. Since you see everything that happens through the narrator's mind, you get to know that person well. In "Of Missing Persons" you learn how Charley sees himself, how he sees others, what he does, and what insights, or understanding, he has into himself.

Charley Ewell is a young man who is disappointed with his life. He tells you that he doesn't like his job and doesn't have many friends. He is lonely and restless, and he wants more from life than what he is getting.

3. Skim the story. What kind of man does Charley say he is? Explain what each of the following actions tells you about his character: (a) visiting the Acme Travel Bureau, (b) buying a ticket to Verna, (c) running out of the barn.

Since the story is written in the first-person, you see the other characters only through Charley's eyes or through their words and actions. You don't find out what they think or feel. Charley gives you his impression of the man at the Acme Travel Bureau and of the people going to Verna with him. But is his view accurate? You can judge the other characters only by what you see or hear of them.

Have you ever looked closely at a stranger on a bus or train? Have you then tried to imagine the person's life from his or her clothing, posture, facial expressions, or actions? That is what Charley does with his fellow passengers en route to Verna. With the man behind the counter at the travel agency, however, he has more information. He talks to the man at some length.

4. What is Charley's impression of the man at the Acme Travel Bureau? Do the man's actions and words support that impression? Explain your answer.

Creating Fantasy

For the most part Charley Ewell tells his story in a simple, matter-of-fact manner. Yet "Of Missing Persons" is science fiction. It goes beyond the real world and requires you to allow your imagination great freedom. It asks you to believe in an idyllic life that exists on the planet Verna. It also expects you to take seriously the possibility of time travel. Through time travel, people move backward or forward in time—or even move into worlds in which time operates differently than it does in our own.

Almost the entire story is told as a flashback. Charley is describing events that took place in the past. The flashback is introduced and concluded by a paragraph in italics. The opening and closing paragraphs of the story are like brackets, enclosing the flashback. The use of flashback contributes to the sense of unreality. While Charley is recalling the past, you wonder, Did this really happen? Could he have experienced what he is describing?

Setting. The setting, characters, and plot of Finney's story work together to make the fantasy believable. What is striking about the story is that it appears to be so ordinary. The setting is ordinary: Charley lives in present-day New York. Through his eyes, you see the "pseudo-modernized office building" on West 42nd Street, where the Acme Travel Bureau is situated. Like any such building, it has glass doors and a directory on the wall listing the occupants. The travel bureau itself is ordinary, with fluorescent lighting and a counter to divide customers from employees. Later, when Charley goes to the Acme Depot, you see a run-down storefront like many others in the city. Finally, the barn is a typical one: an old damp building that smells of cattle.

5. Compare those places to Verna. In what ways is Verna very different?

Characters. On the surface, at least, the characters in "Of Missing Persons" seem to be ordinary people. Charley is a bank teller who is dissatisfied with his life. The man at the travel bureau behaves like any other travel agent helping a customer. To Charley, he appears to be a kindly figure.

> He was a big man, his gray hair crisp and curling, his lined face very intelligent, very kind; he looked the way ministers should look; he looked the way all fathers should look.

Yet the man is not ordinary. He is from the fantastic planet of Verna, where life is simple and serene. He is even willing to sell Charley a ticket to Verna.

At first, the man at the travel bureau refers to the Verna folder as a "little joke." Yet he answers Charley's questions about Verna seriously. After telling Charley more about the place, the man adds, "Amusing fantasy, isn't it?" When Charley later asks, "When does it stop being a joke?" the man replies, "Now. If you want it to."

6. How is the "joke" between the two main characters central to the entire fantasy?

7. None of the characters, aside from Charley, has a name. Why do you think the other characters are nameless?

Plot. Think about how the fantasy develops. In the exposition, the narrator relates the information that the stranger in the bar has given him. You learn about Charley and his life in New York. The rising action takes up much of the story. You feel Charley's tension build—first when he worries about saying the right words to the man at the travel bureau and then when he must decide whether or not to go to Verna.

8. *What is the major conflict in the story? How is it related to the fantasy?*

9. *What is the climax of the story? How is it resolved?*

"Of Missing Persons" ends with a moral—a lesson about the right way to live. Charley addresses you directly. He warns you to avoid his mistake. If you can believe in the fantasy—in the beautiful, ideal world of Verna—then you should "make up your mind and stick to it. Because you won't ever get a second chance." You can smile at the narrator's warning because you do not believe in Verna. Yet you cannot help thinking that maybe he is right. Perhaps you shouldn't give up your belief in the possibility of a better world.

Questions for Thought and Discussion

The questions and activities that follow will help you explore "Of Missing Persons" in more depth and at the same time develop your critical reading skills.

1. **Predicting Alternative Outcomes.** What do you think would have happened if Charley Ewell had remained in the barn? Support your answer with evidence from the story.

2. **Reaching a Consensus.** Do people need conflicts and challenges to get the most out of life, or is a trouble-free world such as Verna the ideal place to live? In small groups, discuss those questions and prepare a statement presenting the opinion of your group. Then, have each group present its statement and try to reach a class consensus, or agreement, on the issue.

3. **Analyzing Character.** Think about the man behind the counter at the Acme Travel Bureau. Do you believe, as Charley Ewell does, that the man knows everything about Charley just by looking at him? Support your answer with evidence from the story.

4. **Comparing.** Compare Charley Ewell to Walter Mitty. How are the two men alike? How are they different?

Writing About Literature

Several suggestions for writing projects follow. You may be asked to complete one or more of these projects. If you have any questions about how to begin a writing assignment, review Using the Writing Process, beginning on page 337.

1. **Creating a Mood.** Invent a story about a weird or unusual experience. The story might be set in a strange underwater land, on a distant planet, or in another time framework. Then write several paragraphs in which you create a mood for the story. Use descriptive details and vivid images to help build the mood.
2. **Writing from the First-Person Point of View.** Imagine that you are one of the people waiting with Charley Ewell in the empty barn. Use the first-person point of view and describe why you went to the barn and what happens after Charley rushes outside.
3. **Describing an Imaginary World.** Charley Ewell's idea of the perfect world is Verna. Create an imaginary world of your own. Describe your imaginary world, showing how it looks, feels, smells, tastes, and sounds. Also tell what people *do* there, how they act, and what they look like.

Chapter 8

Selection *The Rule of Names*

URSULA LE GUIN

Lesson *Foreshadowing and Suspense*

About the Selection

As you learned in the introduction to Unit Two, writers of fantasy and science fiction often invent new worlds in which to set their stories. Some fantasy writers create worlds from the past, from the present, or from what they expect the future will bring. Others make up entirely new worlds that no one has yet imagined. Science fiction writers explore the extraordinary possibilities offered by advances in science. They may set their stories on other planets or rely on imaginary scientific breakthroughs that allow their characters miraculous new ways to travel through time and space. Science fiction writers often invent worlds with more advanced technologies than those we know today.

"The Rule of Names" by Ursula Le Guin is more fantasy than science fiction. The story is set on Sattins Island, an imaginary island in a world that is similar to places you have read about in fairy tales. The plot centers on wizards, dragons, and hidden treasure.

How do writers of fantasy and science fiction get you involved in their stories? One way is by creating settings that you find reasonable even though they are fanciful. In "The Rule of Names" Ursula Le Guin invents a setting that works well as a background for her characters and for the events of the plot.

The people of Sattins Island live simply. They earn their livings by fishing and farming. They send their children to school, and they meet at the local inn to gossip. Yet several features of their lives are unusual.

Magic is part of their daily routine. They have a resident wizard—Mr. Underhill. The people turn to him for such things as charms against warts and spells to make their crops grow. Unfortunately, Mr. Underhill is not a very good wizard and gets little respect from the villagers. Once you have accepted the fanciful world of Sattins Island, Le Guin introduces another character who will bring conflict to the peaceful island.

Although she has written some fantasy, Ursula Le Guin is best known for her science fiction. In fact, her work has a wide audience; both children and adults enjoy her books. In her fantasy stories and science fiction, Le Guin often invents imaginary but true-to-life societies similar to Sattins Island.

Le Guin has been writing science fiction since she was six years old. She has published novels, short stories, poems, and essays, and has won many awards for her work. One of her best-known works is the *Earthsea Trilogy,* made up of three books—*A Wizard of Earthsea, The Tombs of Atuan,* and *The Farthest Shore.* The series is set on a planet called Earthsea, where a struggle takes place between good and evil forces.

Part of Le Guin's appeal is her ability to invent complete worlds. For example, in the *Earthsea Trilogy* and other works, she even creates new languages for her characters. Le Guin bases her imaginary worlds on the real world. She takes what she knows and puts it together in a new way. As Le Guin has pointed out, "I do write about the real world, and I get all my weird ideas from it, too. It is just that reality is much stranger than many people want to admit."

Lesson Preview

The lesson that follows "The Rule of Names" focuses on the use of foreshadowing and suspense. While you are reading a story, or sometimes after you have finished it, you may realize that the author has given hints or clues along the way to what is going to happen. In the lesson you will analyze the various ways in which an author can foreshadow developments, or give you clues.

The clues make you aware that something significant is going to happen. They create a feeling of uncertainty or excitement. That feeling is suspense. Foreshadowing and suspense increase interest in the story, making you say: "I have to find out what will happen next. I can't stand not knowing what will happen."

The questions that follow will help you identify examples of foreshadowing and suspense in "The Rule of Names." As you read, think about how you would answer these questions.

1 Why do magic and supernatural forces seem so natural on Sattins Island? How does Le Guin make that fantasy world believable?

2 What do you learn about Mr. Underhill when he first appears in the story? Is there anything peculiar about his looks or his behavior?

3 Which characters say or do something unusual that causes you to wonder about what they will do next?

4 In which parts of the story do you feel the most suspense? Why?

Vocabulary

Here are some difficult words that appear in the selection that follows. Study the words and their definitions, as well as the sentences that show how the words are used. This will help you get the most from your reading.

disdain contempt; look down on. *The world-famous chef tends to treat the fast-food industry with disdain and scorn.*

walleyed an eye that turns outward, showing an abnormal amount of white. *A walleyed condition can often be corrected with special glasses or surgery on the eye muscle.*

anteroom a waiting room leading to a larger room. *The guests gathered in the anteroom before they were escorted into the dining room.*

cowered huddled, as from fear or shame. *Knowing that he would be punished, the dog cowered under the table.*

The Rule of Names

Ursula Le Guin

Mr. Underhill came out from under his hill, smiling and breathing hard. Each breath shot out of his nostrils as a double puff of steam, snow-white in the morning sunshine. Mr. Underhill looked up at the bright December sky and smiled wider than ever, showing snow-white teeth. Then he went down to the village.

"Morning, Mr. Underhill," said the villagers as he passed them in the narrow street between houses with conical, overhanging roofs like the fat red caps of toadstools. "Morning, morning!" he replied to each. (It was of course bad luck to wish anyone a *good* morning; a simple statement of the time of day was quite enough, in a place so permeated with Influences as Sattins Island, where a careless adjective might change the weather for a week.) All of them spoke to him, some with affection, some with affectionate disdain. He was all the little island had in the way of a wizard, and so deserved respect—but how could you respect a little fat man of fifty who waddled along with his toes turned in, breathing steam and smiling? He was no great shakes as a workman either. His fireworks were fairly elaborate but his elixirs[1] were weak. Warts he charmed off frequently reappeared after three days; tomatoes he enchanted grew no bigger than canteloupes; and those rare times when a strange ship stopped at Sattins Harbor, Mr. Underhill always stayed under his hill—for fear, he explained, of the evil eye. He was, in other words, a wizard the way walleyed Gan was a carpenter: by default. The villagers made do with badly-hung doors and inefficient spells, for this generation, and relieved their annoyance by treating Mr. Underhill quite familiarly, as a mere fellow-villager. They even asked him to dinner. Once he asked some of them to dinner, and served a splendid repast, with silver, crystal, damask,[2] roast goose, sparkling Andrades '639, and plum pudding with hard sauce; but he was so nervous all through the meal that it took the joy out of it, and besides, everybody was hungry again half an hour afterward. He did not like anyone to visit his cave, not even the anteroom, beyond which in fact nobody had ever got. When he saw people approaching the hill he always came trotting out to meet them. "Let's sit out here under the pine trees!" he would say, smiling and waving towards the fir grove, or if it was raining, "Let's go have a drink at the inn, eh?" though everybody knew he drank nothing stronger than well-water.

Some of the village children, teased by that locked cave, poked and pried and made raids while Mr. Underhill was away; but the small door that led into the inner chamber was spell-shut, and it seemed for once to be an effective spell. Once a couple of boys, thinking the wizard was over on the West Shore curing Mrs. Ruuna's sick donkey, brought a crowbar and a hatchet up there, but at the first whack of the hatchet on the door there came a roar of wrath from inside, and a cloud of purple steam. Mr. Underhill had got home early. The boys fled. He did not come out, and the boys came to no harm, though they said you couldn't believe what a huge hooting howling hissing horrible bellow that little fat man could make unless you'd heard it.

1. **elixirs:** medicines used to heal people or brews that supposedly have magical powers.
2. **damask:** a fine linen tablecloth.

His business in town this day was three dozen fresh eggs and a pound of liver; also a stop at Seacaptain Fogeno's cottage to renew the seeing-charm on the old man's eyes (quite useless when applied to a case of detached retina,[3] but Mr. Underhill kept trying), and finally a chat with old Goody Guld, the concertina[4]-maker's widow. Mr. Underhill's friends were mostly old people. He was timid with the strong young men of the village, and the girls were shy of him. "He makes me nervous, he smiles so much," they all said, pouting, twisting silky ringlets round a finger. "Nervous" was a newfangled word, and their mothers all replied grimly, "Nervous my foot, silliness is the word for it. Mr. Underhill is a very respectable wizard!"

After leaving Goody Guld, Mr. Underhill passed by the school, which was being held this day out on the common. Since no one on Sattins Island was literate, there were no books to learn to read from and no desks to carve initials on and no blackboards to erase, and in fact no schoolhouse. On rainy days the children met in the loft of the Communal Barn, and got hay in their pants; on sunny days the schoolteacher, Palani, took them anywhere she felt like. Today, surrounded by thirty interested children under twelve and forty uninterested sheep under five, she was teaching an important item on the curriculum: the Rules of Names. Mr. Underhill, smiling shyly, paused to listen and watch. Palani, a plump, pretty girl of twenty, made a charming picture there in the wintry sunlight, sheep and children around her, a leafless oak above her, and behind her the dunes and sea and clear, pale sky. She spoke earnestly, her face flushed pink by wind and words. "Now you know the Rules of Names already, children. There are two, and they're the same on every island in the world. What's one of them?"

"It ain't polite to ask anybody what his name is," shouted a fat, quick boy, interrupted by a little girl shrieking, "You can't never tell your own name to nobody my ma says!"

---

3. retina: the membrane that lines the back of the eyeball. A detached retina distorts the images that are seen by the eyes.

4. concertina: a musical instrument of the accordian family.

"Yes, Suba. Yes, Popi dear, don't screech. That's right. You never ask anybody his name. You never tell your own. Now think about that a minute and then tell me why we call our wizard Mr. Underhill." She smiled across the curly heads and the woolly backs at Mr. Underhill, who beamed, and nervously clutched his sack of eggs.

" 'Cause he lives under a hill!" said half the children.

"But is it his truename?"

"No!" said the fat boy, echoed by little Popi shrieking, "No!"

"How do you know it's not?"

" 'Cause he came here all alone and so there wasn't anybody knew his truename so they couldn't tell us, and *he* couldn't—"

"Very good, Suba. Popi, don't shout. That's right. Even a wizard can't tell his truename. When you children are through school and go through the Passage, you'll leave your childnames behind and keep only your truenames, which you must never ask for and never give away. Why is that the rule?"

The children were silent. The sheep bleated gently. Mr. Underhill answered the question: "Because the name is the thing," he said in his shy, soft, husky voice, "and the truename is the true thing. To speak the name is to control the thing. Am I right, Schoolmistress?"

She smiled and curtseyed, evidently a little embarrassed by his participation. And he trotted off towards his hill, clutching his eggs to his bosom. Somehow the minute spent watching Palani and the children had made him very hungry. He locked his inner door behind him with a hasty incantation,[5] but there must have been a leak or two in the spell, for soon the bare anteroom of the cave was rich with the smell of frying eggs and sizzling liver.

The wind that day was light and fresh out of the west, and on it at noon a little boat came skimming the bright waves into Sattins Harbor. Even as it rounded the point a sharp-eyed boy spotted it, and knowing, like every child on the island, every sail and spar of the forty boats of the fishing fleet, he ran down the street calling out, "A foreign

5. **incantation:** a magic spell.

boat, a foreign boat!" Very seldom was the lonely isle visited by a boat from some equally lonely isle of the East Reach, or an adventurous trader from the Archipelago.[6] By the time the boat was at the pier half the village was there to greet it, and fishermen were following it homewards, and cowherds and clam-diggers and herb-hunters were puffing up and down all the rocky hills, heading towards the harbor.

But Mr. Underhill's door stayed shut.

There was only one man aboard the boat. Old Seacaptain Fogeno, when they told him that, drew down a bristle of white brows over his unseeing eyes. "There's only one kind of man," he said, "that sails the Outer Reach alone. A wizard, or a warlock, or a Mage . . ."

So the villagers were breathless hoping to see for once in their lives a Mage, one of the mighty White Magicians of the rich, towered, crowded inner islands of the Archipelago. They were disappointed, for the voyager was quite young, a handsome black-bearded fellow who hailed them cheerfully from his boat, and leaped ashore like any sailor glad to have made port. He introduced himself at once as a sea-peddlar. But when they told Seacaptain Fogeno that he carried an oaken walking-stick around with him, the old man nodded. "Two wizards in one town," he said. "Bad!" And his mouth snapped shut like an old carp's.

As the stranger could not give them his name, they gave him one right away: Blackbeard. And they gave him plenty of attention. He had a small mixed cargo of cloth and sandals and piswi feathers for trimming cloaks and cheap incense and levity stones and fine herbs and great glass beads from Venway—the usual peddlar's lot. Everyone on Sattins Island came to look, to chat with the voyager, and perhaps to buy something—"Just to remember him by!" cackled Goody Guld, who like all the women and girls of the village was smitten with Blackbeard's bold good looks. All the boys hung round him too, to hear him tell of his voyages to far, strange islands of the Reach or describe the great rich islands of the Archipelago, the Inner Lanes, the roadsteads[7] white with ships, and the

6. **Archipelago:** a large chain of islands.
7. **roadsteads:** the areas near the shore where ships anchor.

golden roofs of Havnor. The men willingly listened to his tales; but some of them wondered why a trader should sail alone, and kept their eyes thoughtfully upon his oaken staff.

But all this time Mr. Underhill stayed under his hill.

"This is the first island I've ever seen that had no wizard," said Blackbeard one evening to Goody Guld, who had invited him and her nephew and Palani in for a cup of rushwash tea. "What do you do when you get a toothache, or the cow goes dry?"

"Why, we've got Mr. Underhill!" said the old woman.

"For what that's worth," muttered her nephew Birt, and then blushed purple and spilled his tea. Birt was a fisherman, a large, brave, wordless young man. He loved the schoolmistress, but the nearest he had come to telling her of his love was to give baskets of fresh mackerel to her father's cook.

"Oh, you do have a wizard?" Blackbeard asked. "Is he invisible?"

"No, he's just very shy," said Palani. "You've only been here a week, you know, and we see so few strangers here. . . ." She also blushed a little, but did not spill her tea.

Blackbeard smiled at her. "He's a good Sattinsman, then, eh?"

"No," said Goody Guld, "no more than you are. Another cup, nevvy? Keep it in the cup this time. No, my dear, he came in a little bit of a boat, four years ago was it? Just a day after the end of the shad run, I recall, for they was taking up the nets over in East Creek, and Pondi Cowherd broke his leg that very morning—five years ago it must be. No, four. No, five it is, 'twas the year the garlic didn't sprout. So he sails in on a bit of a sloop loaded full up with great chests and boxes and says to Seacaptain Fogeno, who wasn't blind then, though old enough goodness knows to be blind twice over, 'I hear tell,' he says, 'you've got no wizard nor warlock at all, might you be wanting one?' 'Indeed, if the magic's white!'[8] says the Captain, and before you could say cuttlefish Mr. Underhill had settled down in the cave under the hill and was charming the mange[9] off Goody

8. **white magic:** the use of charms, spells, and rituals for good purposes.
9. **mange:** a skin disease of animals that makes the hair fall out.

Beltow's cat. Though the fur grew in grey, and 'twas an orange cat. Queer-looking thing it was after that. It died last winter in the cold spell. Goody Beltow took on so at that cat's death, poor thing, worse than when her man was drowned on the Long Banks, the year of the long herring-runs, when nevvy Birt here was but a babe in petticoats." Here Birt spilled his tea again, and Blackbeard grinned, but Goody Guld proceeded undismayed, and talked on till nightfall.

Next day Blackbeard was down at the pier, seeing after the sprung board in his boat which he seemed to take a long time fixing, and as usual drawing the taciturn Sattinsmen into talk. "Now which of these is your wizard's craft?" he asked. "Or has he got one of those the Mages fold up into a walnut shell when they're not using it?"

"Nay," said a stolid fisherman. "She's oop in his cave, under hill."

"He carried the boat he came in up to his cave?"

"Aye. Clear oop. I helped. Heavier as lead she was. Full oop with great boxes, and they full oop with books o' spells, he says. Heavier as lead she was." And the stolid fisherman turned his back, sighing stolidly. Goody Guld's nephew, mending a net nearby, looked up from his work and asked with equal stolidity, "Would ye like to meet Mr. Underhill, maybe?"

Blackbeard returned Birt's look. Clever black eyes met candid blue ones for a long moment; then Blackbeard smiled and said, "Yes. Will you take me up to the hill, Birt?"

"Aye, when I'm done with this," said the fisherman. And when the net was mended, he and the Archipelagan set off up the village street towards the high green hill above it. But as they crossed the common Blackbeard said, "Hold on a while, friend Birt. I have a tale to tell you, before we meet your wizard."

"Tell away," says Birt, sitting down in the shade of a live-oak.

"It's a story that started a hundred years ago, and isn't finished yet—though it soon will be, very soon. . . . In the very heart of the Archipelago, where the islands crowd thick as flies on honey, there's a little isle called Pendor. The sealords of Pendor were mighty men, in the old days of war before the League. Loot and ransom and tribute came pouring into Pendor, and they gathered a great treasure there, long ago. Then from somewhere away out in the West Reach, where dragons breed on the lava isles, came one day a very mighty dragon. Not one of those overgrown lizards most of you Outer Reach folk call dragons, but a big, black, winged, wise, cunning monster, full of strength and subtlety, and like all dragons loving gold and precious stones above all things. He killed the Sealord and his soldiers, and the people of Pendor fled in their ships by night. They all fled away and left the dragon coiled up in Pendor Towers. And there he stayed for a hundred years, dragging his scaly belly over the emeralds and sapphires and coins of gold, coming forth only once in a year or two when he must eat. He'd raid nearby islands for his food. You know what dragons eat?"

Birt nodded and said in a whisper, "Maidens."

"Right," said Blackbeard. "Well, that couldn't be endured forever, nor the thought of him sitting on all that treasure. So after the League grew strong, and the Archipelago wasn't so busy with wars and piracy, it was decided to attack Pendor, drive out the dragon, and get the gold and jewels for the treasury of the League. They're forever wanting money, the League is. So a huge fleet gathered from fifty islands, and seven Mages stood in the prows of the seven strongest ships, and they sailed towards Pendor. . . . They got there. They landed. Nothing stirred. The houses all stood empty, the dishes on the tables full of a hundred years' dust. The bones of the old Sealord and his men lay about in the castle courts and on the stairs. And the Tower rooms reeked of dragon. But there was no dragon. And no treasure, not a diamond the size of a poppyseed, not a single silver bead . . . Knowing that he couldn't stand up to seven Mages, the dragon had skipped out. They tracked him, and found he'd flown to a deserted island up north called Udrath; they followed his trail there, and what did they find? Bones again. His bones—the dragon's. But no treasure. A wizard, some unknown wizard from somewhere, must have met him single-handed, and defeated him—and then made off with the treasure, right under the League's nose!"

The fisherman listened, attentive and expressionless.

"Now that must have been a powerful wizard and a clever one, first to kill a dragon, and second to get off without leaving a trace. The lords and Mages of the Archipelago couldn't track him at all, neither where he'd come from nor where he'd made off to. They were about to give up. That was last spring; I'd been off on a three-year voyage up in the North Reach, and got back about that time. And they asked me to help them find the unknown wizard. That was clever of them. Because I'm not only a wizard myself, as I think some of the oafs here have guessed, but I am also a descendant of the Lords of Pendor. That treasure is mine. It's mine, and knows that it's mine. Those fools of the League couldn't find it, because it's not theirs. It belongs to the House of Pendor, and the great emerald, the star of the hoard, Inalkil the Greenstone, knows its master. Behold!" Blackbeard raised his oaken staff and cried aloud, "Inalkil!" The tip of the staff began to glow green, a fiery green radiance, a dazzling haze the color of April grass, and at the same moment the staff tipped in the wizard's hand, leaning, slanting till it pointed straight at the side of the hill above them.

"It wasn't so bright a glow, far away in Havnor," Blackbeard murmured, "but the staff pointed true. Inalkil answered when I called. The jewel knows its master. And I know the thief, and I shall conquer him. He's a mighty wizard, who could overcome a dragon. But I am mightier. Do you want to know why, oaf? Because I know his name!"

As Blackbeard's tone got more arrogant, Birt had looked duller and duller, blanker and blanker; but at this he gave a twitch, shut his mouth, and stared at the Archipelagan. "How did you . . . learn it?" he asked very slowly.

Blackbeard grinned, and did not answer.

"Black magic?"

"How else?"

Birt looked pale, and said nothing.

"I am the Sealord of Pendor, oaf, and I will have the gold my fathers won, and the jewels my mothers wore, and the Greenstone! For they are mine.—Now, you can tell your village boobies the whole story after I have defeated this wizard and gone. Wait here. Or you can come and watch, if you're not afraid. You'll never get the chance again to see a great wizard in all his power." Blackbeard turned, and without a backward glance strode off up the hill towards the entrance to the cave.

Very slowly, Birt followed. A good distance from the cave he stopped, sat down under a hawthorn tree, and watched. The Archipelagan had stopped; a stiff, dark figure alone on the green swell of the hill before the gaping cave-mouth, he stood perfectly still. All at once he swung his staff up over his head, and the emerald radiance shone about him as he shouted, "Thief, thief of the Hoard of Pendor, come forth!"

There was a crash, as of dropped crockery, from inside the cave, and a lot of dust came spewing out. Scared, Birt ducked. When he looked again he saw Blackbeard still standing motionless, and at the mouth of the cave, dusty and dishevelled, stood Mr. Underhill. He looked small and pitiful, with his toes turned in as usual, and his little bowlegs in black tights, and no staff—he never had had one, Birt suddenly thought. Mr. Underhill spoke. "Who are you?" he said in his husky little voice.

"I am the Sealord of Pendor, thief, come to claim my treasure!"

At that, Mr. Underhill slowly turned pink, as he always did when people were rude to him. But he then turned something else. He turned yellow. His hair bristled out, he gave a coughing roar—and was a yellow lion leaping down the hill at Blackbeard, white fangs gleaming.

But Blackbeard no longer stood there. A gigantic tiger, color of night and lightning, bounded to meet the lion. . . .

The lion was gone. Below the cave all of a sudden stood a high grove of trees, black in the winter sunshine. The tiger, checking himself in mid-leap just before he entered the shadow of trees, caught fire in the air, became a tongue of flame lashing out at the dry black branches. . . .

But where the trees had stood a sudden cataract[10] leaped from the hillside, an arch of silvery crashing water, thundering down upon the fire. But the fire was gone. . . .

10. cataract: a large waterfall.

For just a moment before the fisherman's staring eyes two hills rose—the green one he knew, and a new one, a bare, brown hillock ready to drink up the rushing waterfall. That passed so quickly it made Birt blink, and after blinking he blinked again, and moaned, for what he saw now was a great deal worse. Where the cataract had been there hovered a dragon. Black wings darkened all the hill, steel claws reached groping, and from the dark, scaly, gaping lips fire and steam shot out.

Beneath the monstrous creature stood Blackbeard, laughing.

"Take any shape you please, little Mr. Underhill!" he taunted. "I can match you. But the game grows tiresome. I want to look upon my treasure, upon Inalkil. Now, big dragon, little wizard, take your true shape. I command you by the power of your true name—Yevaud!"

Birt could not move at all, not even to blink. He cowered, staring whether he would or not. He saw the black dragon hang there in the air above Blackbeard. He saw the fire lick like many tongues from the scaly mouth, the steam jet from the red nostrils. He saw Blackbeard's face grow white, white as chalk, and the beard-fringed lips trembling.

"Your name is Yevaud!"

"Yes," said a great, husky, hissing voice. "My truename is Yevaud, and my true shape is this shape."

"But the dragon was killed—they found dragon-bones on Udrath Island—"

"That was another dragon," said the dragon, and then stopped like a hawk, talons outstretched. And Birt shut his eyes.

When he opened them the sky was clear, the hillside empty, except for a reddish-blackish trampled spot, and a few talon-marks in the grass.

Birt the fisherman got to his feet and ran. He ran across the common, scattering sheep to right and left, and straight down the village street to Palani's father's house. Palani was out in the garden weeding the nasturtiums. "Come with me!" Birt gasped. She stared. He grabbed her wrist and dragged her with him. She screeched a little, but did not resist. He ran with her straight to the pier, pushed her into his fishing-sloop the

Queenie, untied the painter,[11] took up the oars and set off rowing like a demon. The last that Sattins Island saw of him and Palani was the *Queenie*'s sail vanishing in the direction of the nearest island westward.

The villagers thought they would never stop talking about it, how Goody Guld's nephew Birt had lost his mind and sailed off with the schoolmistress on the very same day that that peddlar Blackbeard disappeared without a trace, leaving all his feathers and beads behind. But they did stop talking about it, three days later. They had other things to talk about, when Mr. Underhill finally came out of his cave.

Mr. Underhill had decided that since his truename was no longer a secret, he might as well drop his disguise. Walking was a lot harder than flying, and besides, it was a long, long time since he had had a real meal.

11. painter: a line used for securing or towing a boat.

Reviewing the Selection

Answer each of the following questions without looking back at the story.

Recalling Facts

1. How does old Seacaptain Fogeno know right away that Blackbeard is a wizard?
   - ☐ a. Blackbeard makes Fogeno's eyesight better.
   - ☑ b. Blackbeard sails to the island by himself and carries an oaken staff.
   - ☐ c. Blackbeard comes from the rich islands of the Archipelago, where all the wizards live.
   - ☐ d. Blackbeard tells Fogeno that he is a wizard.

Understanding Main Ideas

2. In "The Rule of Names" Mr. Underhill is a
   - ☐ a. splendid magician.
   - ☐ b. weak old man.
   - ☑ c. dragon in disguise.
   - ☐ d. force working against evil.

Placing Events in Order

3. Birt grabs Palani and makes her sail away with him after
   - ☐ a. he hears that Blackbeard is a wizard.
   - ☐ b. Mr. Underhill threatens to eat the schoolchildren.
   - ☑ c. Mr. Underhill destroys Blackbeard.
   - ☐ d. the people of Sattins Island learn about the stolen treasure of Pendor.

Finding Supporting Details

4. Blackbeard believes that he can defeat Mr. Underhill because he
   - ☐ a. is a powerful wizard himself.
   - ☑ b. knows Mr. Underhill's "truename."
   - ☐ c. is the sealord of Pendor.
   - ☐ d. is one of the Mages.

Recognizing Words in Context

5. "Once he asked some of them to dinner, and served a splendid repast, with silver, crystal, damask, roast goose, sparkling Andrades '639, and plum pudding with hard sauce. . . ." In this context *repast* means
   - ☐ a. dessert.
   - ☐ b. gift.
   - ☑ c. meal.
   - ☐ d. memory.

Interpreting the Selection

Answer each of the following questions. You may look back at the story if necessary.

Making Inferences

6. From the way that the villagers react to Blackbeard's arrival, you can tell that they
   - ☐ a. dislike strangers.
   - ☐ b. are afraid of an invasion of wizards.
   - ☐ c. have no knowledge of the outside world.
   - ☑ d. are curious about newcomers.

Generalizing

7. What kind of magic did Mr. Underhill practice?
   - ☑ a. white magic
   - ☐ b. black magic
   - ☐ c. magic only to heal cats
   - ☐ d. magic against dragons

Analyzing Character

8. Which of the following adjectives best describes Blackbeard's character?
   - ☐ a. arrogant
   - ☐ b. thoughtful
   - ☐ c. courageous
   - ☐ d. clever

Comparing

9. How is Blackbeard similar to Mr. Underhill?
   - ☐ a. Both are dragons.
   - ☐ b. Both have ordinary powers.
   - ☐ c. Both can change their shapes.
   - ☐ d. Both are ordered about by others.

Drawing Conclusions

10. Mr. Underhill probably came to Sattins Island because he
    - ☐ a. knew that the Sattins Islanders were peaceful people.
    - ☐ b. wanted to try being a wizard.
    - ☐ c. wanted a safe place to hide himself and the Hoard of Pendor.
    - ☐ d. knew that the villagers would help him fight the League if necessary.

Foreshadowing and Suspense

In cartoons, television programs, or movies, you have probably noticed that music is used to warn you of danger. You might hear a sinister-sounding melody or drumbeats when the villain first appears. The music is a clue. Later in the show, you might hear the same melody or drumbeats, even though the villain is not in sight. The music signals that something evil is about to happen.

The use of music to warn you of danger is an example of foreshadowing. In fiction <u>foreshadowing</u> is the use of hints or clues to suggest events that are going to happen later in the story. Foreshadowing is often used in fiction writing to build suspense. As you have read, suspense is the anxiety, excitement, or uncertainty that you feel while you wait for the conflict to be resolved. Foreshadowing is one way of building suspense, which in turn makes you eager to learn what lies ahead.

Fantasy and Reality

In the opening pages of "The Rule of Names," Le Guin creates a fantasy world of wizards and magic. Yet she makes the world sound almost normal so that you can accept the presence of the wizard without too much trouble. One reason why it is easy to accept the fantasy world of Sattins Island is that the people there seem to be ordinary folk. Even though they have a wizard living in their midst, they behave in ways that you recognize from your own life.

For example, you see the main character, Mr. Underhill, come out "from under his hill, smiling and breathing hard." Although you soon learn that he is a wizard, he is still someone whom the villagers greet, " 'Morning, Mr. Underhill.' " Early in the story, you also discover that Mr. Underhill is not a very good wizard. The story implies that just as there are both competent and incompetent people in other crafts, there are some people who do well as wizards and others who do not do so well. The mixture of fantasy—represented by the wizard, and reality—suggested by his incompetence, helps to make the story closer to real life.

Le Guin makes the story more believable by creating characters that behave in ordinary ways. They treat Mr. Underhill more or less like one of themselves. They either complain or laugh at his incompetence. Some feel affection for him; others do not. Despite his shortcomings, they accept his services as they might those of a not-very-good carpenter. They are not demanding because they do not have much hope of finding a better wizard.

1. Review the first few pages of the story. Describe two ways in which the people of Sattins Island are like ordinary people. Describe two ways in which their way of life is unusual.

Foreshadowing

Within this world of wizards and magic, Le Guin plants clues along the way as to what will happen. This is called foreshadowing. You might not notice all of the clues as you are reading, but as events unfold, you may realize that things that were said or done earlier were leading up to those events. Some clues are more obvious than others. An author foreshadows events in several ways. Clues might be included in descriptions, in the behavior of certain characters, or in the dialogue.

Description. Ursula Le Guin begins "The Rule of Names" with a description of Mr. Underhill. In the description, he seems perfectly normal except in one detail.

> Mr. Underhill came out from under his hill, smiling and breathing hard. Each breath shot out of his nostrils as a double puff of steam, snow-white in the morning sunshine.

The second sentence contains a bit of foreshadowing—a clue—that you might easily miss. On a December morning, a person's breath might look like puffs of steam, but the description of the steam is a bit odd. The unusual puffs of steam are a clue to Mr. Underhill's identity, as you learn later.

2. In the first two paragraphs of the story, find at least one other detail about Mr. Underhill that foreshadows future developments.

Character's Behavior. Le Guin gives other hints that Mr. Underhill is not what he appears to be. At times his behavior is very odd. The wizard does not like anyone entering his cave. When the village boys try to break through the locked door in the cave, they are frightened away by "a roar of wrath from inside, and a cloud of purple steam." Such a response might be acceptable from a wizard. After all, wizards cast spells and create fireworks. Yet what appears to be a normal act of self-defense by a shy wizard has far more importance. You don't know its importance at first. It is only as the story reaches its climax that you begin to put together the many clues that the author has left along the way.

3. Find another example of Mr. Underhill's behavior that is a clue to his identity.

Dialogue. Writers often foreshadow major events through dialogue. In "The Big Wave," the first selection in this book, Jiya tells Kino, "The sea is our enemy." That statement foreshadows a major event of the story, the terrible tidal wave that kills Jiya's parents and destroys the tiny fishing village.

On several occasions Le Guin uses dialogue to suggest events that will take place later. The old people of the village are friendly toward

Mr. Underhill. The younger people, especially the girls, are shy of him. "He makes me nervous, he smiles so much," the girls say. Yet their parents scoff at the girls' nervousness. That dialogue hints that perhaps Mr. Underhill is not as harmless as he appears.

Le Guin again foreshadows events in the scene in which Mr. Underhill listens to the children discuss the Rule of Names. The teacher, Palani, asks her class to recall the two Rules of Names. Two students answer that you cannot ask anyone his name and that you can never tell your own name. The class then discusses why a person, even Mr. Underhill, cannot tell his "truename." When Palani asks why that is the rule, no one answers until Mr. Underhill interrupts the silence:

> "Because the name is the thing," he said in his shy, soft, husky voice, "and the truename is the true thing. To speak the name is to control the thing. Am I right, Schoolmistress?"

Mr. Underhill's answer foreshadows the confrontation between him and Blackbeard when the latter shouts Mr. Underhill's "truename," Yevaud. By doing so, Blackbeard hopes to control Mr. Underhill, whom he believes to be a powerful wizard. Ironically, Blackbeard's strategy fails because Mr. Underhill—Yevaud—is not a wizard but a dragon.

4. Look at the description of Blackbeard's landing on Sattins Island and Seacaptain Fogeno's response to the news of his arrival. What does the seacaptain say? How do his words foreshadow events?

Suspense

Foreshadowing, as we have said, contributes to the suspense in a story. The author's hints or clues create tension, excitement, and uncertainty. In the examples of foreshadowing you have looked at so far, the author has created uncertainty about Mr. Underhill. She has hinted that names are going to play an important role in the story. With Seacaptain Fogeno's dialogue, she suggests a conflict between Mr. Underhill and Blackbeard.

With those early clues, Le Guin builds suspense. For example, when

Blackbeard inquires about Mr. Underhill, our uncertainties about the wizard increase, as does the suspense.

> Blackbeard smiled at her. "He's a good Sattinsman, then, eh?"
> "No," said Goody Guld, "no more than you are."

It turns out that Mr. Underhill is a relative newcomer. Like Blackbeard, Mr. Underhill suddenly appeared one day. Where did he come from? Why did he choose to stay on Sattins Island?

The author further increases the suspense by telling a story within a story—a brief tale, with its own setting, characters, and plot, told as part of the overall story. When Birt offers to take the newcomer to meet Mr. Underhill, Blackbeard insists on telling him a story. In the tale, Blackbeard talks about a distant place, Pendor, and about the lords of Pendor, whose treasure was seized by a dragon. Why is he going into all that ancient history? There must be a reason, but what is it?

Suddenly, Blackbeard interrupts his narrative, saying to Birt:

> "He'd raid nearby islands for his food. You know what dragons eat?"
> Birt nodded and said in a whisper, "Maidens."
> "Right," said Blackbeard.

5. How does that exchange help to build suspense? (Think back to the description of Mr. Underhill after he answered Palani's question about the Rule of Names: "Somehow the minute spent watching Palani and the children had made him very hungry.")

The story makes the conflict between Blackbeard and Mr. Underhill clear. Even before Blackbeard reveals his identity, you know that he believes Mr. Underhill has the treasure of Pendor and that he, Blackbeard, has come to claim it. The excitement increases as he openly declares that he is the Sealord of Pendor, and then threatens Mr. Underhill. Blackbeard thinks he is going to fight a mighty wizard when he tells Birt, "But I am mightier. Do you know why, oaf? Because I know his name!"

6. How does the battle between Blackbeard and Mr. Underhill create suspense? What is the outcome of the battle?

After the battle, Le Guin adds a surprise ending that creates new suspense.

> Mr. Underhill had decided that since his truename was no longer a secret, he might as well drop his disguise. Walking was a lot harder than flying, and besides, it was a long, long time since he had had a real meal.

7. What questions do those last lines raise? What do you think will happen next?

Sources of Humor

Even during the most suspenseful moments, Le Guin's story is full of humor. Some of the humor comes from the use of imagery—language that appeals to the senses. Although most of Le Guin's images are visual, creating vivid pictures in your mind, she also creates images that appeal to the senses of touch, smell, sound, and taste.

Look again at the last line of the story. Mr. Underhill, whom you now know is a dragon, decides to drop his disguise because "walking was a lot harder than flying." That line recalls the earlier humorous description of Mr. Underhill when he was in disguise. As you will remember, Mr. Underhill used to waddle around Sattins Island "with his toes turned in." Now he is free to fly.

8. Describe two other humorous images of Mr. Underhill.

Another source of humor is Le Guin's tone—the writer's attitude toward his or her subject or toward the audience. In "The Rule of Names" Le Guin makes gentle fun of traditional fairy tales in which wizards and dragons are all-powerful. In this story the wizard/dragon Mr. Underhill is both a figure of fun and a powerful force.

When Blackbeard appears, you sense that the newcomer might be a hero. But he turns out to be a failure. Only the oafish Birt really succeeds. He grabs his true love, the schoolmistress, and saves her from the dragon.

reversal fairytale.

9. Explain another way in which "The Rule of Names" makes fun of traditional fairy tales.

The protagnist achieve his goal.
bad guy.

A third source of humor is Le Guin's use of language. Throughout the story, the narrator and the characters use idioms—accepted phrases and expressions whose meanings cannot be understood from the ordinary meanings of the words. For example, when Blackbeard tells Birt to "hold on a while," he does not mean, as the words literally say, to cling to something. Rather, he means be patient. Because everyone understands and accepts that meaning of the phrase, it is an idiom. Le Guin often uses idioms to describe people in humorous ways. Mr. Underhill, for instance, is described as "no great shakes as a workman either. His fireworks were fairly elaborate but his elixirs were weak." "No great shakes" is an idiom meaning "not very good," but the use of that idiom to describe a wizard is humorous.

Le Guin also uses alliteration—the repetition of consonant sounds at the beginnings of words. Look at the description of the sound the boys heard when they pried into Mr. Underhill's house. They said "you couldn't believe what a huge hooting howling hissing horrible bellow that little fat man could make unless you'd heard it." The repetition of *h*'s imitates the sound of the dragon's breath.

10. Skim the story to find at least two other examples of humor. Explain what makes each of them funny.

Questions for Thought and Discussion

The questions and activities that follow will help you explore "The Rule of Names" in more depth and at the same time develop your critical thinking skills.

1. **Interpreting.** Make a list of all the names of people and places in "The Rule of Names." Do you think any of those names have special meaning? If so, what might they be?

2. **Judging the Evidence.** Organize a trial at which Blackbeard appears as the plaintiff and Mr. Underhill as the defendant in the case of the jewels of Pendor. You will need a judge, a jury, and lawyers. Have each side present its evidence, based on the story. Then have the jury decide who has the right to the jewels of Pendor.

3. **Analyzing Character.** Choose one of the characters in "The Rule of Names" and describe what kind of person he or she is. Remember that in Chapter 4 you learned to analyze a character through his or her words, thoughts, and actions, as well as through what others say about him or her.

4. **Comparing.** In both "The Rule of Names" and "Of Missing Persons," Ursula Le Guin and Jack Finney create fantasy worlds—Sattins Island and Verna. Compare those two worlds. How are they similar? How are they different? If you had to choose to live in one of them, which would you choose? Why?

Writing About Literature

Several suggestions for writing projects are given below. You may be asked to complete one or more of these projects. If you have any questions about how to begin a writing assignment, review Using the Writing Process, beginning on page 337.

1. **Taking Another Point of View.** In Chapter 7 you learned about first- and third-person narration. Rewrite the battle between Blackbeard and Mr. Underhill in the first person. You could be showing the scene from the point of view of Birt, Blackbeard, Mr. Underhill, or some other character.

2. **Using Alliteration.** You have seen how Ursula Le Guin uses alliteration to describe the sounds made by Mr. Underhill in his cave. Write a paragraph in which you use alliteration at least once to emphasize a word, an idea, or a sound.

3. **Creating Suspense.** Imagine that you are asked to add another page to "The Rule of Names." Write a description or use dialogue to create additional suspense about the final outcome of the story. For example, in your dialogue the speakers could be Birt and Palani as they flee Sattins Island, or some Sattins Islanders when they see Mr. Underhill in his true form.

UNIT THREE

Stories from Around the World

As the Night, the Day

Abioseh Nicol

Theme

The Necklace

Guy de Maupassant

Irony

Zlateh the Goat

Isaac Bashevis Singer

Imagery and Figurative Language

Men in a Storm

Jorge Ferretis

Description, Narration, and Dialogue

The stories in this unit come from around the world—West Africa, France, Eastern Europe, and Mexico. Even though you are reading about people whose lives are very different from your own, the stories explore experiences and emotions that are universal. In other words, they deal with feelings and ideas that everyone can recognize and understand. Like the stories you have already read, the selections in this unit are centered around people—what they are like, how they behave toward one another, what ideas and values they hold.

In Abioseh Nicol's "As the Night, the Day," a secondary school student faces a wrenching conflict over right and wrong. In Guy de Maupassant's story "The Necklace," a young woman suffers terribly for her misplaced values. The last two stories involve people who must continually struggle against poverty, famine, and the destructive forces of nature.

The stories throughout this book deal with a variety of situations and characters. You have read the realistic fiction of Unit One, the fantasy worlds of Unit Two, and you are about to read four stories from around the world. Although the stories are very different from each other, they all have one element in common—the characters and settings seem believable. In each of the stories, the author has created a world that might actually have existed. In each, the characters face difficult and very real problems.

Reading stories from other lands offers you an opportunity to see how writers from other cultures see the world. It allows you to compare cultures and to understand that people everywhere confront and cope with difficulties. In addition, by comparing your own culture and experiences with those portrayed in the stories, you can gain new insights into the world in which you live.

Chapter 9

Selection *As the Night, the Day*

ABIOSEH NICOL

Lesson *Theme*

About the Selection

Have you ever kept quiet after doing something wrong, and let someone else take the blame? Or have you ever taken the blame for someone else? Most people dread hearing the words, Everyone will suffer if the guilty person doesn't come forward.

In "As the Night, the Day," a fifteen-year-old boy named Kojo watches his friend Bandele attempt to measure the temperature of a Bunsen burner flame. When the thermometer he is using breaks, Bandele hides the broken parts and tells Kojo not to tell anyone.

Often when you try to hide your guilt, you are found out. In this story the laboratory attendant finds the broken thermometer. The whole class is kept after school to force the culprit to confess. The tension builds for Kojo, who must decide what to do. He faces a moral dilemma.

On the one hand, he wants to be honest and tell the truth. He has already done one wrong by keeping quiet about the accident in the first place. On the other hand, he does not want to betray his friend Bandele, a domineering character who demands that he keep silent. What does Kojo owe to his own standards of honesty? What does he owe to Bandele as a loyal friend?

Kojo's anxiety increases because the other boys in the class blame another student and they attack him. Again, Kojo faces a moment of decision. Will he speak out and and save the other boy, or will he remain silent and save himself?

Even though "As the Night, the Day" is set in an unfamiliar West African country, the dilemma faced by Kojo is universal. That is, it is one that any person anywhere might face.

Abioseh Nicol, the author of this story, was born in Freetown, Sierra Leone, a country on the west coast of Africa. Nicol is also known by the name Davidson Nicol. He has earned fame as a West African poet, critic, and short-story writer.

When Nicol was born in 1924, Sierra Leone was under British rule. It gained its independence in 1961. Nicol was educated first in Nigeria, a nearby British colony, and then at Cambridge University in England. There, he studied medicine. He became a physician and won recognition as a biochemist. Since 1961 Nicol has served Sierra Leone as ambassador to the United Nations as well as to several European countries.

Although Nicol is a doctor and a biochemist, he has pursued a writing career as well. In his writings, he tries to show the true character of the average African. His characters are often middle-class or working people. In addition to writing stories, Nicol writes poetry, for which he is perhaps best known. In his most famous poem, "The Meaning of Africa," he describes the continent of his birth as a "concept," as "happiness, contentment, and fulfillment."

Lesson Preview

The lesson that follows "As the Night, the Day" focuses on the story's theme, or underlying message. Most short stories are written not only to entertain you but also to carry a message about life in general. However, few authors state their themes outright. Instead, they develop the theme through the various elements of the story.

The theme of "As the Night, the Day," like Kojo's dilemma, is not limited to one country or continent; it is universal. It reveals something about human nature that applies to people everywhere. Abioseh Nicol helps you to understand his message through the plot, conflict, setting, and characters in the story. The questions that follow will help you find the theme in this story. As you read, think about how you would answer these questions.

1 To what does Nicol's title "As the Night, the Day" refer? What clue does the title give to the story's theme?

2 Who is the main character? What conflict does he face? How does he resolve the conflict?

3 How does the main character change during the story? What other characters are important to the story? In what ways are they important?

4 What message does Nicol seem to be suggesting about human behavior through the various incidents in the story? What do you think is the main theme, or message, of the story?

Vocabulary

Here are some difficult words that appear in the selection that follows. Study the words and their definitions, as well as the sentences that show how the words are used. This will help you get the most from your reading.

malevolence spite; the wish that harm or evil may happen to others. *He knew that his speech was controversial and would anger some people, but the malevolence of the audience surprised and shocked him.*

coalesced united. *Many nations coalesced to form the United Nations.*

imperiously intensely compelling; urgent. *"Call the ambulance! Quickly!" the doctor shouted imperiously.*

enigmatically mysteriously; in a baffling manner. *The reporter smiled enigmatically, leading us to believe that he knew more than he was saying.*

dispersed broken up; scattered. *The gardener sighed wearily as the wind dispersed the dandelion seeds across the lawn.*

impartiality fairness; justice. *The projects entered in the Science Fair were so impressive that we had to rely on the impartiality of the judges to pick a winner.*

inconsolable brokenhearted; unable to be comforted. *After their dog disappeared, the children were inconsolable for days.*

As the Night, the Day

ABIOSEH NICOL

Kojo and Bandele walked slowly across the hot green lawn, holding their science manuals with moist fingers. In the distance they could hear the junior school collecting in the hall of the main school building, for singing practice. Nearer, but still farther enough, their classmates were strolling toward them. The two reached the science block and entered it. It was a low building set apart from the rest of the high school which sprawled on the hillside of the African savanna. The laboratory was a longish room and at one end they saw Basu, another boy, looking out of the window, his back turned to them. Mr. Abu, the ferocious laboratory attendant, was not about. The rows of multicolored bottles looked inviting. A Bunsen burner soughed[1] loudly in the heavy weary heat. Where the tip of the light blue triangle of flame ended, a shimmering plastic transparency started. One could see the restless hot air moving in the minute tornado. The two African

1. **Bunsen burner soughed:** a small gas burner, used in chemistry, sighed or murmured.

boys watched it, interestedly, holding hands.

"They say it is hotter inside the flame than on its surface," Kojo said, doubtfully. "I wonder how they know?"

"I think you mean the opposite; let's try it ourselves," Bandele answered.

"How?"

"Let's take the temperature inside."

"All right, here is a thermometer. You do it."

"It says ninety degrees now. I shall take the temperature of the outer flame first, then you can take the inner yellow one."

Bandele held the thermometer gently forward to the flame and Kojo craned to see. The thin thread of quicksilver[2] shot upward within the stem of the instrument with swift malevolence and there was a slight crack. The stem had broken. On the bench the small bulbous drops of mercury which had spilled from it shivered with glinting, playful malice and shuddered down to the cement floor, dashing themselves into a thousand shining pieces, some of which coalesced again and shook gaily as if with silent laughter.

"Oh my God!" whispered Kojo hoarsely.

"Shut up!" Bandele said, imperiously in a low voice.

Bandele swept the few drops on the bench into his cupped hand and threw the blob of mercury down the sink. He swept those on the floor under an adjoining cupboard with his bare feet. Then, picking up the broken halves of the thermometer, he tiptoed to the waste bin and dropped them in. He tiptoed back to Kojo, who was standing petrified by the blackboard.

"See no evil, hear no evil, speak no evil," he whispered to Kojo.

It all took place in a few seconds. Then the rest of the class started pouring in, chattering and pushing each other. Basu, who had been at the end of the room with his back turned to them all the time, now turned round and limped laboriously across to join the class, his eyes screwed up as they always were.

2. **quicksilver:** the metal mercury.

The class ranged itself loosely in a semicircle around the demonstration platform. They were dressed in the school uniform of white shirt and khaki shorts. Their official age was around sixteen although, in fact, it ranged from Kojo's fifteen years to one or two boys of twenty-one.

Mr. Abu, the laboratory attendant, came in from the adjoining store and briskly cleaned the blackboard. He was a retired African sergeant from the Army Medical Corps and was feared by the boys. If he caught any of them in any petty thieving, he offered them the choice of a hard smack on the bottom or of being reported to the science masters. Most boys chose the former as they knew the matter would end there with no protracted interviews, moral recrimination, and an entry in the conduct book.

The science master stepped in and stood on his small platform. A tall, thin, dignified Negro with graying hair and silver-rimmed spectacles badly fitting on his broad nose and always slipping down, making him look avuncular.[3] "Vernier" was his nickname as he insisted on exact measurement and exact speech "as fine as a vernier scale," he would say, which measured, of course, things in thousandths of a millimeter. Vernier set the experiments for the day and demonstrated them, then retired behind the *Church Times* which he read seriously in between walking quickly down the aisles of lab benches advising boys. It was a simple heat experiment to show that a dark surface gave out more heat by radiation than a bright surface.

During the class, Vernier was called away to the telephone and Abu was not about, having retired to the lavatory for a smoke. As soon as a posted sentinel announced that he was out of sight, minor pandemonium broke out. Some of the boys raided the store. The wealthier ones swiped rubber tubing to make catapults and to repair bicycles, and helped themselves to chemicals for developing photographic films. The poorer boys were in deadlier earnest and took only things of strict commercial interest which could be sold easily in the market. They emptied

3. **avuncular:** like an uncle.

stuff into bottles in their pockets. Soda for making soap, magnesium sulfate for opening-medicine,[4] salt for cooking, liquid paraffin for women's hairdressing, and fine yellow iodoform powder much in demand for sprinkling on sores.

Kojo protested mildly against all this. "Oh, shut up!" a few boys said. Sorie, a huge boy who always wore a fez[5] indoors and who, rumor said, had already fathered a child, commanded respect and some leadership in the class. He was sipping his favorite mixture of dilute alcohol and bicarbonate—which he called "gin and fizz"—from a beaker. "Look here, Kojo, you are getting out of hand. What do you think our parents pay taxes and school fees for? For us to enjoy—or to buy a new car every year for Simpson?" The other boys laughed. Simpson was the European headmaster, feared by the small boys, adored by the boys in the middle school, and liked, in a critical fashion, with reservations, by some of the senior boys and African masters. He had a passion for new motorcars, buying one yearly.

"Come to think of it," Sorie continued to Kojo, "you must take something yourself, then we'll know we are safe." "Yes, you must," the other boys insisted. Kojo gave in and, unwillingly, took a little nitrate for some gunpowder experiments which he was carrying out at home.

"Someone!" the lookout called.

The boys dispersed in a moment. Sorie swilled out his mouth at the sink with some water. Mr. Abu, the lab attendant, entered and observed the innocent collective expression of the class. He glared round suspiciously and sniffed the air. It was a physics experiment, but the place smelled chemical. However, Vernier came in then. After asking if anyone was in difficulties, and finding that no one could momentarily think up anything, he retired to his chair and settled down to an article on Christian reunion, adjusting his spectacles and thoughtfully sucking an empty tooth-socket.

Towards the end of the period, the class collected around Vernier

4. **opening-medicine:** a laxative.
5. **fez:** a brimless cap, usually red with a black tassel, that was once worn by Turkish men.

and gave in their results, which were then discussed. One of the more political boys asked Vernier if dark surfaces gave out more heat, was that why they all had black faces in West Africa. A few boys giggled. Basu looked down and tapped his clubfoot embarrassedly on the floor. Vernier was used to questions of this sort from the senior boys. He never committed himself as he was getting near retirement and his pension, and became more guarded each year. He sometimes even feared that Simpson had spies among the boys.

"That may be so, although the opposite might be more convenient."

Everything in science had a loophole, the boys thought, and said so to Vernier.

"Ah! that is what is called research," he replied, enigmatically.

Sorie asked a question. Last time, they had been shown that an electric spark with hydrogen and oxygen atoms formed water. Why was not this method used to provide water in town at the height of the dry season when there was an acute water shortage?

"It would be too expensive," Vernier replied, shortly. He disliked Sorie, not because of his different religion, but because he thought that Sorie was a bad influence and also asked ridiculous questions.

Sorie persisted. There was plenty of water during the rainy season. It could be split by lightning to hydrogen and oxygen in October and the gases compressed and stored, then changed back to water in March during the shortage. There was a faint ripple of applause from Sorie's admirers.

"It is an impracticable idea," Vernier snapped.

The class dispersed and started walking back across the hot grass. Kojo and Bandele heaved sighs of relief and joined Sorie's crowd, which was always the largest.

"Science is a bit of a swindle," Sorie was saying. "I do not for a moment think that Vernier believes any of it himself," he continued. "Because if he does, why is he always reading religious books?"

"Come back, all of you, come back!" Mr. Abu's stentorian[6] voice rang out, across to them.

6. stentorian: very loud.

They wavered and stopped. Kojo kept walking on in a blind panic. "Stop," Bandele hissed across. "You fool." He stopped, turned and joined the returning crowd, closely followed by Bandele. Abu joined Vernier on the platform. The loose semicircle of boys faced them.

"Mr. Abu has just found this in the waste bin," Vernier announced, gray with anger. He held up the two broken halves of the thermometer. "It must be due to someone from this class as the number of thermometers was checked before being put out."

A little wind gusted in through the window and blew the silence heavily this way and that.

"Who?"

No one answered. Vernier looked round and waited.

"Since no one has owned up, I am afraid I shall have to detain you for an hour after school as punishment," said Vernier.

There was a murmur of dismay and anger. An important soccer house-match was scheduled for that afternoon. Some boys put their hands up and said that they had to play in the match.

"I don't care," Vernier shouted. He felt, in any case, that too much time was devoted to games and not enough to work.

He left Mr. Abu in charge and went off to fetch his things from the main building.

"We shall play 'Bible and Key,' " Abu announced as soon as Vernier had left. Kojo had been afraid of this and new beads of perspiration sprang from his troubled brow. All the boys knew the details. It was a method of finding out a culprit by divination.[7] A large doorkey was placed between the leaves of a Bible at the new Testament passage where Ananias and Sapphira were struck dead before the Apostles for lying,[8] and the Bible suspended by two bits of string tied to both ends of the key. The combination was held up by someone and the names of all present were called out in turn. When that of the sinner was called,

7. **divination:** the art of trying to foretell the future or the unknown by means of magic.
8. **Ananias and Sapphira:** a husband and wife who were struck dead for lying. Their story is told in Acts 5:1–10 of the New Testament.

the Bible was expected to turn round and round violently and fall.

Now Abu asked for a Bible. Someone produced a copy. He opened the first page and then shook his head and handed it back. "This won't do," he said, "it's a Revised Version; only the genuine Word of God will give us the answer."

An Authorized King James Version was then produced and he was satisfied. Soon he had the contraption fixed up. He looked round the semicircle from Sorie at one end, through the others, to Bandele, Basu, and Kojo at the other, near the door.

"You seem to have an honest face," he said to Kojo, "Come and hold it." Kojo took the ends of the string gingerly with both hands, trembling slightly.

Abu moved over to the low window and stood at attention, his sharp profile outlined against the red hibiscus flowers, the green trees, and the molten sky. The boys watched anxiously. A black-bodied lizard scurried up a wall and started nodding its pink head with grave impartiality.

Abu fixed his aging bloodshot eyes on the suspended Bible. He spoke hoarsely and slowly:

> "Oh Bible, Bible, on a key,
> Kindly tell it unto me,
> By swinging slowly round and true,
> To whom this sinful act is due. . . ."

He turned to the boys and barked out their names in a parade-ground voice beginning with Sorie and working his way round, looking at the Bible after each name.

To Kojo, trembling and shivering as if ice-cold water had been thrown over him, it seemed as if he had lost all power and that some gigantic being stood behind him holding up his tired aching elbows. It seemed to him as if the key and Bible had taken on a life of their own, and he watched with fascination the whole combination moving slowly, jerking, and rhythmically in short arcs as if it had acquired a heart-beat.

"Ayo Sogbenri, Sonnir Kargbo, Oji Ndebu." Abu was coming to the end now. "Tommy Longe, Ajayi Cole, Bandele Fagb . . ."

Kojo dropped the Bible. "I am tired," he said, in a small scream. "I am tired."

"Yes, he is," Abu agreed, "but we are almost finished; only Bandele and Basu are left."

"Pick up that book, Kojo, and hold it up again." Bandele's voice whipped through the air with cold fury. It sobered Kojo and he picked it up.

"Will you continue please with my name, Mr. Abu?" Bandele asked, turning to the window.

"Go back to your place quickly, Kojo," Abu said. "Vernier is coming. He might be vexed. He is a strongly religious man and so does not believe in the Bible-and-key ceremony."

Kojo slipped back with sick relief, just before Vernier entered.

In the distance the rest of the school were assembling for closing prayers. The class sat and stood around the blackboard and demonstration bench in attitudes of exasperation, resignation, and self-righteous indignation. Kojo's heart was beating so loudly that he was surprised no one else heard it.

"Once to every man and nation
  Comes the moment to decide . . ."

The closing hymn floated across to them, interrupting the still afternoon.

Kojo got up. He felt now that he must speak the truth or life would be intolerable ever afterwards. Bandele got up swiftly before him. In fact, several things seemed to happen all at the same time. The rest of the class stirred. Vernier looked up from a book review which he had started reading. A butterfly, with black and gold wings, flew in and sat on the edge of the blackboard, flapping its wings quietly and waiting too.

"Basu was here first before any of the class," Bandele said firmly.

Everyone turned to Basu, who cleared his throat.

"I was just going to say so myself, Sir," Basu replied to Vernier's enquiring glance.

"Pity you had not thought of it before," Vernier said, drily. "What were you doing here?"

"I missed the previous class, so I came straight to the lab and waited. I was over there by the window trying to look at the blue sky. I did not break the thermometer, Sir."

A few boys tittered. Some looked away. The others muttered. Basu's breath always smelt of onions, but although he could play no games, some boys liked him and were kind to him in a tolerant way.

"Well, if you did not, someone did. We shall continue with the detention."

Vernier noticed Abu standing by. "You need not stay, Mr. Abu," he said to him. "I shall close up. In fact, come with me now and I shall let you out through the back gate."

He went out with Abu.

When he had left, Sorie turned to Basu and asked mildly:

"You are sure you did not break it?"

"No, I didn't."

"He did it," someone shouted.

"But what about the Bible and key?" Basu protested. "It did not finish. Look at him." He pointed to Bandele.

"I was quite willing for it to go on," said Bandele. "You were the only one left."

Someone threw a book at Basu and said, "Confess!"

Basu backed on to a wall. "To God, I shall call the police if anyone strikes me," he cried fiercely.

"He thinks he can buy the police," a voice called.

"That proves it," someone shouted from the back.

"Yes, he must have done it," the others said, and they started throwing books at Basu. Sorie waved his arm for them to stop, but they did not. Books, corks, boxes of matches rained on Basu. He bent his head and shielded his face with his bent arm.

"I did not do it, I swear I did not do it. Stop it, you fellows," he moaned over and over again. A small cut had appeared on his temple and he was bleeding. Kojo sat quietly for a while. Then a curious hum started to pass through him, and his hands began to tremble, his arm-pits to feel curiously wetter. He turned round and picked up a book and flung it with desperate force at Basu, and then another. He felt somehow that there was an awful swelling of guilt which he could only shed by punishing himself through hurting someone. Anger and rage against everything different seized him, because if everything and everyone had been the same, somehow he felt nothing would have been wrong and they would all have been happy. He was carried away now by a torrent which swirled and pounded. He felt that somehow Basu was in the wrong, must be in the wrong, and if he hurt him hard enough he would convince the others and therefore himself that he had not broken the thermometer and that he had never done anything wrong. He groped for something bulky enough to throw, and picked up the Bible.

"Stop it," Vernier shouted through the open doorway. "Stop it, you hooligans, you beasts."

They all became quiet and shamefacedly put down what they were going to throw. Basu was crying quietly and hopelessly, his thin body shaking.

"Go home, all of you, go home. I am ashamed of you." His black face shone with anger. "You are an utter disgrace to your nation and to your race."

They crept away, quietly, uneasily, avoiding each other's eyes, like people caught in secret passion.

Vernier went to the first-aid cupboard and started dressing Basu's wounds.

Kojo and Bandele came back and hid behind the door, listening. Bandele insisted that they should.

Vernier put Basu's bandaged head against his waistcoat and dried the boy's tears with his handkerchief, gently patting his shaking shoulders.

"It wouldn't have been so bad if I had done it, Sir," he mumbled, snuggling his head against Vernier, "but I did not do it. I swear to God I did not."

"Hush, hush," said Vernier comfortingly.

"Now they will hate me even more," he moaned.

"Hush, hush."

"I don't mind the wounds so much, they will heal."

"Hush, hush."

"They've missed the football match and now they will never talk to me again, oh-ee, oh-ee, why have I been so punished?"

"As you grow older," Vernier advised, "you must learn that men are punished not always for what they do, but often for what people think they will do, or for what they are. Remember that and you will find it easier to forgive them. 'To thine own self be true!' " Vernier ended with a flourish, holding up his clenched fist in a mock dramatic gesture, quoting from the Shakespeare examination set-book for the year and declaiming to the dripping taps and empty benches and still afternoon, to make Basu laugh.

Basu dried his eyes and smiled wanly and replied: " 'And it shall follow as the night the day.' Hamlet, Act One, Scene Three, Polonius to Laertes."

"There's a good chap. First class, Grade One. I shall give you a lift home."

Kojo and Bandele walked down the red laterite road together, Kojo dispiritedly kicking stones into the gutter.

"The fuss they made over a silly old thermometer," Bandele began.

"I don't know, old man, I don't know," Kojo said impatiently.

They had both been shaken by the scene in the empty lab. A thin invisible wall of hostility and mistrust was slowly rising between them.

"Basu did not do it, of course," Bandele said.

Kojo stopped dead in his tracks. "Of course he did not do it," he shouted, "we did it."

"No need to shout, old man. After all, it was your idea."

"It wasn't," Kojo said furiously. "You suggested we try it."

"Well, you started the argument. Don't be childish." They tramped on silently, raising small clouds of dust with their bare feet.

"I should not take it too much to heart," Bandele continued. "That chap Basu's father hoards foodstuff like rice and palm oil until there is a shortage and then sells them at high prices. The police are watching him."

"What has that got to do with it?" Kojo asked.

"Don't you see, Basu might quite easily have broken that thermometer. I bet he has done things before that we have all been punished for." Bandele was emphatic.

They walked on steadily down the main road of the town, past the Syrian and Lebanese shops crammed with knickknacks and rolls of cloth, past a large Indian shop with dull red carpets and brass trays displayed in its windows, carefully stepping aside in the narrow road as the British officials sped by in cars to their hill-station bungalows for lunch and siesta.

Kojo reached home at last. He washed his feet and ate his main meal for the day. He sat about heavily and restlessly for some hours. Night soon fell with its usual swiftness, at six, and he finished his homework early and went to bed.

Lying in bed he rehearsed again what he was determined to do the next day. He would go up to Vernier:

"Sir," he would begin, "I wish to speak with you privately."

"Can it wait?" Vernier would ask.

"No, Sir," he would say firmly, "as a matter of fact it is rather urgent."

Vernier would take him to an empty classroom and say, "What is troubling you, Kojo Ananse?"

"I wish to make a confession, Sir. I broke the thermometer

yesterday." He had decided he would not name Bandele; it was up to the latter to decide whether he would lead a pure life.

Vernier would adjust his slipping glasses up his nose and think. Then he would say:

"This is a serious matter, Kojo. You realize you should have confessed yesterday."

"Yes, Sir, I am very sorry."

"You have done great harm, but better late than never. You will, of course, apologize in front of the class and particularly to Basu who has shown himself a finer chap than all of you."

"I shall do so, Sir."

"Why have you come to me now to apologize? Were you hoping that I would simply forgive you?"

"I was hoping you would, Sir. I was hoping you would show your forgiveness by beating me."

Vernier would pull his glasses up his nose again. He would move his tongue inside his mouth reflectively. "I think you are right. Do you feel you deserve six strokes or nine?"

"Nine, Sir."

"Bend over!"

Kojo had decided he would not cry because he was almost a man.

Whack! Whack!

Lying in bed in the dark thinking about it all as it would happen tomorrow, he clenched his teeth and tensed his buttocks in imaginary pain.

Whack! Whack!! Whack!!!

Suddenly, in his little room, under his thin cotton sheet, he began to cry. Because he felt the sharp lancing pain already cutting into him. Because of Basu and Simpson and the thermometer. For all the things he wanted to do and be which would never happen. For all the good men they had told them about, Jesus Christ, Mohammed, and George Washington who never told a lie. For Florence Nightingale and David

Livingstone. For Kagawa, the Japanese man, for Gandhi, and for Kwegyir Aggrey, the African. Oh-ee, oh-ee. Because he knew he would never be as straight and strong and true as the school song said they should be. He saw, for the first time, what this thing would be like, becoming a man. He touched the edge of an inconsolable eternal grief. Oh-ee, oh-ee; always, he felt, always I shall be a disgrace to the nation and the race.

His mother passed by his bedroom door slowly dragging her slippered feet as she always did. He pushed his face into his wet pillow to stifle his sobs, but she had heard him. She came in and switched on the light.

"What *is* the matter with you, my son?"

He pushed his face further into his pillow.

"Nothing," he said, muffled and choking.

"You have been looking like a sick fowl all afternoon," she continued.

She advanced and put the back of her moist cool fingers against the side of his neck.

"You have got fever," she exclaimed. "I'll get something from the kitchen."

When she had gone out, Kojo dried his tears and turned the dry side of the pillow up. His mother reappeared with a thermometer in one hand and some quinine[9] mixture in the other.

"Oh, take it away, take it away," he shouted, pointing to her right hand and shutting his eyes tightly.

"All right, all right," she said, slipping the thermometer into her bosom.

He is a queer boy, she thought, with pride and a little fear as she watched him drink the clear bitter fluid.

She then stood by him and held his head against her broad thigh as he sat up on the low bed, and she stroked his face. She knew he had been crying but did not ask him why, because she was sure he would not tell her. She knew he was learning, first slowly and now quickly, and

9. **quinine:** a bitter substance from the cinchona tree that is used in treating malaria.

she would soon cease to be his mother and be only one of the womenfolk in the family. Such a short time, she thought, when they are really yours and tell you everything. She sighed and slowly eased his sleeping head down gently.

The next day Kojo got to school early, and set to things briskly. He told Bandele that he was going to confess but would not name him. He half hoped he would join him. But Bandele had said, threateningly, that he had better not mention his name, let him go and be a Boy Scout on his own. The sneer strengthened him and he went off to the lab. He met Mr. Abu and asked for Vernier. Abu said Vernier was busy and what was the matter, anyhow.

"I broke the thermometer yesterday," Kojo said in a businesslike manner.

Abu put down the glassware he was carrying.

"Well, I never!" he said. "What do you think you will gain by this?"

"I broke it," Kojo repeated.

"Basu broke it," Abu said impatiently. "Sorie got him to confess and Basu himself came here this morning and told the science master and myself that he knew now that he had knocked the thermometer over by mistake when he came in early yesterday afternoon. He had not turned round to look, but he had definitely heard a tinkle as he walked by. Someone must have picked it up and put it in the waste bin. The whole matter is settled, the palaver[10] finished."

He tapped a barometer on the wall and, squinting, read the pressure. He turned again to Kojo.

"I should normally have expected him to say so yesterday and save you boys missing the game. But there you are," he added, shrugging and trying to look reasonable, "you cannot hope for too much from a Syrian boy."

10. palaver: a discussion.

Reviewing the Selection

Answer each of the following questions without looking back at the story.

Recalling Facts

1. The person who actually broke the thermometer was
   - ☐ a. Kojo.
   - ☐ b. Bandele.
   - ☐ c. Basu.
   - ☐ d. Sorie.

Understanding Main Ideas

2. The boys turn on Basu and blame him for breaking the thermometer because he is
   - ☐ a. the youngest student.
   - ☐ b. the oldest student.
   - ☐ c. different from the others.
   - ☐ d. the teacher's pet.

Placing Events in Order

3. Kojo finally confesses after he
   - ☐ a. hears the hymn.
   - ☐ b. learns that Basu has confessed.
   - ☐ c. sees that the 'Bible and Key' will prove him to be guilty.
   - ☐ d. returns to school the day after the incident.

Finding Supporting Details

4. When Kojo and Bandele arrive early at the lab, the other person they see in the classroom is
   - ☐ a. Mr. Abu.
   - ☐ b. Basu.
   - ☐ c. Sorie.
   - ☐ d. Vernier.

Recognizing Words in Context

5. "As soon as a posted sentinel announced that he was out of sight, minor pandemonium broke out." In this context *sentinel* means
   - ☐ a. teacher.
   - ☐ b. guard.
   - ☐ c. official.
   - ☐ d. director.

Interpreting the Selection

Answer each of the following questions. You may look back at the story if necessary.

Making Inferences

6. Kojo and Bandele hide their guilt because they
   - ☐ a. do not like Basu.
   - ☐ b. are afraid of being punished.
   - ☐ c. dislike school.
   - ☐ d. want to get Vernier in trouble.

Generalizing

7. The boys treat Vernier with
   - ☐ a. both respect and scorn.
   - ☐ b. admiration.
   - ☐ c. resentment.
   - ☐ d. both friendliness and sympathy.

Analyzing Character

8. Kojo feels bad about keeping silent because he
   - ☐ a. has never broken anything before.
   - ☐ b. knows that Abu will get in trouble.
   - ☐ c. has gone against what he believes is right.
   - ☐ d. likes Basu, who is taking the blame.

Comparing

9. Compared to Bandele, Kojo is
   - ☐ a. more frightened of punishment.
   - ☐ b. more troubled by his conscience.
   - ☐ c. less honest.
   - ☐ d. more irresponsible.

Drawing Conclusions

10. Abu doesn't believe Kojo's confession because he
    - ☐ a. likes Kojo.
    - ☐ b. has already accepted that Basu is guilty.
    - ☐ c. thinks Kojo is trying to make trouble for the school.
    - ☐ d. knows that Bandele has forced Kojo to confess.

Theme

Authors of short stories develop themes to express their comments on or insights into life and human nature. The theme of a story is different from its subject, although the two may be connected. For example, the subject of "As the Night, the Day" is about the behavior of a group of African students accused of breaking equipment in a science laboratory. The theme, or underlying message, is that a person should be true to himself or herself even though that may involve conflict with another.

Authors seldom state their themes directly. In most stories you must search for the theme by carefully examining all the elements of a story and thinking about its meaning. One of the pleasures of reading short stories is realizing the authors' underlying messages.

In some stories the theme is simple. It can be explained in a sentence. In other stories the theme is complicated, or there may be more than one theme. To discover a story's theme, you must look at all the elements of the story—plot, setting, conflict, and characters. In this lesson you will see how the theme is woven into Abioseh Nicol's story "As the Night, the Day."

Interpreting the Title

An author sometimes gives a clue to a story's theme in the title. You learn in this story that Nicol's title, "As the Night, the Day," comes from a speech in *Hamlet,* a play written by William Shakespeare. In this well-known speech, a young man named Laertes is about to leave on a journey. Before he departs, his father, Polonius, advises his son on how to act and behave. At the end of his speech, Polonius cautions Laertes:

> This above all: To thine own self be true,
> And it must follow, as the night the day,
> Thou canst not then be false to any man.

1. *In your own words, what do you think Polonius means by those lines?*

Nicol has chosen his title deliberately. It alludes to a work by Shakespeare. An allusion is an indirect reference to a work of literature or to a person, place, or event that you are expected to recognize. Shakespeare is well known to most people, and the allusion to Polonius's advice relates closely to the struggle faced by Kojo, the main character in Nicol's story. Should the boy be "true to himself"? What will happen if he does what he thinks is right? Those questions are at the heart of Kojo's conflict, as you will see.

Conflict and Theme

In short stories, the conflict helps to express the theme. "As the Night, the Day" has several conflicts. Two external ones are (1) the conflict between the boys and the master, and (2) the conflict between individual boys. The central conflict, however, is the internal one that Kojo faces as he struggles with his conscience.

Bandele puts the thermometer into the flames, and Kojo is horrified when it breaks. He knows that they should confess. Yet he says nothing when Bandele cleans up the pieces without telling anyone about the accident. Kojo remains silent when the class begins. He is frightened throughout the lesson and heaves a sigh of relief when it is over. However, his troubles have just begun, because Mr. Abu, the laboratory attendant, soon finds the broken thermometer.

2. When the boys are called back to the classroom, what conflict does Kojo face?

3. How does Kojo's internal conflict intensify when (a) Abu insists that the boys play "Bible and Key", (b) Kojo hears the students singing the hymn "Once to Every Man and Nation", and (c) the boys start attacking Basu?

By not confessing at the first opportunity, Kojo is drawn into deeper trouble. The entire class must suffer for his silence, and an innocent student, Basu, is made to take the blame. Kojo feels bad, but he is overwhelmed by "an awful swelling of guilt which he could only shed by punishing himself through hurting someone." So he joins the attack on Basu and hurls several books at him.

Lying in bed that night, Kojo resolves to confess. He even pictures the scene in which he admits his guilt.

4. What do you think Kojo hopes to gain by his confession? Why does he choose nine strokes as a punishment instead of six?

Kojo's conflict over whether or not to confess leads him to face other truths. Alone in his room, Kojo feels that no matter how hard he may try he can never be as good as he would like to be. In school he has learned about many great people whose examples he hopes to follow. After Kojo has had time alone, he understands how difficult it is to follow those examples. Now Kojo understands that becoming responsible, true, and strong won't be easy: "He saw, for the first time, what this thing would be like, becoming a man." Part of "becoming a man" is understanding Polonius's advice—Kojo must first be true to himself before he can hope to be honest and true with others.

Theme and Character

Several characters help develop the theme in "As the Night, the Day." As you have seen, Kojo is a boy with a strong moral conscience. He knows that what he and Bandele have done is wrong. Bandele, by contrast, suffers no pangs of conscience. He is a boy who will do whatever is necessary to avoid blame.

After breaking the thermometer, Bandele orders Kojo to be silent and then whispers, " 'See no evil, hear no evil, speak no evil.' "

5. What does Bandele mean by that old saying?

Kojo goes along with Bandele but he agonizes over the decision. More than once Bandele forces Kojo to remain silent. During the Bible and Key incident, Bandele orders his friend to pick up the Bible after Kojo has dropped it. Then when Kojo hears the hymn and decides he must speak, Bandele diverts everyone's attention. He reminds the class that Basu, the Syrian boy, was the first one in the room.

Kojo's internal and external conflicts show how hard it is for a person to follow the path of truth and honesty. Kojo doesn't want to be punished at school, nor does he want to lose Bandele's friendship. Kojo suffers for a time in agonizing uncertainty. He wants to do what is right, but he is frightened and easily swayed by Bandele, who insists that they deny responsibility for the incident. In the end Kojo decides to be true to himself. He rejects Bandele's selfish attitude and chooses to confess.

6. Early in the story, what evidence shows that Kojo is basically an honest boy? How do you think Kojo's character changes as a result of the conflicts in the story?

When Kojo finally makes up his mind to confess, the story takes an ironic twist. Irony, as you learned in Chapter 6, is the contrast between what is expected to happen and what actually happens. Kojo wants to confess to Vernier. But because the master teacher is busy, the boy confesses to Abu instead. Abu impatiently dismisses Kojo's confession. Basu, it seems, has already told the science master that he was the guilty one.

By using an abrupt, unresolved ending, the author raises some important moral questions, or dilemmas for you to answer. After all Kojo's agonizing, his confession is seen as a trifle—even a lie. If he had confessed immediately, Basu would never have been punished.

7. How do you think Kojo felt about Abu's response to his confession? How do you think Kojo felt when he realized that Basu had confessed?

Minor Themes

Like many stories, "As the Night, the Day" has more than one theme. The major theme is the most fully developed one. However, Nicol offers other insights into life.

One minor theme centers on the treatment of Basu by his fellow students and by the teachers. Because he has a clubfoot, he cannot play sports. He is isolated from the other students because he is different. Perhaps for this reason, he is alone in the laboratory at the beginning of the story. At the end of the story you learn another fact about Basu. He is Syrian—a foreigner in this classroom of young African students. Basu is singled out by the other boys, and even by Abu, as an object of scorn.

8. When Vernier is comforting Basu, he tells the boy, " 'you must learn that men are punished not always for what they do, but often for what people think they will do, or for what they are.' " How does that passage help explain why the boys and Abu find it easy to place the blame on Basu?

9. Why do you think Basu decides to confess to Vernier and Abu even though he is not guilty of breaking the thermometer?

Another minor theme concerns the relationship between people in authority and those they control. In this story you have two sets of authority figures: the British colonial rulers and the school authorities, including Vernier and Abu.

You get a vague glimpse of the European headmaster, Simpson, who "had a passion for motorcars, buying one yearly." You also see "the British officials [who] sped by in cars to their hill-station bungalows for lunch and siesta." The older African students like Simpson in some ways. They have little response to the more distant British officials, although their presence as a foreign, occupying power is felt constantly.

The students have a much stronger reaction, however, to the science master, Vernier, and the laboratory attendant, Abu. Those men have a greater impact on their daily lives than either Simpson or the colonial officials do. Vernier and Abu are symbols of real authority, whom the students treat with a mixture of fear, limited respect, and contempt. They fear Abu's position as the disciplinarian. They respect Vernier for his insistence on careful measurement and speech, although they challenge him with difficult or political questions whenever they can.

10. How do the boys behave toward Vernier and Abu when they are in the classroom? How do they behave when Abu and Vernier are not present in the classroom?

11. What do you think is the underlying message in the relationship between the boys and their teachers?

Questions for Thought and Discussion

The questions and activities that follow will help you explore "As the Night, the Day" in more depth and at the same time develop your critical thinking skills.

1. **Taking a Stand.** Hold a panel discussion in which students take different stands on this statement: Kojo waited too long for his confession to be of any value. Each panel member should justify his or her position with examples from the story or from real life.

2. **Analyzing Character.** Is Abu or Vernier the stronger character in the story? Give reasons for your answer based on their words, thoughts, actions, or what others think of them.

3. **Inferring.** Do you think that Vernier believed Basu's confession? Give reasons for your answer.

4. **Comparing.** Both Basu and Jerry in "A Mother in Mannville" tell a lie. How is the behavior of the two boys similar? How is it different?

Writing About Literature

Several suggestions for writing projects are given below. You may be asked to complete one or more of these projects. If you have any questions about how to begin a writing assignment, review Using the Writing Process, beginning on page 337.

1. **Creating a New Ending.** Imagine what would have happened if Abu had believed Kojo's story. Write a new ending showing Kojo apologizing to the class and to Basu. In your ending, indicate how the class might behave toward Basu after Kojo's confession. Show also how the friendship between Bandele and Kojo might be affected.

2. **Developing an Argument.** Imagine that you have to give a speech to a group of students on the following topic: Honesty is the best policy. Write a short speech explaining your views on the topic. Support your argument with strong examples.

3. **Writing from Another Point of View.** "As the Night, the Day" is told from a third-person narrator's point of view. Choose one scene in the story and rewrite it from the first-person point of view of one of the characters. For example, you could re-create from Basu's point of view the scene in which the boys attack Basu.

4. **Reporting on Research.** In the story, Kojo remembers learning about "good men," such as Jesus Christ, Mohammed, George Washington, and several others. Find out more about one of the "good men" that Kojo thought of during the night when he decided to confess. Then write a report explaining how that person might have served as an example to Kojo.

Chapter 10

Selection *The Necklace*

GUY DE MAUPASSANT

Lesson *Irony*

About the Selection

In every age and in every culture, people have had dreams of achieving wealth or fame, or both. A person might dream of becoming a famous scientist, actor, or sports figure. In "The Secret Life of Walter Mitty" you read about an average middle-aged man who dreamed of being a gallant hero. Although his daydreams were excessive, they were easy for us to recognize and understand.

"The Necklace," by the French writer Guy de Maupassant, centers on a young woman who yearns to live in wealth and luxury and to be accepted into upper-class society.

De Maupassant lived in France in the late 1800s. At that time a person's place in society was largely determined by birth. Class divisions were fixed. Rarely could a person from the lower classes become rich enough to rise into the upper class, or marry into a higher class. Most people remained in the class into which they were born.

Mathilde Loisel, the main character in "The Necklace," is desperately unhappy because she and her husband are members of the *petite bourgeoisie* which is the lower middle class. Members of the *petite bourgeoisie* are respectable but have very little social standing. Madame Loisel is a pretty young woman with dreams of wealth and status that seem unlikely to come true.

One day, however, her husband comes home with an invitation to a grand ball. He is a low-level government clerk, and the ball is being given by the minister who heads his department. The invitation offers Madame Loisel her chance to enter society. She scrapes together enough money to buy a lovely gown, and she borrows a beautiful diamond necklace from a wealthy friend. The scene is set for her dream to come true. As with so many dreams, however, reality interrupts, and Madame Loisel must face the results.

Guy de Maupassant is recognized as one of the world's greatest short-story writers. He wrote more than three hundred stories, most of them between 1880 and 1890. He often wrote about the middle class, government officials, and peasants.

De Maupassant came from a noble family in northern France. His family was not wealthy, but like many sons of the nobility, he received his education at a seminary. He disliked the school so much that he managed to get himself expelled. He then attended a lycée, or French secondary school, and later studied law.

After completing his education, de Maupassant settled in Paris, where he supported himself by becoming a civil servant, or government official. For almost ten years he worked in various government offices. The work was dull, and the pay was low. De Maupassant felt like an outsider in the sophisticated, free-spending Paris society. After working long hours at the office, he would return home and write long into the night. His experiences at work gave him material for many of his stories.

In 1867, soon after going to Paris, de Maupassant met his godfather, Gustave Flaubert, a famous French novelist. Flaubert helped train his godson as a writer. He taught the young man about literary style and introduced him to the leading writers of Europe.

De Maupassant's work began to be noticed in 1876, but it was not until 1880 that he could support himself entirely by writing. Within a few years he became one of the most widely read French authors. In recent years his appeal in France has declined, but his popularity in the English-speaking world has grown.

Lesson Preview

The lesson that follows "The Necklace" focuses on irony in the story. As you learned in Chapter 6, irony refers to the contrast between what is expected and what actually happens. It can also be a contrast between what a person says and what he or she means. A writer often uses irony to comment on a person's character, situation, or to criticize society.

"The Necklace" is told in the third person. As the narrator describes the characters and events in the story, the various examples of irony become apparent to the reader. The questions that follow will help you see the irony in the story. As you read, think about how you would answer these questions.

1 What is Mathilde Loisel's life really like? How would she like it to be?

2 How does the invitation to the ball offer Mme. Loisel a chance to achieve her dreams? What actually happens?

3 Why is the necklace important to Mme. Loisel before the ball? During the ball? After the ball?

4 What is the theme of the story? How is the theme related to the irony in the story?

5 What attitude do you think the author takes toward Mathilde Loisel and her husband?

Vocabulary

Here are some difficult words that appear in the selection that follows. Study the words and their definitions, as well as the sentences that show how the words are used. This will help you get the most from your reading.

hierarchy any group in which there are higher and lower positions of importance or power. *Because of his youth and inexperience, he ranked very low in the company's hierarchy.*

salons large drawing rooms for entertaining guests. *The ambassador hired different chamber orchestras to play in each of the salons at the embassy.*

coquettish flirtatious. *The young woman, laughing in a coquettish manner, insisted that she must leave the party.*

boudoirs women's private sitting rooms. *In the 1800s, wealthy women entertained in their boudoirs, welcoming friends and admirers there almost every day.*

quail a game bird of the pheasant family. *Quail has been popular for centuries as both a game bird and a source of food.*

colleague an associate or fellow worker. *Another colleague and I went to an important lecture sponsored by our company.*

immoderate excessive; more than is proper. *The labor union, feeling that their demands were not immoderate, decided to strike the company.*

vestibule a small entrance hall or room. *The woman left her dripping umbrella in the stand in the vestibule.*

chagrin feeling of disappointment, failure, or humiliation. *With a feeling of despair and chagrin, the boy realized that he didn't pass his chemistry exam.*

garret attic. *The students couldn't afford to spend much money on living quarters, so they decided to rent the inexpensive garret.*

The Necklace

GUY DE MAUPASSANT

She was one of those pretty and charming girls who are sometimes, as if by a mistake of destiny, born in a family of clerks. She had no dowry,[1] no expectations, no means of being known, understood, loved, wedded, by any rich and distinguished man; and she let herself be married to a little clerk at the Ministry of Public Instruction.

She dressed plainly because she could not dress well, but she was as unhappy as though she had really fallen from her proper station; since with women there is neither caste nor rank; and beauty, grace, and charm act instead of family and birth. Natural fineness, instinct for what is elegant, suppleness of wit, are the sole hierarchy, and make from women of the people the equals of the very greatest ladies.

She suffered ceaselessly, feeling herself born for all the delicacies and all the luxuries. She suffered from the poverty of her dwelling, from the wretched look of the walls, from the worn-out chairs, from the ugliness of the curtains. All those things, of which another woman of her

1. **dowry:** the property that a bride brings to her husband at marriage.

rank would never even have been conscious, tortured her and made her angry. The sight of the little Breton peasant who did her humble housework aroused in her regrets which were despairing, and distracted dreams. She thought of the silent antechambers hung with Oriental tapestry, lit by tall bronze candelabra, and of the two great footmen in knee breeches who sleep in the big armchairs, made drowsy by the heavy warmth of the hot-air stove. She thought of the long *salons* fitted up with ancient silk, of the delicate furniture carrying priceless curiosities, and of the coquettish perfumed boudoirs made for talks at five o'clock with intimate friends, with men famous and sought after, whom all women envy and whose attention they all desire.

When she sat down to dinner, before the round table covered with a tablecloth three days old, opposite her husband, who uncovered the soup tureen and declared with an enchanted air, "Ah, the good *pot-au-feu!* [2] I don't know anything better than that," she thought of dainty dinners, of shining silverware, of tapestry which peopled the walls with ancient personages and with strange birds flying in the midst of a fairy forest; and she thought of delicious dishes served on marvelous plates, and of the whispered gallantries which you listen to with a sphinx-like smile, while you are eating the pink flesh of a trout or the wings of a quail.

She had no dresses, no jewels, nothing. And she loved nothing but that; she felt made for that. She would so have liked to please, to be envied, to be charming, to be sought after.

She had a friend, a former schoolmate at the convent, who was rich, and whom she did not like to go and see any more, because she suffered so much when she came back.

But, one evening, her husband returned home with a triumphant air, and holding a large envelope in his hand.

"There," said he, "here is something for you."

She tore the paper sharply, and drew out a printed card which bore these words:

"The Minister of Public Instruction and Mme. Georges Ramponneau

2. ***pot-au-feu:*** French dish made by boiling meat and vegetables.

request the honor of M. and Mme.[3] Loisel's company at the palace of the Ministry on Monday evening, January 18th."

Instead of being delighted, as her husband hoped, she threw the invitation on the table with disdain, murmuring:

"What do you want me to do with that?"

"But, my dear, I thought you would be glad. You never go out, and this is such a fine opportunity. I had awful trouble to get it. Every one wants to go; it is very select, and they are not giving many invitations to clerks. The whole official world will be there."

She looked at him with an irritated eye and she said, impatiently:

"And what do you want me to put on my back?"

He had not thought of that; he stammered.

"Why, the dress you go to the theater in. It looks very well, to me."

He stopped, distracted, seeing that his wife was crying. Two great tears descended slowly from the corners of her eyes towards the corners of her mouth. He muttered:

"What's the matter? What's the matter?"

But, by a violent effort, she had conquered her grief, and she replied, with a calm voice, while she wiped her wet cheeks:

"Nothing. Only I have no dress, and therefore I can't go to this ball. Give your card to some colleague whose wife is better equipped than I."

He was in despair. He resumed:

"Come, let us see, Mathilde. How much would it cost, a suitable dress, which you could use on other occasions, something very simple?"

She reflected several seconds, making her calculations and wondering also what sum she could ask without drawing on herself an immediate refusal and a frightened exclamation from the economical clerk.

Finally, she replied, hesitantly:

"I don't know exactly, but I think I could manage it with four hundred francs."

He had grown a little pale, because he was laying aside just that

3. **M., Mme.:** abbreviations for the French words *Monsieur* and *Madame,* meaning Mr. and Mrs.

amount to buy a gun and treat himself to a little shooting next summer on the plain of Nanterre, with several friends who went to shoot larks down there, of a Sunday.

But he said:

"All right. I will give you four hundred francs. And try to have a pretty dress."

The day of the ball drew near, and Mme. Loisel seemed sad, uneasy, anxious. Her dress was ready, however. Her husband said to her one evening:

"What is the matter? Come, you've been so queer these last three days."

And she answered:

"It annoys me not to have a single jewel, not a single stone, nothing to put on. I shall look like distress. I should almost rather not go at all."

He resumed:

"You might wear natural flowers. It's very stylish at this time of year. For ten francs you can get two or three magnificent roses."

She was not convinced.

"No; there's nothing more humiliating than to look poor among other women who are rich."

But her husband cried:

"How stupid you are! Go look up your friend Mme. Forestier, and ask her to lend you some jewels. You're quite thick enough with her to do that."

She uttered a cry of joy:

"It's true. I never thought of it."

The next day she went to her friend and told of her distress.

Mme. Forestier went to a wardrobe with a glass door, took out a large jewel-box, brought it back, opened it, and said to Mme. Loisel:

"Choose, my dear."

She saw first of all some bracelets, then a pearl necklace, then a Venetian cross, gold and precious stones of admirable workmanship. She tried on the ornaments before the glass, hesitated, could not make up her mind to part with them, to give them back. She kept asking:

"Haven't you any more?"

"Why, yes. Look. I don't know what you like."

All of a sudden she discovered, in a black satin box, a superb necklace of diamonds and her heart began to beat with an immoderate desire. Her hands trembled as she took it. She fastened it around her throat, outside her highnecked dress, and remained lost in ecstasy at the sight of herself.

Then she asked, hesitating, filled with anguish:

"Can you lend me that, only that?"

"Why, yes, certainly."

She sprang upon the neck of her friend, kissed her passionately, then fled with her treasure.

The day of the ball arrived. Mme. Loisel made a great success. She was prettier than them all, elegant, gracious, smiling, and crazy with joy. All the men looked at her, asked her name, endeavored to be introduced. All the attachés of the Cabinet wanted to waltz with her. She was remarked by the minister himself.

She danced with intoxication, with passion, made drunk by pleasure, forgetting all, in the triumph of her beauty, in the glory of her success, in a sort of cloud of happiness composed of all this homage, of all this admiration, of all these awakened desires, and of that sense of complete victory which is so sweet to woman's heart.

She went away about four o'clock in the morning. Her husband had been sleeping since midnight, in a little deserted anteroom, with three other gentlemen whose wives were having a very good time.

He threw over her shoulders the wraps which he had brought, modest wraps of common life, whose poverty contrasted with the elegance of the ball dress. She felt this and wanted to escape so as not to be remarked by the other women, who were enveloping themselves in costly furs.

Loisel held her back.

"Wait a bit. You will catch cold outside. I will go and call a cab."

But she did not listen to him, and rapidly descended the stairs. When they were in the street they did not find a carriage; and they began to look for one, shouting after the cabmen whom they saw passing by at a distance.

They went down towards the Seine, in despair, shivering with cold. At last they found on the quay one of those ancient noctambulant coupés[4] which, exactly as if they were ashamed to show their misery during the day, are never seen round Paris until after nightfall.

It took them to their door in the Rue des Martyrs, and once more, sadly, they climbed up homeward. All was ended, for her. And as to him, he reflected that he must be at the Ministry at ten o'clock.

She removed the wraps, which covered her shoulders, before the glass, so as once more to see herself in all her glory. But suddenly she uttered a cry. She had no longer the necklace around her neck!

Her husband, already half undressed, demanded:

"What is the matter with you?"

She turned madly toward him:

"I have—I have—I've lost Mme. Forestier's necklace."

He stood up, distracted.

"What!—how?—Impossible!"

And they looked in the folds of her dress, in the folds of her cloak, in her pockets, everywhere. They did not find it.

He asked:

"You're sure you had it on when you left the ball?"

"Yes, I felt it in the vestibule of the palace."

"But if you had lost it in the street we should have heard it fall. It must be in the cab."

"Yes. Probably. Did you take his number?"

"No. And you, didn't you notice it?"

"No."

4. noctambulant coupés: carriages that seemed to be sleepwalking.

They looked, thunderstruck, at one another. At last Loisel put on his clothes.

"I shall go back on foot," said he, "over the whole route which we have taken, to see if I can't find it."

And he went out. She sat waiting on a chair in her ball dress, without strength to go to bed, overwhelmed, without fire, without a thought.

Her husband came back about seven o'clock. He had found nothing.

He went to Police Headquarters, to the newspaper offices, to offer a reward; he went to the cab companies—everywhere, in fact, whither he was urged by the least suspicion of hope.

She waited all day, in the same condition of mad fear before this terrible calamity.

Loisel returned at night with a hollow, pale face; he had discovered nothing.

"You must write to your friend," said he, "that you have broken the clasp of her necklace and that you are having it mended. That will give us time to turn round."

She wrote at his dictation.

At the end of a week they had lost all hope.

And Loisel, who had aged five years, declared:

"We must consider how to replace that ornament."

The next day they took the box which had contained it, and they went to the jeweler whose name was found within. He consulted his books.

"It was not I, madame, who sold that necklace; I must simply have furnished the case."

Then they went from jeweler to jeweler, searching for a necklace like the other, consulting their memories, sick both of them with chagrin and with anguish.

They found, in a shop at the Palais Royal, a string of diamonds which seemed to them exactly like the one they looked for. It was worth forty thousand francs. They could have it for thirty-six.

So they begged the jeweler not to sell it for three days yet. And they made a bargain that he should buy it back for thirty-four thousand francs, in case they found the other one before the end of February.

Loisel possessed eighteen thousand francs which his father had left him. He would borrow the rest.

He did borrow, asking a thousand francs of one, five hundred of another, five louis[5] here, three louis there. He gave notes, took up ruinous obligations, dealt with usurers,[6] and all the race of lenders. He compromised all the rest of his life, risked his signature without even knowing if he could meet it; and, frightened by the pains yet to come, by the black misery which was about to fall upon him, by the prospect of all the physical privations and of all the moral tortures which he was to suffer, he went to get the new necklace, putting down upon the merchant's counter thirty-six thousand francs.

When Mme. Loisel took back the necklace, Mme. Forestier said to her, with a chilly manner:

"You should have returned it sooner, I might have needed it."

She did not open the case, as her friend had so much feared. If she had detected the substitution, what would she have thought, what would she have said? Would she not have taken Mme. Loisel for a thief?

Mme. Loisel now knew the horrible existence of the needy. She took her part, moreover, all of a sudden, with heroism. That dreadful debt must be paid. She would pay it. They dismissed their servant; they changed their lodgings; they rented a garret under the roof.

She came to know what heavy housework meant and the odious cares of the kitchen. She washed the dishes, using her rosy nails on the greasy pots and pans. She washed the dirty linen, the shirts, and the dishcloths, which she dried upon a line; she carried the slops down to the street every morning, and carried up the water, stopping for breath at every landing. And, dressed like a woman of the people, she went to

5. louis: a French coin worth twenty francs.
6. usurers: money lenders who charged very high interest rates.

the fruiterer, the grocer, the butcher, her basket on her arm, bargaining, insulted, defending her miserable money sou by sou.[7]

Each month they had to meet some notes, renew others, obtain more time.

Her husband worked in the evening making a fair copy of some tradesman's accounts, and late at night he often copied manuscript for five sous a page.

And this life lasted ten years.

At the end of ten years they had paid everything, everything, with the rates of usury, and the accumulations of the compound interest.

Mme. Loisel looked old now. She had become the woman of impoverished households—strong and hard and rough. With frowsy hair, skirts askew, and red hands, she talked loud while washing the floor with great swishes of water. But sometimes, when her husband was at the office, she sat down near the window, and she thought of that gay evening of long ago, of that ball where she had been so beautiful and so fêted.[8]

What would have happened if she had not lost that necklace? Who knows? who knows? How life is strange and changeful! How little a thing is needed for us to be lost or to be saved!

But, one Sunday, having gone to take a walk in the Champs Élysées to refresh herself from the labors of the week, she suddenly perceived a woman who was leading a child. It was Mme. Forestier, still young, still beautiful, still charming.

Mme. Loisel felt moved. Was she going to speak to her? Yes, certainly. And now that she had paid, she was going to tell her all about it. Why not?

She went up.

"Good day, Jeanne."

The other, astonished to be familiarly addressed by this plain goodwife, did not recognize her at all, and stammered:

---

7. **sou by sou:** penny by penny.
8. **fêted:** honored.

"But—madame!—I do not know—You must have mistaken."

"No. I am Mathilde Loisel."

Her friend uttered a cry.

"Oh, my poor Mathilde! How you are changed!"

"Yes, I have had days hard enough, since I have seen you, days wretched enough—and that because of you!"

"Of me! How so?"

"Do you remember that diamond necklace which you lent me to wear at the ministerial ball?"

"Yes. Well?"

"Well, I lost it."

"What do you mean? You brought it back."

"I brought you back another just like it. And for this we have been ten years paying. You can understand that it was not easy for us, us who had nothing. At last it is ended, and I am very glad."

Mme. Forestier had stopped.

"You say that you bought a necklace of diamonds to replace mine?"

"Yes. You never noticed it, then! They were very like."

And she smiled with a joy which was proud and naive at once.

Mme. Forestier, strongly moved, took her two hands.

"Oh, my poor Mathilde! Why, my necklace was paste.[9] It was worth at most five hundred francs!"

9. paste: a hard, shiny glass used to make artificial gems.

Reviewing the Selection

Answer each of the following questions without looking back at the story.

Recalling Facts

1. How much money did the Loisels have to pay for the replacement necklace?
   - ☐ a. 5,000 francs
   - ☐ b. 10,000 francs
   - ☐ c. 18,000 francs
   - ☑ d. 36,000 francs

Understanding Main Ideas

2. Mme. Loisel is unhappy with her life because she
   - ☐ a. wishes she could live in Paris.
   - ☑ b. wants to be spoiled and admired.
   - ☐ c. is not as pretty as the women she admires.
   - ☐ d. hates her husband.

Placing Events in Order

3. Which of the following events takes place before all the others?
   - ☐ a. Mme. Loisel borrows her friend's diamond necklace.
   - ☐ b. Mme. Forestier tells Mme. Loisel that the necklace is paste.
   - ☐ c. Mme. Loisel returns the necklace to Mme. Forestier.
   - ☑ d. M. Loisel brings home the invitation to the ball.

Finding Supporting Details

4. At the beginning of the story, Mme. Loisel does not like visiting her friend Mme. Forestier because
   - ☐ a. Mme. Forestier is angry with her for returning the necklace late.
   - ☐ b. Mme. Forestier lives in a distant part of Paris.
   - ☑ c. Mme. Loisel cannot have the luxuries her friend has.
   - ☐ d. Mme. Loisel dislikes Mme. Forestier.

Recognizing Words in Context

5. "She had no dowry, no expectations, no means of being known, understood, loved, wedded, by any rich and distinguished man; and she let herself be married to a little clerk at the Ministry of Public Instruction." In this context *little* means
   - ☐ a. short.
   - ☐ b. selfish.
   - ☐ c. narrow-minded.
   - ☑ d. unimportant.

Interpreting the Selection

Answer each of the following questions. You may look back at the story if necessary.

Making Inferences

6. What feelings does M. Loisel have toward his wife?
   - ☐ a. He resents her constant dreaming.
   - ☐ b. He is jealous of her success at the ball.
   - ☑ c. He wishes he could give her what she wants.
   - ☐ d. He doesn't care about her much.

Generalizing

7. What type of people does Mme. Loisel envy?
   - ☐ a. well-educated, intelligent people
   - ☐ b. hardworking people
   - ☑ c. wealthy, fashionable people
   - ☐ d. country people such as peasants

Analyzing Character

8. After the first few days of looking for the necklace, why don't the Loisels tell Mme. Forestier that they have lost it?
   - ☐ a. They are sure they will find it.
   - ☑ b. They are afraid of what Mme. Forestier will think of them.
   - ☐ c. They are afraid M. Loisel will lose his job.
   - ☐ d. They think the police will accuse them of stealing the necklace.

Comparing

9. How does the Loisels' life after the ball differ from their life before it?
   - ☐ a. Their life is easier and more fashionable.
   - ☐ b. Mme. Loisel is happier because she has been admired at the ball.
   - ☑ c. Their life is a constant misery because they have to repay their debt.
   - ☐ d. M. Loisel is happier because he has bought a gun and can hunt with his friends.

Drawing Conclusions

10. By the end of the story, Mme. Loisel
   - ☑ a. has more or less learned to accept her life.
   - ☐ b. has come to hate Mme. Forestier.
   - ☐ c. still dreams of becoming wealthy.
   - ☐ d. regrets her foolish dreams.

protaganist: the main character

antaganist: Her mind.

Irony

In earlier chapters you saw examples of irony—the contrast between what is expected and what actually happens. Irony is also a contrast between appearance and reality or between expectation and outcome. "How ironic," a person may sigh, "I always wanted to win a prize. But what do I win? An ugly lamp I can't use." What is the irony there? The person has often anticipated the excitement of winning a prize, but what the person actually experiences upon becoming a winner is disappointment.

In literature you can find three kinds of irony: verbal irony, dramatic irony, and situational irony. Verbal irony occurs in a story when a writer or a character says one thing but means something entirely different. Have you ever seen someone shoot a basket, miss by a lot, and mutter, "Good shot"? That is an example of verbal irony. The speaker's words may sound like a compliment, but in fact, they are the opposite because the speaker really means, What a terrible shot.

Dramatic irony occurs in a story when you have information or an understanding of events that a character does not have. Therefore, a character's words or actions mean one thing to him or her, but they mean much more to you. An example of dramatic irony is found in the folktale "Little Red Riding Hood." The little girl thinks she sees her grandmother, but you know it is the wolf. You have important information about the grandmother/wolf that Red Riding Hood does not have.

Situational irony occurs in a story when what happens is different from what you expect or what the characters expect. In this lesson you will see how Guy de Maupassant uses situational irony in "The Necklace."

Situational Irony

"The Necklace" has many examples of situational irony. The irony is closely related to Mme. Loisel's character and to the elements of the plot.

Character. In the opening paragraphs, de Maupassant introduces you to Mathilde Loisel, the main character in the story. She is a pretty young woman who is married to a low-level clerk in the Ministry of Public Instruction. She is extremely discontented with her situation because she feels she was "born for all the delicacies and all the luxuries" in life. Both her family background and her husband's low-level job deny her the opportunity to live the kind of life she desires.

De Maupassant carefully describes Mme. Loisel's sufferings and details the reasons for her misery. However, you can clearly see that the causes of Mme. Loisel's unhappiness are not so much her physical situation as much as her unrealistic expectations.

1. List three reasons that Mme. Loisel would give as the causes of her unhappiness. As the reader, do you see those causes in the same way that Mme. Loisel sees them? Explain your answer.

Mme. Loisel's overpowering desire to become a part of a world more graceful and splendid than her own is the spark that sets off the couple's true suffering.

Rising Action. Early in the rising action you find an example of situational irony. M. Loisel expects his wife to be delighted with the invitation to the ball. Instead, she is grief-stricken because she has nothing to wear. In order to provide her with four hundred francs for a dress, M. Loisel must give up his own dream of buying a gun to go shooting with his friends. M. Loisel never expected that his hard-won invitation would cost him that anticipated pleasure.

Climax. The story reaches a climax on the night of the ball. The narrator observes, "Mme. Loisel made a great success." She enjoyed the kind of triumph she had always dreamed would be hers.

2. Why is Mme. Loisel so happy during the ball? What happens to destroy her happiness on that same night? What is the irony in that situation?

Notice a further irony as the story builds to the climax. When the young couple leave the ball, they are suddenly thrust into the real world. They must hunt for a carriage to drive them home.

> [The carriage] took them to their door in the Rue des Martyrs, and once more, sadly, they climbed homeward. All was ended, for her. And as to him, he reflected that he must be at the Ministry at ten o'clock.

3. How does the phrase, "All was ended, for her," foreshadow what is about to happen? What is the verbal irony in that phrase?

The passage above contains yet another irony. The Loisels live on the Rue des Martyrs—the Street of Martyrs. As you learn, they become martyrs in a way, suffering for ten years to pay for the lost necklace. They suffer in silence but without real cause, as you discover later. If they had spoken to Mme. Forestier and not just assumed that they must spend 36,000 francs for the replacement necklace, they would have been spared their sufferings.

Falling Action. After the loss of the necklace, the Loisels are burdened with a huge debt. They sacrifice their youth and what little social position they have to repay their loans. In the process a further irony develops. De Maupassant describes it in this passage:

> Mme. Loisel now knew the horrible existence of the needy. She took her part, moreover, all of a sudden, with heroism. That dreadful debt must be paid. She would pay it.

4. What is ironic about Mme. Loisel's life during the time she and her husband are repaying the debt?

Resolution. The most startling example of situational irony occurs at the end of the story. After finally repaying the awful debt, Mme. Loisel meets her friend Mme. Forestier again. Mathilde feels proud of her achievement and decides to tell her friend about it.

5. What terrible irony results from that situation? Why is it so terrible?

Irony and Theme

As you have seen, irony is woven into the plot of "The Necklace." By using irony, Guy de Maupassant expresses the theme of the story. The theme is not directly stated but is gradually revealed as the story develops.

As you learned in Chapter 9, a clue to the theme of a story can sometimes be found in the title. In "The Necklace," Mme. Forestier's diamond necklace helps to focus attention on the story's theme. The necklace becomes a symbol. A symbol is an object, a person, a place, or an action that stands for or suggests something else.

Mme. Loisel wants to borrow just the right piece of jewelry from her friend. The jewelry will put the finishing touch to her dream come true—the ministerial ball. She chooses what she believes is a beautiful diamond necklace.

6. What does the necklace symbolize, or represent, to Mme. Loisel when she chooses it from among her friend's jewels? What does she learn about the necklace in the end? How does the symbolism of the necklace change?

After the necklace is lost, Mme. Loisel tries to find out how valuable a piece of jewelry it was. She and her husband discover that "a string of diamonds which seemed to them exactly like the one they looked for" would cost them 36,000 francs. For ten years they must sacrifice, scrimp, and save to pay for the replacement diamonds. The necklace is the reason for their hardships. Yet when their sacrifice is over, Mme. Loisel learns that the diamonds she lost were fake.

different: { Moral -
Theme -

7. What do you think Mme. Loisel feels at the moment she hears the truth about the necklace?

The situational irony builds the story's theme. All her life Mme. Loisel has been discontented because she doesn't have the dresses, jewels, and luxuries she desires. On the night of the ball she seems to have everything. However, appearances can deceive. Superficial things, such as dresses, jewelry, or even social invitations, may seem more important than they really are.

8. What do you think the Loisels have learned from their sacrifice?

Things are not always what they seem.

Author's Tone

De Maupassant's tone, or attitude toward his characters, is also expressed through the irony of the story. Reread the first three paragraphs of "The Necklace."

9. What are two adjectives you would use to describe de Maupassant's attitude toward Mme. Loisel? Why did you choose each?

In this story de Maupassant is commenting not only on the Loisels but also on the social world in which Mme. Loisel dreams of living. M. Loisel knows of his wife's ambitions, so he is triumphant when he gets the invitation to the ball. He is proud of his achievement and hopes it will please his unhappy wife.

> I had awful trouble to get it. Every one wants to go; it is very select, and they are not giving many invitations to clerks. The whole official world will be there.

The young couple attend the ball, where Mme. Loisel is a great success. "All the men looked at her, asked her name, endeavored to be introduced. . . . She was remarked by the minister himself." Despite her triumph, she never hears another word from any of those people after the ball.

10. What do you think de Maupassant thinks of the "official world"? How does his attitude toward that world reinforce the story's theme?

"The Necklace" is a satire in which de Maupassant criticizes the shallow, foolish dreams of Mme. Loisel, as well as her husband's acceptance of her ambitions. Although you may feel some sympathy for the misguided young couple, de Maupassant exposes the consequences of their weaknesses.

11. Do you consider de Maupassant's satire to be gentle or harsh? Explain your answer.

Questions for Thought and Discussion

The questions and activities that follow will help you explore "The Necklace" in more depth and at the same time develop your critical thinking skills.

1. **Predicting Alternative Outcomes.** Near the end of the story, the narrator observes, "What would have happened if she had not lost that necklace?" Think about the character of the Loisels and about the society in which they lived. What do you think would have happened to the Loisels if the necklace had not been lost?

2. **Analyzing Character.** How would you describe Mme. Loisel's character at the beginning of the story? How do you think she changes as a result of the loss of the necklace? What do you think she will be like in later years?

3. **Comparing.** In "The Necklace" a supposedly valuable necklace is lost. In "As the Night, the Day" a laboratory thermometer is broken. Compare and contrast the responses of the main characters to the loss in each story.

4. **Organizing a Debate.** Organize a debate around this topic: Mme. Loisel should have told her friend right after the ball that she had lost the necklace. Each side in the debate should base its position on the nature of the particular characters in the story.

Writing About Literature

Several suggestions for writing projects are given below. You may be asked to complete one or more of these projects. If you have any questions about how to begin a writing assignment, review Using the Writing Process, beginning on page 337.

1. **Describing an Ironic Situation.** Think of an ironic situation that involved you or someone you knew. Describe the situation so that the irony is clear.

2. **Creating Dialogue.** Imagine what could have happened at the end of the story if Mme. Loisel had asked Mme. Forestier to return the real diamond necklace. Think about the kind of person you think Mme. Forestier is and the hardships the Loisels suffered. Then create a dialogue between Mme. Loisel and Mme. Forestier in which they discuss the return of the necklace.

3. **Writing from Another Point of View.** Think of Mme. Forestier's reaction to Mme. Loisel's story at the end of "The Necklace." Then create a scene in which Mme. Forestier tells the story of her friend's sacrifice to her husband. Use description and dialogue to show what you imagine Mme. Forestier thinks of Mme. Loisel and her ten-year ordeal.

4. **Writing a Detailed Description.** Guy de Maupassant describes Mme. Forestier's necklace simply as "a superb necklace of diamonds." In two or three paragraphs, write a vivid and detailed description of what you think the necklace looked like.

Chapter 11

Selection *Zlateh the Goat*

ISAAC BASHEVIS SINGER

Lesson *Imagery and Figurative Language*

About the Selection

Do you remember reading folktales as a child? A folktale is a simple, timeless story that deals with the customs, traditions, and beliefs of ordinary people. Probably the best-known folktales are fairy tales or the stories of Davy Crockett or Paul Bunyan.

Isaac Bashevis Singer's story "Zlateh the Goat" resembles a folktale. It is a simple, short, direct tale that teaches a certain kind of wisdom. And it can be enjoyed by people of all ages.

The story is set in a rural village, where Reuven, a poor furrier, lives with his family. The household includes Zlateh, a goat that everyone loves. Sadly, Reuven decides that Zlateh must be sold so that the family can have enough money to celebrate Hanukkah, an important Jewish religious festival. Aaron, Reuven's twelve-year-old son, must take Zlateh to the butcher in a neighboring town.

Think of how you would feel if a pet your family loved had to be destroyed! Zlateh is even more than a pet since she has provided milk as well as companionship to the family. Despite his sadness, Aaron sets out on his mission. On the road, fate—in the form of a snowstorm—intervenes and changes the course of the story.

Isaac Bashevis Singer was sixty-two years old and a world-famous author when he wrote "Zlateh the Goat." As a child, he had heard many tales about animals from his mother. Some were about goats, cows, or birds. Like Aesop in ancient Greece, Singer fashioned these tales into his own stories.

Singer's background has greatly influenced his writing. He was born in the small town of Leoncin in Poland and later moved to Warsaw. His family was Jewish. His father and both of his grandfathers were rabbis. They, along with the rest of the Jews of Eastern Europe, had been restricted to living in certain areas called ghettos. For hundreds of years within the major towns and cities, the Jewish ghettos developed a lively culture that preserved Jewish learning and traditions.

Singer wrote in Yiddish, the everyday language of Polish Jews. Yiddish is based on the German language. By the early 1900s, when Singer was born, Yiddish was an international language that included words and phrases from many European languages.

In his short stories, Singer drew on the people and scenes he knew in Warsaw and those he remembered from Leoncin. Although several of his stories and one novel were published in Poland, it was not until he moved to the United States in 1935 that his writing career flourished. Even then, he did not become well known until his books were translated from Yiddish into English.

At first, Singer had to rely on others to translate his stories. Today, he does a rough translation and gets help from someone to perfect his English. "Zlateh the Goat" was translated by Elizabeth Shub, who worked closely with the author. If a word or phrase seemed untranslatable, Singer would come up with a solution.

Singer feels that all good writers must know their roots. As a result, many of his stories explore the Jewish experience of the past few hundred years. They re-create the Poland of the past. In the introduction to a book of his short stories, he once wrote that he wanted to "reveal a world that is little known to you but which is rich in comedy and tragedy; rich in its individuality, wisdom, foolishness, and goodness."

Lesson Preview

The lesson that follows "Zlateh the Goat" focuses on imagery and figurative language. Writers use comparisons to make you see things in new ways. Sometimes they describe experiences, places, or objects in a way that you can feel through all five senses. Like all writers, Singer chooses his words carefully to create strong images for his readers.

"Zlateh the Goat" is a short, simple story. From the very beginning you get a strong impression of the setting and the landscape. The questions that follow will help you see how Singer uses imagery and figurative language in the story. As you read, think about how you would answer these questions.

1 At the beginning of the story, what does the landscape look like? How does it change?

2 Which of the five senses—sight, sound, touch, taste, smell—are used in Singer's descriptions?

3 What comparisons does Singer use when describing experiences, places, or objects?

4 What role does Zlateh play in the story? Is Zlateh more like a person than a goat? Explain your answer.

Vocabulary

Here are some difficult words that appear in the selection that follows. Study the words and their definitions, as well as the sentences that show how the words are used. This will help you get the most from your reading.

sprouted began to grow. *The seeds that we planted weeks ago have finally sprouted.*

cleft divided. *The small cleft in the rocky ledge provided a nesting site for the bird.*

Zlateh the Goat

Isaac Bashevis Singer

At Hanukkah[1] time the road from the village to the town is usually covered with snow, but this year the winter had been a mild one. Hanukkah had almost come, yet little snow had fallen. The sun shone most of the time. The peasants complained that because of the dry weather there would be a poor harvest of winter grain. New grass sprouted, and the peasants sent their cattle out to pasture.

For Reuven the furrier it was a bad year, and after long hesitation he decided to sell Zlateh the goat. She was old and gave little milk. Feyvel the town butcher had offered eight gulden[2] for her. Such a sum would buy Hanukkah candles, potatoes and oil for pancakes, gifts for the children, and other holiday necessaries for the house. Reuven told his oldest boy Aaron to take the goat to town.

Aaron understood what taking the goat to Feyvel meant, but he had to obey his father. Leah, his mother, wiped the tears from her eyes when

1. **Hanukkah:** a Jewish holiday that celebrates the successful uprising of the Jews against the Syrians in 165 B.C. Hanukkah usually falls in December.
2. **gulden:** coins once used as money.

she heard the news. Aaron's younger sisters, Anna and Miriam, cried loudly. Aaron put on his quilted jacket and a cap with earmuffs, bound a rope around Zlateh's neck, and took along two slices of bread with cheese to eat on the road. Aaron was supposed to deliver the goat by evening, spend the night at the butcher's, and return the next day with the money.

While the family said goodbye to the goat, and Aaron placed the rope around her neck, Zlateh stood as patiently and good-naturedly as ever. She licked Reuven's hand. She shook her small white beard. Zlateh trusted human beings. She knew that they always fed her and never did her any harm.

When Aaron brought her out on the road to town, she seemed somewhat astonished. She'd never been led in that direction before. She looked back at him questioningly, as if to say, "Where are you taking me?" But after a while she seemed to come to the conclusion that a goat shouldn't ask questions. Still, the road was different. They passed new fields, pastures, and huts with thatched roofs. Here and there a dog barked and came running after them, but Aaron chased it away with his stick.

The sun was shining when Aaron left the village. Suddenly the weather changed. A large black cloud with a bluish center appeared in the east and spread itself rapidly over the sky. A cold wind blew in with it. The crows flew low, croaking. At first it looked as if it would rain, but instead it began to hail as in summer. It was early in the day, but it became dark as dusk. After a while the hail turned to snow.

In his twelve years Aaron had seen all kinds of weather, but he had never experienced a snow like this one. It was so dense it shut out the light of the day. In a short time their path was completely covered. The wind became as cold as ice. The road to town was narrow and winding. Aaron no longer knew where he was. He could not see through the snow. The cold soon penetrated his quilted jacket.

At first Zlateh didn't seem to mind the change in weather. She too was twelve years old and knew what winter meant. But when her legs sank deeper and deeper into the snow, she began to turn her head and look at Aaron in wonderment. Her mild eyes seemed to ask, "Why are we out in such a storm?" Aaron hoped that a peasant would come along with his cart, but no one passed by.

The snow grew thicker, falling to the ground in large, whirling flakes. Beneath it Aaron's boots touched the softness of a plowed field. He realized that he was no longer on the road. He had gone astray. He could no longer figure out which was east or west, which way was the village, the town. The wind whistled, howled, whirled the snow about in eddies. It looked as if white imps were playing tag on the fields. A white dust rose above the ground. Zlateh stopped. She could walk no longer. Stubbornly she anchored her cleft hooves in the earth and bleated as if pleading to be taken home. Icicles hung from her white beard, and her horns were glazed with frost.

Aaron did not want to admit the danger, but he knew just the same that if they did not find shelter they would freeze to death. This was no ordinary storm. It was a mighty blizzard. The snowfall had reached his knees. His hands were numb, and he could no longer feel his toes. He choked when he breathed. His nose felt like wood, and he rubbed it with snow. Zlateh's bleating began to sound like crying. Those humans in whom she had so much confidence had dragged her into a trap. Aaron began to pray to God for himself and for the innocent animal.

Suddenly he made out the shape of a hill. He wondered what it could be. Who had piled snow into such a huge heap? He moved toward it, dragging Zlateh after him. When he came near it, he realized that it was a large haystack which the snow had blanketed.

Aaron realized immediately that they were saved. With great effort he dug his way through the snow. He was a village boy and knew what to do. When he reached the hay, he hollowed out a nest for himself and the goat. No matter how cold it may be outside, in the hay it is always warm. And hay was food for Zlateh. The moment she smelled it she became contented and began to eat. Outside the snow continued to fall. It quickly covered the passageway Aaron had dug. But a boy and an animal need to breathe, and there was hardly any air in their hideout. Aaron bored a kind of window through the hay and snow and carefully kept the passage clear.

Zlateh, having eaten her fill, sat down on her hind legs and seemed to have regained her confidence in man. Aaron ate his two slices of bread and cheese, but after the difficult journey he was still hungry. He looked at Zlateh and noticed her udders were full. He lay down next to her, placing himself so that when he milked her he could squirt the milk into his mouth. It was rich and sweet. Zlateh was not accustomed to being milked that way, but she did not resist. On the contrary, she seemed eager to reward Aaron for bringing her to a shelter whose very walls, floor, and ceiling were made of food.

Through the window Aaron could catch a glimpse of the chaos outside. The wind carried before it whole drifts of snow. It was completely dark, and he did not know whether night had already come or whether it was the darkness of the storm. Thank God that in the hay it was not cold. The dried hay, grass, and field flowers exuded the warmth of the summer sun. Zlateh ate frequently; she nibbled from above, below, from the left and right. Her body gave forth an animal warmth, and Aaron cuddled up to her. He had always loved Zlateh, but now she was like a sister. He was alone, cut off from his family, and wanted to talk. He began to talk to Zlateh. "Zlateh, what do you think about what has happened to us?" he asked.

"Maaaa," Zlateh answered.

"If we hadn't found this stack of hay, we would both be frozen stiff by now," Aaron said.

"Maaaa," was the goat's reply.

"If the snow keeps on falling like this, we may have to stay here for days," Aaron explained.

"Maaaa," Zlateh bleated.

"What does 'Maaaa' mean?" Aaron asked. "You'd better speak up clearly."

"Maaaa, Maaaa," Zlateh tried.

"Well, let it be 'Maaaa' then," Aaron said patiently, "You can't speak, but I know you understand. I need you and you need me. Isn't that right?"

"Maaaa."

Aaron became sleepy. He made a pillow out of some hay, leaned his head on it, and dozed off. Zlateh too fell asleep.

When Aaron opened his eyes, he didn't know whether it was morning or night. The snow had blocked up his window. He tried to clear it, but when he had bored through to the length of his arm, he still hadn't reached the outside. Luckily he had his stick with him and was able to break through to the open air. It was still dark outside. The snow continued to fall and the wind wailed, first with one voice and then with many. Sometimes it had the sound of devilish laughter. Zlateh too awoke, and when Aaron greeted her, she answered, "Maaaa." Yes, Zlateh's language consisted of only one word, but it meant many things. Now she was saying, "We must accept all that God gives us—heat, cold, hunger, satisfaction, light and darkness."

Aaron had awakened hungry. He had eaten up his food, but Zlateh had plenty of milk.

For three days Aaron and Zlateh stayed in the haystack. Aaron had always loved Zlateh, but in these three days he loved her more and more. She fed him with her milk and helped him keep warm. She comforted him with her patience. He told her many stories, and she always cocked her ears and listened. When he patted her, she licked his hand and his face. Then she said, "Maaaa," and he knew it meant, I love you too.

The snow fell for three days, though after the first day it was not as thick and the wind quieted down. Sometimes Aaron felt that there could never have been a summer, that the snow had always fallen, ever since he could remember. He, Aaron, never had a father or mother or sisters. He was a snow child, born of the snow, and so was Zlateh. It was so quiet in the hay that his ears rang in the stillness. Aaron and Zlateh slept all night and a good part of the day. As for Aaron's dreams, they were all about warm weather. He dreamed of green fields, trees covered with blossoms, clear brooks, and singing birds. By the third night the snow had stopped, but Aaron did not dare to find his way home in the darkness. The sky became clear and the moon shone, casting silvery nets on the snow. Aaron dug his way out and looked at the world. It was all white, quiet, dreaming dreams of heavenly splendor. The stars were large and close. The moon swam in the sky as in a sea.

On the morning of the fourth day Aaron heard the ringing of sleigh bells. The haystack was not far from the road. The peasant who drove the sleigh pointed out the way to him—not to the town and Feyvel the butcher, but home to the village. Aaron had decided in the haystack that he would never part with Zlateh.

Aaron's family and their neighbors had searched for the boy and the goat but had found no trace of them during the storm. They feared they were lost. Aaron's mother and sisters cried for him; his father remained silent and gloomy. Suddenly one of the neighbors came running to their house with the news that Aaron and Zlateh were coming up the road.

There was great joy in the family. Aaron told them how he had found the stack of hay and how Zlateh had fed him with her milk. Aaron's sisters kissed and hugged Zlateh and gave her a special treat of chopped carrots and potato peels, which Zlateh gobbled up hungrily.

Nobody ever again thought of selling Zlateh, and now that the cold weather had finally set in, the villagers needed the services of Reuven the furrier once more. When Hanukkah came, Aaron's mother was able to fry pancakes every evening, and Zlateh got her portion too. Even though Zlateh had her own pen, she often came to the kitchen, knocking on the door with her horns to indicate that she was ready to visit, and she was always admitted. In the evening Aaron, Miriam, and Anna played dreidel.[3] Zlateh sat near the stove watching the children and the flickering of the Hanukkah candles.

Once in a while Aaron would ask her, "Zlateh, do you remember the three days we spent together?"

And Zlateh would scratch her neck with a horn, shake her white bearded head and come out with the single sound which expressed all her thoughts, and all her love.

3. **dreidel:** a Hanukkah game played with a top.

Reviewing the Selection

Answer each of the following questions without looking back at the story.

Recalling Facts

1. Both Zlateh and Aaron are
   - ☐ a. twelve years old.
   - ☐ b. afraid of the dark.
   - ☐ c. unhappy about going to town.
   - ☐ d. glad to see the snowstorm.

Understanding Main Ideas

2. Reuven decides to sell Zlateh to the butcher because
   - ☐ a. the family no longer needs a goat.
   - ☐ b. the goat is too old to pull a plow.
   - ☐ c. the family needs money to celebrate Hanukkah.
   - ☐ d. the goat is old and ill tempered.

Placing Events in Order

3. Which of the following events occurs first in the story?
   - ☐ a. Aaron finds the haystack.
   - ☐ b. Zlateh refuses to walk any farther in the snowstorm.
   - ☐ c. Aaron dreams of summer.
   - ☐ d. Zlateh provides milk to keep Aaron alive during the storm.

Finding Supporting Details

4. The story takes place
   - ☐ a. near a large city.
   - ☐ b. in the mountains.
   - ☐ c. near the coast.
   - ☐ d. in the countryside.

Recognizing Words in Context

5. "He tried to clear it, but when he had bored through to the length of his arm, he still hadn't reached the outside." In this context *bored* means
   - ☐ a. eaten.
   - ☐ b. made a hole.
   - ☐ c. become tired of.
   - ☐ d. cleaned.

Interpreting the Selection

Answer each of the following questions. You may look back at the story if necessary.

Making Inferences

6. Aaron's father is "silent and gloomy" during Aaron and Zlateh's absence because he
   - ☐ a. thinks that he may be responsible for his son's death.
   - ☐ b. is always unhappy about life.
   - ☐ c. has had a very bad season selling his furs.
   - ☐ d. is angry that Aaron has taken so long to return from the butcher.

Generalizing

7. The relationship between Zlateh and Aaron in the haystack can best be described as
   - ☐ a. lonely.
   - ☐ b. lacking in communication.
   - ☐ c. uncomfortable.
   - ☐ d. mutually beneficial.

Analyzing Character

8. Which of the following words best describes Aaron's behavior during the blizzard?
   - ☐ a. joyful
   - ☐ b. stubborn
   - ☐ c. lazy
   - ☐ d. resourceful

Comparing

9. How does Reuven's life change after the blizzard?
   - ☐ a. He decides to open a business in the village.
   - ☐ b. He is angry because Aaron didn't take the goat to town.
   - ☐ c. He is busy again because the villagers need a furrier.
   - ☐ d. He decides to move the family to the village.

Drawing Conclusions

10. At the end of the story, the family will never sell Zlateh because
    - ☐ a. Reuven has become rich as a result of the cold weather.
    - ☐ b. the goat has saved Aaron's life.
    - ☐ c. Aaron has taken a job to help support the family.
    - ☐ d. Aaron's sisters and mother would be too unhappy if the goat were sold.

Imagery and Figurative Language

In "Zlateh the Goat" Isaac Bashevis Singer tells a simple story of a poor family's struggle to survive. The plot of "Zlateh the Goat" is straightforward. It contains no twists or surprise ending. In fact, you could summarize the main events in a few sentences. The characters, too, are simple and direct. They are rural people whose lives are grounded in old traditions and customs.

The simplicity is deceptive. In this story Singer brings to life a world that is distant in both time and place from twentieth-century industrial society. For the brief time that you are reading the story, you can see, hear, and feel the world in which Aaron and Zlateh live. How does Singer draw you so completely into the story?

Singer's success is due in part to his use of language. Like the story, his language is generally very simple and straightforward. He does not use hard words or long, complicated sentences. Yet through his use of language, he produces strong images in your mind.

In this lesson you will study how Singer uses imagery and figurative language to create vivid, lasting impressions of a way of life that no longer exists.

Imagery

In Chapter 8, "The Rule of Names," you saw how Ursula Le Guin used imagery to add humor to the story. Imagery is language that appeals to the senses. In everyday life, you experience events through your five senses—sight, hearing, taste, touch, and smell. The more senses a description appeals to, the more real the image becomes.

"Zlateh the Goat" begins with a description of the unusually mild winter in the village. The first paragraph gives many details that let you see, hear, and feel the unusual weather and the problems it causes.

1. *Look at the first paragraph. What do you see? Hear? Feel?*

Because of the mild winter, Reuven the furrier has no business and no income, so he decides to sell Zlateh, the family goat. Because the family loves Zlateh, they are miserable about his decision. However, Reuven feels he has no other choice.

When Aaron and Zlateh set off for town, the weather is mild and unthreatening. Suddenly, a winter storm develops. In describing the storm, Singer not only makes you see, feel, and hear its force, but he also makes you aware of its danger.

2. *Read the following sentences. Tell which sense each image appeals to. How does each image suggest danger?*

a. *It [the snow] was so dense it shut out the light of day.*

b. *The cold soon penetrated his quilted jacket.*

c. *The snow grew thicker, falling to the ground in large, whirling flakes.*

d. *The wind whistled, howled, whirled the snow about in eddies.*

e. *Icicles hung from her [Zlateh's] white beard, and her horns were glazed with frost.*

During the storm, Aaron and Zlateh find safety in a huge haystack. Although the snow and wind threaten outside, they are protected within.

Zlateh's milk keeps Aaron alive, and her presence comforts him. At one point, Aaron dreams about summer.

3. Reread the paragraph near the end of the story (page 300) that begins, "The snow fell for three days. . . ." What images of summer does Singer create? Compare those images of summer to the wintry landscape Aaron sees when he digs his way out of the haystack.

Figurative Language

In Chapter 4, "A Mother in Mannville," you learned that writers often use figurative language to help you see the world—or some aspect of the world—in new and different ways. Isaac Bashevis Singer employs several kinds of figures of speech, including similes, metaphors, and personification.

Simile. A simile, you will recall, directly compares unlike things using the word *like, as,* or *resembles.* The contrast in the comparison makes you stop and think about why the comparison is being made. For example, suppose someone said, "Sarah's eyes were as bright as exploding stars." The simile is startling. It does not mean that Sarah's eyes were literally exploding, but it does let you see how full of light and energy her eyes were.

In "Zlateh the Goat" Singer uses several similes. However, his similes are generally quite simple ones.

When he is describing the blizzard, Singer uses several similes that help you to see, hear, and feel the storm. Look at the following passage: "The wind whistled, howled, whirled the snow about in eddies. It looked as if white imps were playing tag on the fields."

In the second sentence Singer uses a simile to compare the snow whirling about the field to imps playing tag. The image is intriguing because it suggests that the blizzard has given birth to a supernatural world. With the whirling white snow blocking out the real world, strange creatures—white imps—appear to play games in the fields.

4. Read the following similes. How does each create a strong image or focus on a particular idea?

a. His nose felt like wood, and he rubbed it with snow.

b. He had always loved Zlateh, but now she was like a sister.

The words *like* and *as* do not always signal similes. "In his twelve years Aaron had seen all kinds of weather, but he had never experienced a snow like this one." In that sentence the word *like* shows a comparison, but it is not a simile because the word *snow* is not compared to another word in the sentence.

Metaphor. Another kind of figure of speech, you will remember, is a metaphor. A metaphor can be thought of as a cousin of a simile. It is an implied comparison between unlike things, but it does not use the word *like, as,* or *resembles.* Instead, a metaphor suggests that one thing *is* another.

In "Zlateh the Goat" Singer uses a metaphor to show how Aaron felt during the time he spent in the haystack: "He, Aaron, never had a father or mother or sisters. He was a snow child, born of the snow, and so was Zlateh." You know that the description is not meant to be taken literally. Neither Aaron nor Zlateh is made of snow, but the metaphor creates a vivid picture of the world in which they existed—a totally snow-covered world.

Often, metaphors are not as obvious as, "He was a snow child. . . ." For example, in the sentence, The children flocked around the magician, a comparison is implied between two things that are unlike, or different. The word *flocked* is metaphoric; you get the impression that the children are like a flock of sheep.

5. Read the following passage and explain the metaphor: "She [Zlateh] could walk no longer. Stubbornly she anchored her cleft hooves in the earth and bleated as if pleading to be taken home."

Personification. A third kind of figurative language is personification, in which an animal, an object, or an idea is described as though it were human. The animal, object, or idea is thus given human qualities. Like similes and metaphors, personification is used by a writer to arouse certain feelings or responses in the reader.

6. In the following passage, notice how the wind is personified. Read the passage and explain two ways in which it is given human qualities.

> *The snow continued to fall and the wind wailed, first with one voice and then with many. Sometimes it had the sound of devilish laughter.*

In "Zlateh the Goat" Singer often writes about the goat as though she were a person and a member of the family. At the same time, the author never lets you forget that Zlateh is a goat. When Aaron first leads Zlateh on the road to town, the goat is puzzled.

> She looked back at him questioningly, as if to say, "Where are you taking me?" But after a while she seemed to come to the conclusion that a goat shouldn't ask questions.

In that passage the goat seems to think and to reason—two qualities that are considered human. The goat's questioning look and acceptance of her fate make her a sympathetic character. In fact, you begin to see her as more than the family goat. In your mind, she becomes an individual with human thoughts and feelings.

7. Skim the story. Find at least three other examples of personification concerning Zlateh. Explain (a) what human quality each example gives the goat, and (b) how each creates a feeling, or response, toward the goat.

All writers of short stories want to make their characters and settings come to life. By using powerful imagery and figurative language, they draw you into their stories.

Questions for Thought and Discussion

The questions and activities that follow will help you explore "Zlateh the Goat" in more depth and at the same time develop your critical thinking skills.

1. **Recognizing Themes.** In "Zlateh the Goat" Isaac Bashevis Singer states the theme directly. What is the theme of the story? When and how is it stated? Why do you think Singer expresses it in that manner?

2. **Taking a Stand.** Organize a class discussion around this question: Do animals feel emotions such as love, anger, and bewilderment? Encourage people with different views to express their opinions and present supporting evidence from real life or from stories they have read.

3. **Comparing.** The world of Aaron and his family in "Zlateh the Goat" differs greatly from that of families in industrial societies today. What do you think is the greatest difference between the two ways of life? Are there any similarities? Explain your answer.

4. **Analyzing Setting.** In Chapter 5 you learned about the importance of setting. How important do you think the setting is to "Zlateh the Goat"? Explain your answer using examples from the story.

Writing About Literature

Several suggestions for writing projects are given below. You may be asked to complete one or more of these projects. If you have any questions about how to begin a writing assignment, review Using the Writing Process, beginning on page 337.

1. **Inventing Similes.** Write a paragraph or two in which you use at least one simile to describe a person, a place, or an object. Remember that a simile helps to create a vivid picture of the subject you are describing by comparing it to something very different. Be as original as you can.

2. **Using Metaphors.** Write a metaphor to describe each of the following scenes.

   a. a full moon in winter

   b. a TV newsroom minutes before airtime

3. **Analyzing Character.** In a page or two, explain what kind of person you think Aaron is. Use what you have learned about Aaron from his words, thoughts, and actions in the story.

4. **Writing from Another Point of View.** Imagine that Zlateh actually could talk instead of just bleating "Maaa." Re-create one incident in the story from Zlateh's first-person point of view. You might choose the walk along the road to town, the time in the haystack, or the reunion with the family.

Chapter 12

Selection *Men in a Storm*

JORGE FERRETIS

Lesson *Description, Narration, and Dialogue*

About the Selection

You have probably heard the term *flash flood.* Do you know what it means? A flash flood occurs when heavy rains or melting snows suddenly fill rivers to overflowing. Almost without warning, huge cascades of water cause rivers to flood their banks, destroying everything in their paths.

A flash flood is the natural disaster that threatens the people in Jorge Ferretis's story "Men in a Storm." Like the tidal wave in "The Big Wave," it is one of the forces of nature over which people have no control.

"Men in a Storm" is set in Mexico in the 1930s. In some ways "Men in a Storm" resembles "Zlateh the Goat." Although Ferretis's Mexico is distant from Isaac Bashevis Singer's Poland, the two stories have some similarities. The characters in both stories are poor people who struggle each day to make a living. In both, an animal is important to the family's survival.

In "Men in a Storm," Jorge Ferretis presents the harsh life faced by Mexican peasants. He is interested in realism, showing life as it really is, rather than as an ideal, or romanticized, picture. The story focuses on Tata José, an elderly peasant, who lends his prized ox to his brother Jesús. While Jesús is out plowing, a flash flood sweeps down on him, washing both man and beast into the turbulent river.

In the story Ferretis seems more concerned with portraying the condition of the peasants rather than developing the individual characters. This concern for the peasants was part of Ferretis's cultural heritage.

For hundreds of years peasants in Mexico had suffered many hardships brought about by nature and by wealthy landowners. In 1910 there was a revolt against the dictator, Porfirio Díaz, who had ruled Mexico for many years. The revolutionaries proclaimed noble goals. Most important, they promised to improve life for the long-suffering peasants.

Although the revolutionaries soon forced Díaz out of power, the fighting between political groups raged on for many years. Rival leaders and factions emerged. Marauding armies swept through the countryside. They stole the peasants' food, animals, and personal belongings. Sometimes, they burned crops to keep food from falling into the hands of their enemies. Often, they forced peasants to join them in the fighting. In 1924 Mexico finally experienced an uneasy peace.

The years of fighting took their toll. Thousands of peasants were killed. Many of those who survived were poor, undernourished, and resigned to their condition.

Jorge Ferretis was only eight years old when the Mexican Revolution began. As a teenager, however, he fought in its later struggles. He saw the hardships heaped on the poor by the years of fighting. In the years after the revolution, Ferretis worked as a journalist and observed the ways in which the revolution failed to live up to its ideals.

In the novels and stories that Ferretis wrote in the 1930s and 1940s, his subject was the plight of the poor. He showed the peasants as they were, without romanticizing, or making their lives look better than they were. In his stories Ferretis did not comment directly on the revolution's failure. However, the stories themselves were a strong criticism of the conditions in which the peasants were forced to live.

Lesson Preview

The lesson that follows "Men in a Storm" looks at the blend of description, narration, and dialogue in a story. Each of those elements plays an important role in a short story. Through description the author lets you see a person, place, or event. Through narration you learn about the actions or events in the story. Through dialogue you get a chance to hear what the characters say and how they say it.

Jorge Ferretis uses "Men in a Storm" to show the condition of Mexican peasants. The questions that follow will help you identify how he uses description, narration, and dialogue to make his point. As you read, think about how you would answer these questions.

1 Where does the author use description? What is he describing? What kind of language does he use in his description?

2 What is the narrative, or story, that the author is telling?

3 Does the story have a lot of dialogue or only a little? When does the author use dialogue? What kind of language do the characters in the story use in conversation?

4 How do the words the author chooses let you know what he feels about his characters?

Vocabulary

Here are some difficult words that appear in the selection that follows. Study the words and their definitions, as well as the sentences that show how the words are used. This will help you get the most from your reading.

diligently painstakingly; industriously. *The detectives diligently searched the house for clues.*

encrusted to form a crust on the surface. *The old garden gate was encrusted with years of rust.*

reproachfully in a scolding or blaming manner. *The boy knew it was time to clean up his room when his mother pointed reproachfully to a pile of dirty laundry.*

savory pleasing in taste or smell. *The savory smell of freshly brewed coffee floated throughout the house.*

turbulent causing disturbance; unruly. *The turbulent waves violently knocked the boat from side to side.*

immobile not moveable; firmly fixed. *The deer, immobile with fright, seemed unable to move out of the road.*

disconsolate without hope; cheerless. *She was disconsolate over the loss of the final swim meet.*

flailed to wave or swing about wildly; thrash. *As he flailed his arms about in the water, he realized that learning to swim was more difficult than he thought.*

recede to go or move backward; withdraw. *As the swollen river began to recede, the townspeople started cleaning up the debris left by the flood.*

resurrection the coming back into use; revival; rising from the dead. *The resurrection of the city's shelter program should help many homeless families this year.*

figurines small statues. *We admired the delicate porcelain figurines that Liu Tai brought with her from China.*

Men in a Storm

JORGE FERRETIS

Translated by Antonia García

Few trees, large, still. Dark trunks of fluted stone.

The world begins to take shape with the approach of daybreak.

An unseen cow moos, as if the moo was diluted in the shade.

At the foot of one of those solitary trees, there is a form, like a protuberance[1] of the trunk, darker than the color of the bark. But that form is soft, warm. It's Tata José, wrapped in his woolen blanket, squatting next to the trunk. An early riser, one of those old men who get up before the lazy hens.

Before sitting down there, next to the trunk, he had already fed the ox.

In a nearby hut, a light becomes visible through the reed walls. You can picture a woman seated on her heels, on the floor. Diligently she

1. **protuberance:** a large bulge or swelling.

fans the embers until the dried branches which she broke with her hands catch fire.

A moment later, from the same hut, a shivering shadow emerges. It's Tata José's son.

He comes out, wrapped up to his eyes in his blanket, like his father.

He walks up to the old man, and stops, silent, like a piece of wood. The less men speak, the better they understand each other.

However, after several moments, the latecomer says: "Las' night I heard Uncle Jesús."

"Yep," responds the form encrusted in the trunk.

"I heard 'm outside askin' to borrow an ox."

"Yep," repeats the old man's dry voice.

And after a pause, the boy insists: "And dya lend it to 'im?"

" 'Course, so as he kin complete the team."

" 'n now what'll we use to plow?"

The old man, in an even drier tone, responds almost reproachfully: "Jesús is a lot more behind 'n us. He ain't even got the field ready fer plowin'. And I wasn't about to deny 'm the use of my Josco."

Again they fell silent, like two dark blocks. And on those two blocks, the dawn, with its light, begins to chisel human faces, hardened, silent.

Suddenly the voice of a woman is heard. It's almost as if she was the power to bring statues to life. A sturdy old woman, sticking her head out of the hut's one window, shouts her incantation;[2] she calls them to breakfast.

Breakfast! The two men go sit down near the fire. Oh, those tortillas[3] that puff up, one by one, on the pan! That whiteness which is thinned between the darkened hands of that woman, only to turn golden on that warm earthenware pan. And some strips of dried meat which for a couple of seconds twitch among the red hot coals. And a few gulps of coffee, that coffee, which before being served, may be heard bubbling

2. incantation: the chanting of special words believed to have magic power.
3. tortilla: a round, thin pancake made of cornmeal. Tortillas are a basic food in Mexico.

in the pot. That coffee which warms up people from the inside. Aaah! So nice and hot, that when it is served, a savory mist comes out of the cup, and also provides outside warmth.

Now that it was light outside, the two left the hut. Surely they hadn't eaten their fill; but their stomachs were half-full with the sweetened watered-down coffee, boiled corn, and strips of meat with chile. Enough to fool their guts. And make them hang on (though their stomachs might growl) until past sundown. Their guts! They sure were aware of the price of corn. They sure were aware, by the moderate or abundant way in which the woman served them tortillas.

Tata José and his boy weren't in a hurry, and even less so that day. Of course they couldn't have refused to lend Josco to Uncle Jesús.

Each of them shouldered a hoe and made his way uphill.

Little patches of mist rose from the hills leaving them clear, and spotted with cornfields.

Sun. Noontime. The air was hot. But there, over the northern range, black clouds were beginning to pile up. Tata José, with his small eyes shining amidst his wrinkles, stood silent for a moment, contemplating the thunderheads in the distance.

The son, also looking, remarked: "It's sure rainin' hard up there!"

And they continued hoeing at the clods of dirt.

But behind them, a thunderclap made the air tremble and then vibrate over the fields. If the sky had been made of blue crystal, that enormous thunderbolt would have shattered it. And it would have fallen on the people in bits and pieces.

"Let's go," Tata said, shouldering his hoe. "That storm is goin' to catch us."

But the boy, behind, stopped with a shout, pointing to a hill below where the river twisted: "Look, Tata!"

The two felt as though they were being strangled by the same apprehension.[4] The storm still hadn't arrived, and nevertheless, the river

4. **apprehension:** dread of something.

had already risen, catching them by surprise. The men who were working on the other side of the river could no longer ford it. And Uncle Jesús' farmlands were on that side!

The old man and his son trotted downhill. On the banks of the river, the rising waters were beginning to uproot entire banana groves. The waters dug away at the roots of the big trees, bending them over, causing a racket of breaking branches.

Far away, on the other side of the river, you could tell that several men were shouting from a small hilltop. They were waving their arms and shouting themselves hoarse, but the roar of the current drowned out their voices.

The water continued to rise minute by minute. By now, two or three huts had been swept away from the bottomlands.

Women and chickens, pigs and children, were screeching everywhere.

Tata José and his son, running to where the water leveled off, arrived panting opposite Uncle Jesús' land. There, the bottomlands had turned into a large, turbulent lake.

About a kilometer away, they saw Uncle Jesús. The team of unyoked oxen stayed close to him and looked at the flood fearfully. The old man stood immobile, erect, with his long goad[5] in his hand, stuck into the ground next to his feet. The mound where they were standing kept getting smaller and smaller, as if it were melting away. It was even useless to yell.

Enormous drops began to fall on a slant, from the blotchy sky. It was barely starting to rain over there and Josco was going to be carried away by the current! Their ox!

The father and his son began running again. The downpour grew heavier! Running at full speed, they felt as if the clouds were stoning them. The drops were so big and strong that they almost seemed aimed at smashing their eyes. Suddenly it looked as if, among the gushing torrents of lukewarm water, buckets of alcohol or gasoline had been mixed,

5. goad: a stick with a sharp point, used in driving oxen.

which would catch fire in the midst of the storm because in the soaked sky noisy flashes of fire appeared. Bursts of laughter from a sky drunk with darkness.

Only after an hour did the downpour abate.

The father and his son, like two desperate goblins, were still walking in the mud of the hillside, peering at the swollen river. Surely the current had dragged away their Josco.

When the sky had grown completely calm, it was almost night. And the two anguished goblins opened their eyes wider in the darkness.

"There ain't nothin', Tata."

"There ain't nothin'," replied the disconsolate old man, his shirt and trousers clinging to his body, drenched in the rain and perspiration.

But suddenly, among pieces of floating garbage and sticks, they made out a form thrashing weakly in the water.

"Could it be Uncle?"

"Jesúuus!" Tata shouted from the shore.

"Unncle!" shouted the boy.

Barely treading water to keep from drowning, the man jerked his head up from the water.

"EEEH!" he replied with a muted cry.

"Where's the ox?" the boy shouted as loud as he could.

"He's coming along," he answered, gathering up strength to make a feeble cry, pointing back with his arm.

And then he was barely able to add: "Wait for 'm at the bend."

Father and son, indeed, noticed a large form farther away. And with their hearts beating wildly, they guessed that it was their ox.

Moved by the same impulse, before thinking about jumping into the water to help Uncle Jesús reach the shore, they started running toward the bend.

The sky was now clear. But the moon was only gradually lighting up the crests of the hills.

And by the dim light of a few stars, the boy threw himself into the current, which swelled up as though it were the ocean.

He flailed away in the darkness until he reached the shadow of the ox. And swimming alongside it, he kept pushing and pushing. He had to get it to the shore before both of them were sucked into a rocky gorge where, in the distance, the floodwaters continued to roar.

Tata José, up to his knees in the water, shouted hoarsely in the darkness to his son and to his ox.

Toward midnight, the moon came out. Toward midnight also, the boy, almost faint, managed to push the ox up against the bank. But the spot was rocky, and the animal, benumbed by so many hours in the water, couldn't get out.

Amidst the shadows, far off, muffled human cries could be heard from time to time.

From the bank, as though he were a large branch, the old man plunged into the water next to the ox, which was so numb that it didn't even bellow. After the splash, the old man could be seen groping until he finally clutched onto the branches of a tree which was still pretty well rooted to the rocky embankment. And in that way, the dark body tightly linked to the branches served as a retaining wall for the animal. That large black floating hulk could have slid slowly away toward the mouth of the river if Tata José hadn't been there, wrapped into a knot, mooring it with his feet.

The son came out drenched and battered, and began to climb the hills. Maybe in the village he would find people who would want to come down to help them.

It was daybreak when the water level began to recede. The boy returned running followed right behind by his mother and by another little man, eleven years old, who more than wanted to help, but who lacked the strength. And with the panting efforts of the four of them, the ox at last was safe, although unable to get up on its feet.

Daybreak found it lying there in the mud, waterlogged with its eyes even sadder than is normal for an ox, and its snout in the ground. It didn't even want to eat. It was useless for the boy to go up and cut fresh grass for it.

It didn't move all morning long, and Tata José stayed to care for it, crouching nearby, distressed and still.

In the early afternoon, the animal, with trembly legs, attempted to get up. And the old man sighed with relief.

They didn't find Uncle Jesús until later in the afternoon, lifeless, far downstream. He had been deposited on the bank as the floodwaters subsided. Surely he must have struggled, swimming hard, until the end.

They found him before he had grown stiff, with his stomach swollen. And they began to shake him.

"He must've swallowed a lot of water," someone said.

And with a round, heavy stone, they began to rub hard on that swelling. Others moved his arms, as if they were working on a pump. Others shouted in his ears, for a long, long time. Later they twisted his head. And in that way, between squeezing and shouting, they brought him back to life. When he started to breathe heavily and half opened one eye, everyone there let out a sacred cry. It was as if each one had worked, in part, that miracle of resurrection.

A few days passed.

In their village there was still no end to the comments about the losses each man had sustained. One, his red pepper field; another, three pigs and a little girl. The one from down below, his banana trees full of bunches. Another, his shack and his pregnant wife. That one, his black goat. Still another one, his jug without handles, where he kept his loose money.

A few days passed.

One afternoon, they saw Uncle Jesús leaving his hut. It was his first time out since that fateful night.

And his first steps were toward José's hut.

Tata went out to meet him.

It was as if they hadn't seen each other in a long time. On their weather-beaten faces, a strong brotherly joy shone. Their four hands clasped each other in a wonderful greeting.

Then, they both went to sit down in front of the hut, close to the tree.

Uncle Jesús had come to thank him. He was grateful that Tata had lent him the ox.

Tata José, a bit embarrassed, would have preferred not to talk about it.

"I thought you'd be mad," he said without looking him in the face.

"Mad?" Jesús asked, bewildered.

"Well, yeah! 'Cause me and my boy went to save our Josco before you. . . ."

"Well, now!" Uncle Jesús exclaimed. "I'd 've done the same! A human being ain't worth as much as an ox. I'd 've done the same!"

And his face truly did not show the slightest trace of reproach or anger. He was really grateful to the man who had been so generous as to lend him what he treasured so much.

Seated on the ground, Tata and Uncle were quiet for a long time.

The clouds, soaked in sunset, were burning. The horizon was spectacularly on fire, but it didn't impress these two old men, even though they were blinded by the brightness. They were thinking of the bliss of having two oxen. Like Tata José, an old man could die in peace knowing he hadn't wasted his life. He could bequeath that fortune of horns and tails to his son.

In those parts, men hacked each other to death with machetes[6] for the slightest reason. Or the army patrols would execute them on the basis of a piece of gossip. For the most insignificant theft they could be hung. An animal, on the other hand, wasn't sacrificed just like that. One would have to think about it. A cow, even if it had spent a night damaging somebody's cornfield, was captured delicately. Who would bother fighting to take possession of a man? A cow, on the other hand . . .

6. **machetes:** large knives with heavy blades, often used for cutting back underbrush or sugar cane.

Uncle Jesús, indifferent to the sky, and sitting on the soft earth, was becoming a sociologist.[7]

And he said: "Ya know what I'd do to make people worth more?"

"What?"

"Well, if I was the boss of Mexico, I would order people killed in slaughterhouses, and their meat to be sold! About five pesos a pound, until we got to like eating one another."

"And why?" asked Tata eyeing him fixedly.

"Well, in that way don't ya figure people wouldn't waste people? I'll bet you've never seen 'm waste a goat anywhere."

"Well, no. . . ."

And the two old men fell silent again. In the distance they looked like two figurines of dried mud, illuminated by the burning of those large black clouds, ignited by the sunset as though they were rags in the sky.

7. **sociologist:** one who studies society and social relationships.

Reviewing the Selection

Answer each of the following questions without looking back at the story.

Recalling Facts

1. Why does Tata José lend Uncle Jesús his ox when Jesús already has an ox?
   - ☐ a. Jesús's ox is sick.
   - ☐ b. Two oxen are needed to pull the plow.
   - ☐ c. Jesús is using his ox for another job.
   - ☐ d. Tata's ox is stronger.

Understanding Main Ideas

2. In "Men in a Storm" Jorge Ferretis shows that
   - ☐ a. violent storms are a common occurrence in Mexico.
   - ☐ b. an ox is a better swimmer than a person.
   - ☐ c. the Mexican peasants scarcely see themselves as human beings.
   - ☐ d. the Mexican peasants do not care much for their relatives.

Placing Events in Order

3. Which of the following events occurs last?
   - ☐ a. Tata and his son see Jesús swimming in the river.
   - ☐ b. Tata and his son bring Jesús back to life.
   - ☐ c. Tata and his son see Jesús with the two oxen.
   - ☐ d. Tata and his son save their bull.

Finding Supporting Details

4. Tata saves his ox by
   - ☐ a. leading it to safety on a patch of high ground.
   - ☐ b. feeding it fresh grass after the storm.
   - ☐ c. breathing life back into the ox and forcing water out of its lungs.
   - ☐ d. holding on to the ox all night to keep it from floating downriver.

Recognizing Words in Context

5. "Only after an hour did the downpour abate."
   In this context *abate* means to
   - ☐ a. lessen.
   - ☐ b. increase.
   - ☐ c. begin.
   - ☐ d. end.

Interpreting the Selection

Answer each of the following questions. You may look back at the story if necessary.

Making Inferences

6. Why doesn't Tata José pull Jesús out of the water when he first finds him?
   - ☐ a. Uncle Jesús tells him to leave.
   - ☐ b. Tata must find the ox.
   - ☐ c. Tata is too exhausted to help Jesús.
   - ☐ d. The two men dislike each other.

Generalizing

7. You can tell by the description of the family's breakfast that the characters
   - ☐ a. usually don't have enough to eat.
   - ☐ b. eat a balanced diet.
   - ☐ c. eat more in the morning than at other meals.
   - ☐ d. prefer tortillas to meat with chili.

Analyzing Character

8. Which pair of adjectives best describes the Mexican peasants in this story?
   - ☐ a. poor and uncaring
   - ☐ b. selfish and greedy
   - ☐ c. uneducated but practical
   - ☐ d. friendly but uncooperative

Comparing

9. In the story the ox is worth more than a person because an ox
   - ☐ a. lives longer than a human.
   - ☐ b. can swim better.
   - ☐ c. can pull a plow, while people cannot.
   - ☐ d. means the survival of a family.

Drawing Conclusions

10. At the end of the story, Uncle Jesús has an idea for making people worth more. His suggestion
    - ☐ a. expresses an opinion that is widely held among Mexican peasants.
    - ☐ b. is one that many sociologists would make.
    - ☐ c. expresses the author's bitter comment on the peasants' situation.
    - ☐ d. shows that he does not understand what has happened.

Description, Narration, and Dialogue

Like most short stories, "Men in a Storm" includes description, narration, and dialogue. Description is writing that helps you to picture a person, a place, or an event. Narration gives you an account of the actions or events in a story. Dialogue, you will recall, is conversation between two or more characters.

The balance among those elements will vary from story to story. Some writers build their works around a lot of dialogue. Others use very little dialogue but include a lot of description.

Writers use description, narration, and dialogue for different purposes. Through description, for example, they can establish a setting or mood. Dialogue can be used to reveal characters or to build suspense.

In this lesson you will see what roles description, narration, and dialogue play in "Men in a Storm."

Description

In literature, description gives you details so that you can see or understand the person, object, or place that the author is trying to create. Writers use description for various reasons. Sometimes, they want to create sensory impressions. As you learned in Chapter 11, writers use imagery or figurative language, which are kinds of description, to create images that appeal to your senses.

On occasion, short-story writers use description to give direct, factual information. For example, a writer might describe a person's height, weight, age, or coloring in a straightforward, factual manner. More often, writers use description to establish the setting or mood of a story.

In the opening paragraphs of "Men in a Storm," Ferretis carefully details the setting. Through those descriptive details, he establishes the mood of the story.

> Few trees, large, still. Dark trunks of fluted stone.
>
> The world begins to take shape with the approach of daybreak.
>
> An unseen cow moos, as if the moo was diluted in the shade.
>
> At the foot of one of those solitary trees, there is a form, like a protuberance of the trunk, darker than the color of the bark. But that form is soft, warm. It's Tata Josê, wrapped in his woolen blanket, squatting next to the trunk.

1. Where do you think the story is set? What mood, or atmosphere, do you sense?

2. Find another descriptive passage in the story. What mood does the passage create?

The first few paragraphs of the story portray a primitive world. In a way, the first few lines describe a scene resembling the beginning of the world. It has the elements of the Biblical scene of creation. With the light of dawn, "the world begins to take shape." Soon, you hear the sounds and see the sights of an emerging world. That sense of a primitive, Biblical world reappears again in the story, as you will see later in this lesson.

Notice, too, that Ferretis uses imagery and figurative language in the description.

3. To what senses does the description in the first four paragraphs appeal? Identify one simile and one metaphor that Ferretis uses.

Narration

Narration and description are woven closely together in a short story. In fact, the description is part of the overall story. The narration tells you about the characters' actions and what events take place.

As you learned in Chapter 7, the story may be told by either a first-person or a third-person narrator. The narrator in "Men in a Storm" is clearly someone outside the action, so the story has a third-person narrator.

4. Review the story to determine if Ferretis uses an omniscient (all-knowing), a limited omniscient, or an objective point of view. Give examples from the story to support your decision.

Through the narration you learn about the characters and the events of the plot. The people in the story are Mexican peasants, but they could be peasants anywhere in the world. Only the food—the tortillas—and the names of Tata José and Uncle Jesús place the story in Mexico.

Ferretis treats his characters in an unusual way. Only the two old men, José and Jesús, and the ox, Josco, have names. The other characters are nameless. José's wife and his son, who plays a major role in rescuing the ox, are never named.

5. How does the namelessness of the characters add to the primitive feeling of the story?

As you read earlier, the description at the beginning of the story creates an almost Biblical landscape. The narrative itself continues that image. It tells of events such as those in Genesis, the first book of the Old Testament, which describes the beginning of the world. The image is continued when Tata José lends his brother Jesús a valued ox—an act of brotherly kindness, a strong teaching of the Bible.

The central event of "Men in a Storm" is a flash flood that threatens the lives, land, and animals of the peasants. In the Bible a flood destroys everything on earth except for Noah, his family, and the animals Noah brought into the ark.

Finally, Tata José and his son make a significant choice: to save Josco, the ox, rather than Uncle Jesús. The Bible has many stories of people making critical choices. However, unlike many stories in the Bible, the choice made by Tata José and his son has little to do with choosing between good and evil. Instead, it is a matter of survival. In fact, they make their decision without a second thought. They don't even look for Uncle Jesús until late in the afternoon *after* the ox has rallied.

6. Use examples from the story to explain why the men chose to save the ox first.

Dialogue

Like the description and narration, the dialogue in the story reveals a primitive world in which peasants are struggling to survive. Ferretis uses dialogue only occasionally. When the characters speak, they do not say much. They do not have the strength or energy to talk at length.

As you have learned, a writer uses dialogue as a means of characterization, showing what people are like through their words. Look at the first bit of dialogue in "Men in a Storm." That conversation takes place between Tata José and his son.

7. What do you learn about each of the characters from that dialogue? Why do you think the conversation ends when it does?

Use of Dialect. "Men in a Storm" was written in Spanish and translated into English. The translator tried to re-create the sounds of the Spanish original. Ferretis's characters speak in a Spanish dialect, a pattern of speech used by people of a certain group or of a particular region. The characters are uneducated people who use informal language, not the formal language taught in school. Ferretis wanted to create true-to-life characters, showing them as peasants really are. One way he created realistic characters was by writing the dialogue to reflect the actual speech patterns of Mexican peasants.

When the translator began to put the dialogue into English, she had to find some way of re-creating the speech patterns Ferretis had captured. What the translator did was to write the dialogue using slang, poor grammar, and slurred or incomplete pronunciation of certain words. By doing so, she showed you that the peasants spoke in an uneducated way.

8. Skim the various conversations in the story to find examples of (a) slang, (b) poor grammar, and (c) slurred or incomplete pronunciation.

Dialogue and Theme. Although there is little dialogue in the story, Ferretis uses it to express his theme. In the opening dialogue, for example, you learn that Tata José has lent his ox to his brother, who is far behind in his plowing. That dialogue shows that kindness and brotherly love do exist among people struggling to survive.

Later, after the flood, the two brothers speak about the choice Tata José made.

9. What does Jesús think of his brother for saving the ox first? What does Jesús think about the value of human life? In your own words, what theme, or message, do you think Ferretis has developed through that dialogue?

Style

Description, narration, and dialogue are all elements of the author's style. Style refers to the way a piece of literature is written. It does not refer to what the author says but to *how* he or she says it. Other elements that make up an author's unique style are sentence and paragraph length, diction, and tone.

Most sentences in "Men in a Storm" are short. At times, Ferretis uses phrases as though they were complete sentences. His paragraphs are generally short, too.

10. How do the short sentences and paragraphs contribute to the realism of the story?

11. There are several paragraphs that are longer than the rest. Read those paragraphs. What effect do the longer paragraphs have on the story?

Diction is the writer's choice and arrangement of words. Writers decide on which words to use depending on their subject, their audience, and the mood they want to create. You have already seen one example of diction in the peasants' dialect.

Ferretis uses both informal, or colloquial, language and formal language in the story. Look, for example, at the passage after the men have eaten breakfast.

> Surely they hadn't eaten their fill; but their stomachs were half-full with the sweetened, watered-down coffee, boiled corn, and strips of meat with chile. Enough to fool their guts.

12. Is Ferretis using informal or formal language here? Give reasons for your answer.

Through Ferretis's style you can tell his tone, or attitude toward his subject. As you have seen, he creates a realistic portrait of Mexican peasants struggling to survive.

13. Do you think Ferretis is sympathetic or unsympathetic toward Tata José and his family? How can you tell?

Questions for Thought and Discussion

The questions and activities that follow will help you explore "Men in a Storm" in more depth and at the same time develop your critical thinking skills.

1. **Taking a Stand.** If you had been in the situation of Tata José and his son, would you have saved Josco or Uncle Jesús first? Explain your choice.

2. **Identifying Causes.** Why do you think the characters in "Men in a Storm" feel that human life is worth so little? Think of as many reasons as possible. Cite evidence from the story to support your answers.

3. **Evaluating Images.** At the beginning of the story, you see the image of Tata José as part of the tree. At what other points in the story do you see this image of a tree/man? What purpose do you think that image serves?

4. **Comparing.** Both "Men in a Storm" and "Zlateh the Goat" are simple tales about poor and simple people. In what other ways are those stories similar? How do the two stories differ?

5. **Recognizing Figurative Language.** In Chapters 4 and 11, you learned about figures of speech such as simile and metaphor. Find examples of each in "Men in a Storm." Explain the effect of each figure of speech.

Writing About Literature

Several suggestions for writing projects are given below. You may be asked to complete one or more of these projects. If you have any questions about how to begin a writing assignment, review Using the Writing Process, beginning on page 337.

1. **Analyzing Tone.** How does the author of "Men in a Storm" express his attitude toward the characters in his story? Explain how the author's choice of words, expressions, and descriptions contribute to the story's tone.

2. **Writing an Eyewitness Account.** Have you ever witnessed a flood, a fire, or any other disaster? Write an eyewitness account of what happened. Use description, narration, and dialogue in your account.

3. **Developing a Writing Style.** Choose a person whom you admire or respect. First write a description of the person as though you were telling a friend about him or her. Then write a description of the same person as though you were writing a biographical entry for an encyclopedia. For each description, use a style appropriate to your subject and audience.

4. **Creating Dialogue.** Imagine a scene in which Tata José is dying and is passing on his possessions to his son. Write a page or so of dialogue in which the older man reminds his son of his responsibilities.

Using the Writing Process

The lesson that follows is designed to help you with the writing assignments you will meet in this book. It explains the major steps in the writing process. Read the lesson carefully so that you understand the writing process thoroughly. On pages 347–348, following the lesson, is a checklist. Whenever you are asked to complete a writing assignment, you can just refer to the checklist as a reminder of the things you should consider as you're working on the assignment. The lesson can then serve as a reference—an information source. Turn to it whenever you feel that it would be helpful to review part or all of the process.

When presented with a writing assignment, many people's instant response is panic. What will I write about? Do I have anything to say? To ease the panic, remind yourself that writing is something that *no one* simply sits down and does with the words flowing freely and perfectly from first sentence to last. Rather, writing is a *process;* that is, it involves a number of steps. The writing process is not a straightforward, mechanical one, such as that involved in solving a mathematical problem. These pages give you a plan that you can follow to sensibly work through the complex task of presenting your ideas on paper.

Keep in mind that writing is not simply the act of filling a piece of paper with words. It is a sophisticated act of communication. The purpose of writing is to put *ideas* across to other people. Since ideas come from your mind, not your pen, the writing process begins with the work that takes place in your mind: the creation and organization of ideas. The process then proceeds to the expression of ideas—the actual setting down of words on paper. The final stage is the polishing of both the ideas and the words that express them.

As they work, writers engage in a variety of activities—thinking, planning, organizing, writing, revising, rethinking. For clarity, we label the various stages in the process prewriting, writing, and revising. However, the stages are not so straightforward and separate. One blends into the next, and sometimes a writer returns to a previous activity, moving back and forth through the process. When you write, your goal should be to produce a clear and lively work that expresses interesting ideas. The writing process can help you in that effort.

Stage 1: Prewriting

Define Your Task

The first stage in the writing process is prewriting. At this stage, your goal is to choose a topic, to figure out what you are going to say about it, and to decide what style and tone you are going to use. Making these decisions is essential if you are going to write something interesting and to express your ideas clearly and vividly. At this stage you jot down thoughts and ideas—the material that you will eventually organize and write about in detail. During the prewriting stage, you should search for answers to the following questions:

What Will I Write About? This question must be answered before you do anything else. You need to choose a topic. Then you need to *focus* the topic. A focused topic directs your thinking as you write. This is important whether you are writing a brief description, a short story, an essay, or a research paper. Deciding just what issues you want to address, what kind of character you want to develop, or what theme and events you want a story to revolve around will focus your thinking and help you create a bright, strong piece of writing.

A careful decision is called for here. A good topic is neither too broad nor too narrow. The length of what you are writing and your purpose for writing often dictate how broad your focus should be. In an essay or a research paper, for instance, you need to choose a topic that's defined enough to explore in depth. You don't want to choose a topic that's so broad that you can only touch on the main ideas. If your assignment is to write a short story, you'll want to focus on perhaps one main relationship between characters, one important conflict, just a few related events. You can then write in detail to create full, interesting characters and a well-developed story. When you need to focus a topic, think about what would be practical for the given task.

What Do I Want to Say? You need to think about what information you want or need to include, and what ideas you want to communicate.

What Is My Purpose for Writing? Will you try to persuade, to inform, to explain, or to entertain your readers?

What Style Will I Use? Do you want to write formally or in a casual, conversational style? Will you use the first person, I, or the third-person, he, she, or they? Will you write seriously or use jokes and humor? If you are writing a story, will you use dialogue?

How Will I Organize My Ideas? What will you start with? In what order will you present and develop your ideas?

Who Is My Audience? Who will be reading your work? Are you writing for other students? For people who already have some background in the subject? For people who know nothing about the subject? For children or for adults? Your audience will dictate the approach you take—whether you will write in a formal or an informal tone, whether you will provide a lot of background information or very little, what kind of words you will use.

Generate and Organize Ideas

Although most of the writing assignments in this book provide fairly specific directions about the type of writing to be done, they leave lots of room for imagination. By using your imagination, you can discover fresh and exciting ideas that are distinctly yours. How can you come up with those bright ideas? Below are some techniques that can help you tap your creative powers. They can help you at the prewriting stage and any time you need to generate new ideas. You might use them to come up with a topic for a research paper, an essay, or a short story. You might use them to focus a topic or to generate ideas about a topic you've already chosen. Techniques such as outlining and clustering are also useful for organizing ideas. Try each of the techniques, and eventually you'll find the ones that work best for you for a particular purpose.

Free Writing. Have you ever been given a writing assignment and found that you had no idea what to write? Free writing is an activity for getting started—for coming up with ideas to write about. To free write, write anything that comes to mind, no matter how far off the topic it seems. At first it may seem silly, but eventually your mind will start associating ideas. Soon you will be writing complete thoughts about the topic.

Suppose you were asked to write about winter. How to begin? Start writing. Put down the first thought that comes to mind and let ideas begin to flow. You might come up with something like this:

> I don't know what to write. Winter. What can I say that hasn't already been said about winter? It's cold, there's lots of snow . . . well, not in all places I guess. Actually when it's cold here, it's warm on the other side of the world. Do they call that winter then, or summer . . . ?

Can you see how you might go from thoughts that are totally off the track to thoughts that are intriguing? When you have finished, look at all the ideas you've written down. Perhaps there are whole sentences or paragraphs that can go into your story or essay. This exercise will have gotten you started.

Brainstorming. This also is an activity to generate ideas. It can be done alone or in a group. When brainstorming, you want to come up with as many ideas as possible. Each idea will spur a new idea. As you or others in a brainstorming group think of ideas, write them down. After you have come up with all the ideas you can, select several to develop for the assignment.

Clustering. This technique can be useful both to generate ideas and to organize them. In fact, you actually do both at the same time, for as you jot down ideas, you "cluster" the ones that go together.

Begin by putting your main idea—your focused topic—in the center of the page and circling it. As you think of ideas associated with the main idea, write them nearby, circle them, and connect them with a line to the main idea. Then, as you think of ideas related to each of those *subtopics,* attach the ideas to the word they relate to. You can take this process as far as you like. The farther you branch out, the more detailed you get. When you get to the point where you're ready to write your story or your essay, you can use such a diagram as a guide to grouping your ideas. A simple clustering diagram is shown below. The main idea is "symbols in a story."

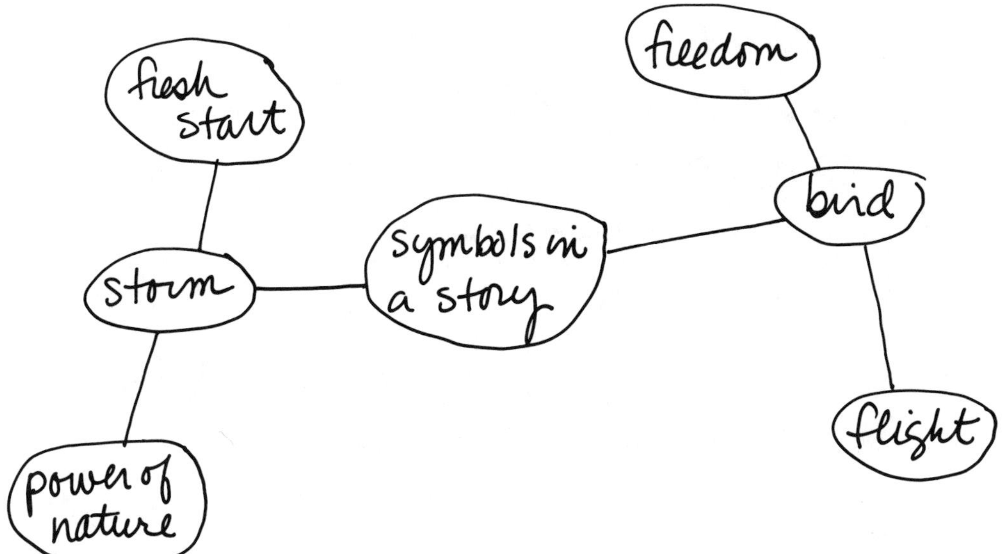

Outlining. Outlining is usually thought of as an organizing tool, but it also provides a useful form in which to write down ideas as you think of them. It gives you a way to group ideas, just as clustering does. In addition, it helps you to organize those groups of ideas—to arrange them in the order in which you think you would like to write about them.

Start by writing down some main ideas that you want to include. Leave space after each one for listing related facts or thoughts—details—that you will want to include about the topic. Each idea you list will probably make you think of another idea. Look at the example below. Imagine that your assignment is to write a character sketch. You think you'd like to write about an old man. That's a main idea, so you write it down. One of the aspects of the man you want to talk about is his lifestyle. That, too, is a main idea, so you leave some space after your first idea and write it down. Okay, you ask yourself, what is the old man like? List each specific detail under the first main idea. Go on and do the same with lifestyle, and whatever other main ideas you may have.

Character Sketch

Old Man
- about 80 years old
- tall, thin, straight
- athletic
- friendly, outgoing

Man's lifestyle
- lives in his own apartment in the city
- involved in theater
- many friends of all ages

You can work back and forth in an outline, adding and deleting, until you're satisfied with the ideas that are there. Your last step will be to arrange the outline in the order in which you think you want to present the ideas in your writing. Then the outline becomes a kind of map for writing. Remember, though, that it's a loose map—you can rearrange, drop, and add ideas even as you are writing.

Outlining is also a good way of organizing the ideas you generate through brainstorming and free writing. It helps you place those ideas in some kind of order.

Stage 2: Writing

The second stage in the writing process is the writing itself. At this stage, you write a first draft of your paper or story, using the notes or outline that you developed in the prewriting stage as a guide. This is the stage at which you turn those loose ideas into sentences and paragraphs that work together.

Get Your Thoughts on Paper. When you begin writing, the most important thing to focus on is saying what you want to say—getting all your ideas down on paper in sentences and paragraphs. Some people find it easiest to write their first drafts without worrying if they have chosen exactly the right words and without checking on spelling. Just put a question mark next to anything you aren't sure of and check it later. You can even put a blank in a sentence if you can't think of the right word to put there. Fill it in when you revise.

As you are writing, you may discover that you sometimes have to go back and do some more thinking and planning. You may need to gather more information or think through an idea again. You may also do some rearranging of ideas.

Develop a Tone. In the writing stage, you need to begin to develop a tone—an attitude toward your subject. How do you want to *sound* to the reader? What impression do you want the reader to have toward the subject? Do you want to sound authoritative, amusing, sad, pleased?

You'll want to establish your tone right away—in the first paragraph. The first paragraph is important because it must grab your reader's interest and show where you are headed.

Organize Your Writing. As you write, you will, of course, be following the basic rules of the language. Sentences should express complete thoughts. They should follow one another in logical order. Each paragraph should focus on one main idea, and it should contain details that support that idea.

As you move from one paragraph to the next, use transition words and phrases to link your ideas. Clearly connect ideas and thoughts that go together so the reader can follow your story, argument, or explanation.

Stage 3: Revising

The third stage in the writing process is revising. This is the point at which you look for ways to polish your writing. Revising is more than just fixing a few errors. It can involve both major and minor changes.

Rethink Ideas and Organization

The first goal in revising is to check for clear, logical expression. Does what I have written make sense? Have I clearly said everything I am trying to say? Have I arranged my ideas in the best order?

Reread the entire draft to see if paragraphs and sentences follow in a logical order. You may find that putting paragraphs in a different order makes your points clearer. Remember that each paragraph is part of a whole, and it should relate to your topic. Sometimes you may write an excellent paragraph, only to discover that it has very little to do with the topic. No matter how good you think a sentence or a paragraph is, drop it if it doesn't belong.

As you read what you have written, you may also want to rewrite sentences and paragraphs, or even add new material. At this stage, you may also want to go back to your prewriting notes to see that you included everything you wanted to include.

Look at Your Language

After you have checked the ideas and organization, review the style and form in which you have written. Think about the language—the words and phrases you have used. Do they say precisely what you mean? Do they create strong images?

If you want your writing to be lively and interesting, write with strong verbs and nouns. They make strong writing. If you find yourself piling on the adjectives and adverbs, you'll know that you're struggling to support weak verbs and nouns. What is a strong verb or noun? It is one that is precise, active, fresh. It paints a clear picture in the mind.

Use Strong Verbs. Some verbs, for instance, are tired, overused, dull. The verb *to be,* for example, is about the weakest verb in the language. It doesn't *do* anything. So look at the sentences in which you use the verbs *is, are, am, was, have been,* etc. Are there action words that you can use instead? Instead of saying "Sam was happy," might you describe an action that *shows* that Sam was happy? "Sam smiled shyly and nodded his head," "Sam beamed," "Sam grinned," "Sam jumped into the air, arms raised above his head, and shouted, YES!"

Use Precise Nouns. Your nouns too should be precise. Whenever possible, create a strong image for the reader. The word *thing,* for instance, is imprecise and overused. What kind of image does it create in your mind? None. Search for the word that *tells.* If you are describing a street scene, for instance, instead of saying that there is a building on the corner, can you tell what kind of building it is? Is it a bank? A three-story Victorian house? A gothic cathedral? An open-air vegetable market? Draw clear pictures with your nouns.

Don't Overuse Adjectives and Adverbs. Adjectives and adverbs have their place, but try not to overdo them. When you do find yourself in need of an adjective, choose one that creates a strong image. Avoid those that are overused and don't really describe. *Beautiful* and *nice,* for instance, are overused adjectives.

Toss Out Unnecessary Words. Have you used more words than you need to say something? This is known as being redundant. Saying that someone is "bright and intelligent," for instance, is redundant because the adjectives are synonyms. Use one or the other. Another example is the phrase "crucially important." Why not just say "crucial"?

As you examine your language, throw out any words that don't serve a purpose—that don't give information, paint a clear picture, or create atmosphere. By taking out unnecessary words, you will have "tight writing"—writing that moves along.

Check the Structure and Rhythm of Your Sentences. Read your work out loud and listen to the rhythm and sounds of the language. Do the sentences all sound the same? If they do, can you vary the structure of your sentences—making some simple, some complex, some long, some short? Correct any sentence fragments, and divide run-on sentences into two or more sentences.

After you've gone through that kind of thinking a few times at the revision stage, you'll find yourself automatically choosing livelier, clearer language as you write. You'll become a better writer. That, too, is a process.

Check for Errors

The final step in the revising process is the all-important "housekeeping" review—checking for correct spelling, grammar, and punctuation, and for readable handwriting. You don't, of course, have to wait until the end of the writing process to pay attention to those details. But before you write your final draft, check carefully for errors in those areas.

Checklist for the Writing Process

- ✓ What is my topic? Is it focused enough? Should I broaden or narrow it?
- ✓ What do I want to say about the topic? What are my thoughts, feelings, and ideas about it?
- ✓ Which prewriting activity or activities would most help me to gather ideas?
- ✓ Do I need to do some research? Some reading? Consult outside sources? What other materials, if any, do I need?
- ✓ What is the main point or idea that I want to communicate? What ideas are secondary? Which of those ideas are most important?
- ✓ What details will I include to support and expand on the main ideas?
- ✓ Should I include examples or anecdotes?
- ✓ How will I organize my ideas?
- ✓ What is my purpose for writing? Do I want to entertain? Inform? Explain? Persuade? Perhaps a combination?
- ✓ Who is my audience?
- ✓ What kind of language will I use? Will I be formal, informal, or casual? Will I use dialogue? Will I speak directly to the reader?
- ✓ What tone do I want to take—what feeling do I want to give the reader about the subject? How can I sustain that tone throughout my writing?
- ✓ How can I effectively begin my first paragraph? Should I use a question? A startling or unusual fact? An amazing statistic? Should I begin with an action or a description? Perhaps a piece of dialogue?
- ✓ How will I end? If writing nonfiction, should I summarize what I have already said, or should I offer a new thought or argument as my conclusion?

- ✓ Have I developed my ideas in the best order possible? Should I move some paragraphs around?
- ✓ Have I covered my topic adequately? Does the writing fulfill its purpose and get the main point across to my audience?
- ✓ Do I need to rewrite parts? Perhaps some ideas need to be clarified or explained further. Perhaps I could write a better description or account of an event?
- ✓ Do I want to add anything?
- ✓ Are there any unnecessary ideas or details that should be deleted?
- ✓ Is each paragraph well developed—are the facts and ideas presented in a good order?
- ✓ Do all the sentences in each paragraph relate to one idea?
- ✓ Are the ideas between sentences and between paragraphs connected with transition words and phrases that make the connections clear?
- ✓ Is the writing vivid? Have I used active, precise, colorful words that create strong images?
- ✓ Does the final paragraph provide a good ending?
- ✓ Are the sentences well constructed? Are there any run-ons or sentence fragments that need fixing? Do I vary the kinds of sentences—some long, some short, some active, some passive?
- ✓ Is the grammar correct?
- ✓ Are all the words spelled correctly?
- ✓ Is all the punctuation correct?
- ✓ Is the final draft clean and legible?
- ✓ Have I read the final draft over one last time to check for any errors that may have crept in as I was copying?

Glossary of Literary Terms

This glossary includes definitions for all the important literary terms introduced in this book. The first time they are defined and discussed in the text, the terms are underlined. Following each term in the glossary is a page reference (in parentheses) that tells the page on which the term is introduced.

Many terms are discussed in more than one chapter, especially as they apply to various stories. This glossary provides the fullest definition of each term. Boldfaced words within the definitions are other terms that appear in the glossary.

alliteration (page 229) the repetition of consonant sounds at the beginnings of words.

allusion (page 259) an indirect reference to a work of literature or to a person, a place, or an event that the reader is expected to recognize.

characterization (page 102) the methods by which a writer develops a character's personality. The five methods of characterization are (1) describing a character's physical appearance, (2) showing the character's actions, (3) revealing the character's thoughts and words, (4) showing what other characters think and say about the character, and (5) telling the reader directly what the writer thinks of the character.

characters (page 25) the people, animals, things, or even machines that act or speak in a story. The word *character* also refers to the personalities of those individuals.

chronological order (page 56) the arrangement of events in the order in which they occur.

cliché (page 168) an expression or an idea that has become stale from overuse.

climax (page 26) the point of greatest interest or highest tension in a story. Usually, the climax is also the turning point in the story.

conflict (page 26) a struggle of some kind that is central to the plot of every story. *See* **external conflict** and **internal conflict.**

description (page 329) the kind of writing that helps readers to picture a person, a place, or an event.

dialect (page 332) the pattern of speech used by people of a certain group or of a particular region. It refers to the special expressions and pronunciations of that region or group.

dialogue (page 24) conversation between two or more characters.

diction (page 333) a writer's choice and arrangement of words.

dramatic irony (page 284) a type of irony that occurs in a story when the reader has information or an understanding of events that a character does not have. *See* **irony.**

exposition (page 52) the part of the **plot** in which important background information is given and the characters and the conflict are introduced. The exposition is usually found at the beginning of a story.

external conflict (page 78) a struggle between a person and an outside force. The four kinds of external conflict are (1) conflict between two people, (2) conflict between a person and society, (3) conflict between groups, and (4) conflict between a person and the forces of nature. *See* **conflict.**

falling action (page 52) the part of the **plot** following the **climax** in which the action begins to slow down. The falling action leads to the **resolution.**

fantasy (page 113) is an imagined reality. Fantasy may include imaginary beasts, magic, ghosts, demons, or other supernatural powers. *See* **science fiction.**

figurative language (page 103) the use of words and phrases in unusual ways to create strong, vivid images, to focus attention on certain ideas, or to compare dissimilar things. When words or phrases are used figuratively, they have meanings other than their usual meanings. *See* **metaphor, personification**, and **simile.**

first-person point of view (page 196) the vantage point in which the narrator is a character in the story and tells the story as he or she experiences or understands it. The narrator uses the "I" vantage point to tell what happens. *See* **point of view.**

flashback (page 56) a scene, a conversation, or an event that interrupts the present action to show something that happened in the past. A flashback is a memory shown through the eyes of one of the characters. Flashbacks can add to the tension of a story by giving the reader new information about the characters or the events.

folktale (page 293) a simple, timeless story that deals with the customs, traditions, and beliefs of ordinary people.

foreshadowing (page 223) the use of hints or clues to suggest events that are going to happen later in the story. Foreshadowing is a device used by fiction writers to build **suspense.**

humor (page 163) whatever is funny or amusing in a situation.

idiom (page 229) an accepted phrase or an expression whose meaning cannot be understood from the ordinary meanings of the words.

imagery (page 228) language that appeals to any of the five senses—sight, sound, touch, taste, or smell.

internal conflict (page 78) a struggle that takes place within a person's mind. *See* **conflict.**

irony (page 164) a contrast between appearance and reality or between what is expected and what actually happens. *See* **dramatic, situational**, and **verbal irony.**

jargon (page 168) special words or phrases, used by people in certain kinds of work. Jargon can have a particular meaning to one group but little or no meaning to people outside of that group.

joke (page 163) something that is said or done on purpose to get a laugh.

limited omniscient point of view (page 197) a third-person point of view in which the narrator's insights are limited to the minds of only a few of the characters, or only one character. *See* **point of view.**

metaphor (page 104) an implied comparison between unlike things. A writer will use a metaphor in order to give readers an unusual way of looking at one of the things. A metaphor is a comparison that suggests one thing *is* another. *See* **figurative language.**

mood (page 106) the general feeling or atmosphere of a scene or a story.

moral (page 201) a lesson about the right way to live. few words

narration (page 329) an account of the actions or events in a story. It tells the reader what is happening in the story.

narrator (page 87) the person who is telling the story.

objective point of view (page 198) a third-person point of view in which the narrator does not comment on or interpret any of the characters or their actions. *See* **point of view.**

omniscient point of view (page 197) a third-person narrator who can see into the minds of all the characters and knows their hidden thoughts and emotions. Nothing escapes the narrator's understanding. *See* **point of view.**

personification (page 308) a figure of speech in which an animal, an object, or an idea is described as though it were human. The animal, object, or idea is given human qualities. Like other figures of speech, personification is used by a writer to arouse certain feelings or responses in the reader. *See* **figurative language.**

plot (page 26) the sequence of events in a story. A plot usually has five sections: **exposition, rising action, climax, falling action,** and **resolution.**

point of view (page 196) the vantage point from which the narrator tells a story. *See* **first-person** and **third-person point of view, omniscient point of view, limited omniscient,** and **objective point of view.**

realistic fiction (page 3) a work of fiction in which the characters and events seem like those of real life.

resolution (page 52) the conclusion of the story in which the **conflict** or conflicts end. *See* **plot.**

rising action (page 52) the part of the **plot** in which the tension of the story builds, complications increase the **conflict,** and the action moves toward the **climax.**

satire (page 163) the kind of writing in which certain ideas, customs, or human weaknesses are ridiculed. A writer often satirizes certain behavior or ideas by using exaggeration. Satire can be gentle or harsh.

science fiction (page 113) a special kind of fantasy writing in which technology, machines, robots, computers, or other scientific inventions play a major role in taking the reader to extraordinary worlds. In science fiction characters can move through time and space in ways that real people cannot. *See* **fantasy.**

setting (page 23) the time and the place of the action of a story.

short story (page 3) a work of fiction that can usually be read at one sitting.

simile (page 104) a direct comparison between unlike things using the word *like, as,* or *resembles* to connect them. Like other figures of speech, a simile is used to offer vivid new ways of looking at things. *See* **figurative language.**

situational irony (page 285) a type of irony in which what happens is different from what the reader expects or what the characters expect. *See* **irony.**

slapstick (page 163) a kind of humor that depends on fast, foolish action to make people laugh.

stereotype (page 165) a character who matches a fixed idea held by a number of people. A stereotype conforms to a certain pattern and lacks individuality.

style (page 333) the way in which a piece of literature is written. How an author writes is part of his or her style. **Description, narration, dialogue, diction,** and **tone** are all elements that go into a writer's style.

surprise ending (page 144) an unexpected twist that concludes a story.

suspense (page 82) the interest, uncertainty, or excitement that a reader feels while waiting for a conflict to be resolved. *See* **foreshadowing.**

symbol (page 287) an object, a person, a place, or an action that stands for or suggests something else.

Should be a complete sentence.

theme (page 27) the underlying message or meaning of a story. Through the theme, a writer can share his or her insights about life. A story often has a major theme and one or more minor themes.

third-person point of view (page 196) the vantage point in which the narrator is someone who stands outside the events of the story. The third-person narrator tells about what happens to the characters, referring to them as "he," "she," and "they." *See* **point of view.**

tone (page 228) a writer's attitude toward his or her subject or toward the audience.

verbal irony (page 284) a type of irony in which a writer or a character in a story says one thing but means something entirely different. *See* **irony.**